Enterprise Application Integration

David S. Linthicum

ADDISON–WESLEY

Boston • San Francisco • New York • Toronto • Montreal
London • Munich • Paris • Madrid
Capetown • Sidney • Tokyo • Singapore • Mexico City

The publisher offers discounts on this book when ordered in quantity for special sales. For more information, please contact:

Pearson Education Corporate Sales Division
One Lake Street
Upper Saddle River, NJ 07458
(800) 382-3419
corpsales@pearsontechgroup.com

Visit AW on the Web: www.awl.com/cseng/

Library of Congress Cataloging-in-Publication Data
Linthicum, David S., 1962–
    Enterprise application integration / David S. Linthicum.
       p. cm.—(Addison-Wesley information technology series)
    Includes bibliographical references and index.
    ISBN 0-201-61583-5
    1. Application software—Development. 2. Business enterprise—Data processing. I. Title.
QA76.76.A65 L56 2000
005.1—dc21   99–046633

ISBN 0-201-61583-5
Text printed on recycled paper
3 4 5 6 7 8 9 10—MA—0403020100
3rd printing, May 2000

For my family. Thanks for everything.

Contents

Contents   ix

CHAPTER 18   MESSAGE BROKERS–THE PREFERRED EAI ENGINE   291

CHAPTER 19   PROCESS AUTOMATION AND EAI   319

Preface

Enterprise Application Integration, or EAI, is a buzzword that gives a name to the informal process that's been going on for years—the integration of various applications so that they may share information and processes freely. However, with a new, intense focus on EAI from both the vendor and analyst community, the opportunity finally exists to get ahead of the curve on a problem—the integration of applications—that costs the Fortune 1000 over $100 billion per year.

Forester Research estimates that more than 30 percent of IT dollars are currently being spent linking systems together for the common good. Perhaps it's time to consider whether that is too great a cost.

The EAI twist to this old story is not so much about system integration as it is about rethinking the technologies and approaches that would allow EAI to become a short-term and cost-effective reality. EAI also represents a technology-business philosophy that focuses on the business issues at hand and suggests that all systems existing either inside or outside an enterprise should be free to share information and logic in ways inconceivable in the past. EAI is the nexus of technology, method, philosophy, and desire to finally address years of architectural neglect.

Make no mistake—this is an emerging space. Now is the time to ask the tough questions. Now is the time to determine the real value of applying EAI in an enterprise. It's time to question which technologies add value, and to determine which problems they solve. And now is the time to reflect on some of the architectural and design decisions that have been made over the years.

Why EAI?

Because enterprise architectures have been poorly planned for the last two decades and longer, it is time to return distributed enterprises into the realm of sanity. Many organizations built systems based on the "cool" technology of the day, suckered into the hype without properly considering how these systems would somehow, someday, share information. For example, there are organizations with dozens, if not hundreds, of different types of open and proprietary systems, each with its own development, database, networking, and operating system religion. The result is a heterogeneous mass (read, chaos) that only the bravest—or most foolhardy—enterprise architects are willing to sort out without gutting the entire enterprise just to get things back on a sane track.

Again, EAI as such is not new. However, the science behind linking varied types of information systems certainly is. EAI has become a sophisticated set of procedures with newly refined technologies, such as message brokers, that allow users to tie systems together using a common glue. The concept of EAI may not be new, but the power of the tools and technology, as well as the techniques available to solve the EAI problem, sure are. Middleware, for example, once clearly a programmer's toy, is now a business tool that allows enterprises to freely move information between any number of systems at will—in many cases, without having to change the source or the target systems. Cutting-edge technology has created the opportunity to solve a problem that has been becoming more intractable for years.

Enter ERPs

Another factor that is driving enterprises toward the promised land of EAI is the broad acceptance of Enterprise Resource Planning (ERP) applications as the new IT infrastructure for the post-millennium corporation. Packaged applications, such as those from SAP, PeopleSoft, and Baan, have revolutionized the way integrated information technology systems are built within most enterprises. Rather than creating new systems from scratch, the modern enterprise is able to leverage existing business rules and processes defined by a single, or several, vendors.

Companies such as SAP have become multibillion dollar entities thanks to the wide acceptance of ERP applications in larger enterprises. What's more, interest in packaged applications has increased in general, with sales automation packages, customer care packages, and vertical market-oriented packages making headlines in the trade publications.

As much as ERP applications can help the integration solution, however, they can also hurt. Organizations are discovering that ERP applications are difficult to install and configure and that, too often, once they are up and running, they turn out not to be all that they were cracked up to be. There is the "little problem" of extracting information from these beasts, information that may be vital to other information systems within the enterprise. For example, if SAP replaces five systems within an enterprise and those five systems supply information to any number of other systems that may also be in place, then the SAP systems must also communicate with these other systems in the enterprise. Making this happen demands an incredible degree of coordination, programming, and testing.

Although coordinating these systems may seem like a minor problem to those who have linked custom systems, it is important to remember that a packaged application typically does not allow for any modification to its source that would enable it to pump information out of a common middleware pipe. This requires interfaces that the ERP application vendor provides. While it would seem like an easy stretch to expect the vendor to have solid and easy-to-use interfaces already in place, the reality is much different. In fact, the major ERP application vendors are beginning to create these interfaces within their products. For the time being, the interfaces are immature and difficult to use.

This immaturity represents another aspect of EAI and its real value within many enterprises. EAI is able to link many disparate systems—including ERP applications. It is not unreasonable to suggest that the growing interest in ERP could very well be driving the interest in EAI as well.

Why Write a Book on EAI?

If EAI has been around for a while in everything but name, why write a book on it now? As we've already suggested, the need for EAI is a result of many years of building distributed computing systems with poor architectural planning. The systems using traditional techniques and technology simply cannot communicate with one another without changing a significant portion of the application. In other words, a logical approach is necessary in order to integrate existing enterprise applications, as well as to address the new breed of technology.

This book is designed to provide the average computer-literate person with enough information to determine if his or her enterprise needs, or would benefit from, EAI—and, if so, how to approach enterprise information planning requirements using the concepts of EAI.

We will present approaches to implementing EAI within typical enterprises, or between two or more enterprises, using the supply chain integration scenarios. We will also discuss the enabling technologies of EAI, technologies such as middleware, system management layers, standards (such as XML), and application development tools that allow applications and databases to share information with one another. Interfaces into complex systems such as SAP and PeopleSoft will not be left out of the mix. We'll also take a look at the future of EAI technology and discuss how you can prepare for it now.

Ultimately, this book is designed to save you money. Because the lack of proper EAI means that many existing information systems cannot coordinate or share information—resulting in a tremendous loss of revenue—then the addition of EAI within most enterprises has the potential of saving that revenue. Much of those savings come either with the automation of processes that are currently being completed through mechanical mechanisms or through viewing all enterprise systems as a single virtual system and thus having access to all relevant data for decision support.

Of course, any number of other types of savings may be derived from EAI; they vary case by case, enterprise by enterprise. In most situations, the value of EAI is apparent.

In addition to the benefit of application integration within the enterprise, a tremendous benefit is also derived from sharing information with applications that exist outside of the enterprise. e-Business integration is a mechanism by which information systems are connected with information systems that are owned and maintained by a trading partner. The result is the ability to share information such as order inventory and sales data. Sharing such information speeds up all aspects of business, including production, sales, order processing, and invoice processing. Increased efficiency in any and all of these areas results in increased profitability.

e-Business is the next frontier of EAI. Analysts have already begun to double the estimates for business-to-business electronic commerce.

Acknowledgments

There are so many people to thank that it's difficult to know where to start. First of all, I want to thank Ursula Kappert, my executive assistant. Ursula diligently took on most of the heavy lifting in creating this book, including editing, gathering and sending chapters and graphics, and also putting up with a grumpy boss after yet another marathon writing session.

I want to thank Steve Johnson, my graphics guy, who was able to take my abstract, modern art–like chicken scratches and turn them into understandable and enjoyable images. Credit also needs to go to Mary O'Brien and Elizabeth Spainhour of Addison-Wesley, who had faith in this book and allowed me to bring it to market. Also, thanks to David Wolfe, who helped edit earlier drafts.

I would also like to thank Christine Sukhenko, my technology analyst, who assisted me in research for the book, and Andre Yee, my VP of R&D, who provided many ideas and felt the impact of mine.

Moreover, I can't leave out the SAGA Software executive team, including CEO Dan Gillis, for the encouragement to take on and complete this project. It's better to lead than to follow.

CHAPTER ONE

Defining EAI

"They have computers, and they may have other weapons of mass destruction."
—Janet Reno, Attorney General,
February 2, 1998

As corporate dependence on technology has grown more complex and far reaching, the need for a method of integrating disparate applications into a unified set of business processes has emerged as a priority. After creating islands of automation through generations of technology, users and business managers are demanding that seamless bridges be built to join them. In effect, they are demanding that ways be found to bind these applications into a single, unified enterprise application. The development of **Enterprise Application Integration (EAI)**, which allows many of the stovepipe applications that exist today to share both processes and data, allows us to finally answer this demand.

Interest in EAI is driven by a number of important factors. With the pressures of a competitive business environment moving IT management to shorter application life cycles, financial prudence demands that IT managers learn to use existing databases and application services rather than recreate the same business processes and data repositories over and over (see Figure 1.1). Ultimately, finances are a prime concern. The integration of applications to save precious development dollars creates a competitive edge for corporations who share application information either within the corporation or with trading partners.

The vast majority of corporations use several generations of systems that rely on a broad range of enabling technology developed over many years. Mainframes, UNIX servers, NT servers, and even proprietary platforms whose names have been forgotten, constitute the technological base for most enterprises. These technologies, new and old, are all providing some value in the enterprise, but their value is diminished if they are unable to leverage other enterprise applications. Moreover, the need to integrate those systems with packaged systems has been intensified by the popularity of packaged applications such as SAP, PeopleSoft, and Baan.

The case for EAI is clear and easy to define. *Accomplishing* EAI, however, is not.

The idea of EAI is something we've been wrestling with over the last several years as the need for a comprehensive integration system has grown more urgent. Forester Research estimates that up to 35 percent of development time is devoted to creating interfaces and points of integration for applications and data sources. Most problems with developing software derive from attempts to integrate it with existing systems. Certainly that has been a significant problem in creating traditional client/server systems—what was inexpensive to build was expensive to integrate and became difficult to maintain.

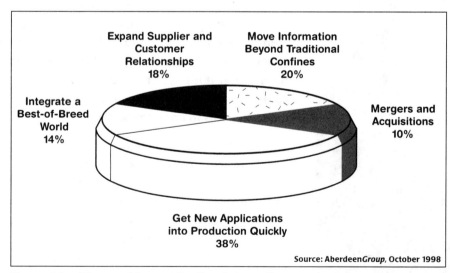

Figure 1.1   **The need for application integration**

What *Is* EAI?

So, if EAI is the solution, what exactly is it? EAI is not simply a buzzword dreamed up by the press and analyst community. It is, at its foundation, a response to decades of creating distributed monolithic, single-purpose applications leveraging a hodgepodge of platforms and development approaches. EAI represents the solution to a problem that has existed since applications first moved from central processors. Put briefly, EAI is the unrestricted sharing of data and business processes among *any* connected applications and data sources in the enterprise.

The demand of the enterprise is to share data and processes *without* having to make sweeping changes to the applications or data structures (see Figure 1.2). Only by creating a method of accomplishing this integration can EAI be both functional and cost effective.

Now that you know what it is, the value of EAI should be obvious. EAI is the solution to the unanticipated outcome of generations of development

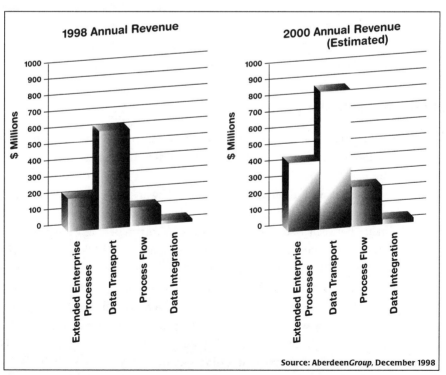

Figure 1.2   The technology that drives EAI is growing quickly.

undertaken without a central vision or strategy. For generations, systems have been built that have served a single purpose for a single set of users without sufficient thought to integrating these systems into larger systems and multiple applications.

Undoubtedly, a number of stovepipe systems are in your enterprise—for example, inventory control, sales automation, general ledger, and human resource systems. These systems typically were custom built with your specific needs in mind, utilizing the technology-of-the-day. Many used nonstandard data storage and application development technology.

While the technology has aged, the value of the applications to your enterprise likely remains fresh. Indeed, that "ancient" technology has probably remained critical to the workings of your enterprise. Unfortunately, many of these business-critical systems are difficult to adapt to allow them to communicate and share information with other, more advanced systems. While there always exists the option of replacing these older systems, the cost of doing so is generally prohibitive.

Packaged applications such as SAP, Baan, and PeopleSoft—which are natural stovepipes themselves—have only compounded the problem. Sharing information among these systems is particularly difficult because many of them were not designed to access anything outside their own proprietary technology.

Applying Technology

If EAI articulates the problem, then traditional middleware has sought to articulate the solution—sort of. Traditional middleware addresses the EAI problem in a limited manner.

The primary limitation is that middleware that uses **message queuing** or **remote procedure calls (RPCs)** only provides point-to-point solutions—that is, linkage between system A and system B. Unfortunately, any attempt to link additional systems quickly becomes a complex tangle of middleware links. Worse still, traditional middleware demands significant alterations to the source and target systems, embedding the middleware layer into the application or data store.

For example, when integrating a custom accounting system running on Windows 2000 with a custom inventory control system running on the mainframe, you may select a message-queuing middleware product to allow both systems to share information. In doing so, however, you generally have to alter the source system (where the information is coming from) with the target system (where the information is going to) in order to make use of the middleware. This is due to the fact that the point-to-point middleware layer only provides a program interface, and thus the programs must change to accommodate the middleware. This is costly and sometimes risky.

What's more, as we use the same or similar technology, as with the previous example, to integrate other applications inside an enterprise, the number of point-to-point solutions may grow to accommodate information movement between various systems. The end result is software pipes running in and out of existing enterprise systems, with no central control and central management, and a limited ability to react to change. The end state looks more like an ill-planned highway system that was built by many small integration projects but with little strategic value.

An additional complication to this scenario is that IT managers must perform integration projects inside fluid environments using rapidly advancing technology. In seeking to integrate links, the manager may also encounter additional problems such as:

- A variety of legacy systems that contain mission-critical applications
- Several packaged applications with both proprietary and open frameworks
- A hodgepodge of hardware and operating system platforms
- A hodgepodge of communication protocols and networking equipment
- Geographically disbursed applications and databases

In addition to these structural limitations, the economics of traditional middleware have placed EAI out of the reach of most IT organizations. Even a simple dual-application linking is financially daunting, running as high as $10 million according to the Aberdeen Group.

Given these significant limitations, it follows that EAI represents a very different method of application integration than that using traditional middleware (see Figure 1.3). EAI provides a set of integration-level application semantics. Put another way, EAI creates a common way for both business processes and data to speak to one another across applications. More importantly, we approach this old problem with a new set of technologies designed specifically for EAI.

So, keeping this information in mind, we can focus on the following differences between traditional approaches and the vision of EAI:

- EAI focuses on the integration of both business-level processes and data, whereas the traditional middleware approach is data oriented.

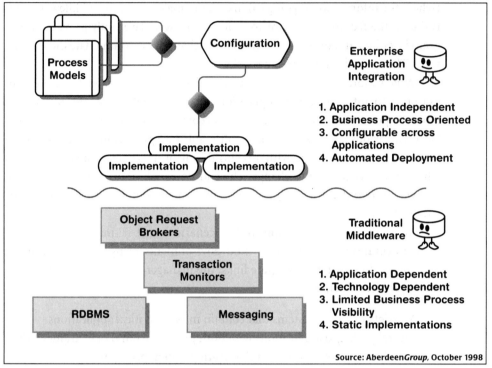

Figure 1.3   EAI versus traditional middleware

- EAI includes the notion of reuse as well as distribution of business processes and data.
- EAI allows users who understand very little about the details of the applications to integrate the applications.

How Did Things Get This Bad?

EAI answers the problem of integrating systems and applications. But how did the problem come about? The answer depends to a great extent on perspective. In the early days of computing, information was processed on centralized platforms. As a result, process and data existed in a homogeneous environment. Integrating applications (both processes and data) within the same machine rarely created a problem beyond some additional coding. As technology developed, platforms changed. Smaller and more open platforms, including UNIX and Windows NT (in addition to new programming paradigms such as object-oriented and component-based development), challenged traditional mainframes, once the backbone of IT.

Whether correctly or not, traditional IT leveraged the power of these newer, more open platforms. A number of factors contributed to this. Users wanted applications that were driven by newer and more attractive graphical user interfaces. Misreading or ignoring this desire, traditional legacy systems lagged in adopting "user-friendly" graphical user interfaces, abandoning the field to the newer platforms. Perhaps more importantly, the press trumpeted the claim that the cost of applying and maintaining the newer platforms was less than traditional systems. Sometimes this claim was correct. Often it was not.

In the rush to incorporate these new systems, most enterprises applied minimal architectural foresight to the selection of platforms and applications. IT managers made many of their decisions based on their perception of the current technology market. For example, when the UNIX platforms were popular in the early 1990s, UNIX was placed in many enterprises, regardless of how well it fit. Today, the same is true of Windows NT.

Clearly, the installation of these systems has been a textbook example of "management-by-magazine." Rather than making sound, business-driven decisions, or evaluating all possible solutions, decisions were made to implement the "coolest" technology.

While acknowledging that smaller and more open systems can hold a very important place in the enterprise, this decision-making process lacked the perspective and foresight that might have minimized, or possibly avoided, many integration problems. The success of these smaller, more open systems was that they met the requirement of commodity computing but with a steep price—the need for integration with the existing, older system.

The need for EAI is the direct result of this architectural foresight, or rather, the lack of it. Until recently, architecture at the enterprise level had been virtually nonexistent. Information technology decisions tended to be made at the department level, with each department selecting technology and solutions around its own needs and belief structures. For example, accounting may have built their information systems around a mainframe, while human resources leveraged the power of distributed objects, and research and development might have used distributed transaction processing technology. The end result could have been a mixing and matching of technologies and paradigms. As a result, the enterprise as a whole was left with a "system" that is nearly impossible to integrate without fundamental re-architecture—and a significant investment of precious funds.

To address the problem of architectural foresight, many organizations have created the role of the enterprise architect. This person or office is responsible for overseeing a centralized architecture and making sure that technology and solutions selected for the enterprise are functionally able to interact well with one another. As a result, departments will be able to share processes and data with a minimum of additional work.

Enterprise architects will be called upon to make some unpopular decisions. They will be charged with making decisions regarding the commitment to a single programming paradigm and technology religion. If the enterprise goes to distributed objects, it must do so as a unified whole. Tough, centralized decisions must be made. The idea of selecting technology for technology's sake is today a proposition that is simply too expensive. Corporate America is finally shutting down the playground that was once information technology.

Chaos Today, Order Tomorrow

The establishment of enterprise architects is a significant and positive development. Often, in addition to developing a central long-term strategy for the future, the role of the architect is to coordinate the technology that is already in place.

Most enterprises leverage many different technologies. The integration of these technologies is almost always a difficult and chaotic proposition. Traditional middleware technology, such as message-queuing software, ties applications together, but these "point-to-point" solutions create single links between many applications, as we mentioned previously. As a result, the integration solution itself may become more expensive to maintain than the applications it's connecting.

When using the point-to-point approach, integrating applications comes down to altering each application to be able to send and receive messages. This can be accomplished with any number of **message-oriented middleware (MOM)** products (e.g., IBM's MQSeries). While this is easily managed within the context of integrating two applications, integrating additional applications demands additional pipes. If you have successfully integrated application A with application B and would like to include applications C and D, you will have to create a pipe between each involved application. In no time, the process will grow so complex as to render it almost unmanageable. (See Figure 1.4.)

This "solution" is absurd. However, traditional middleware leaves no other choice but to leverage this type of architecture.

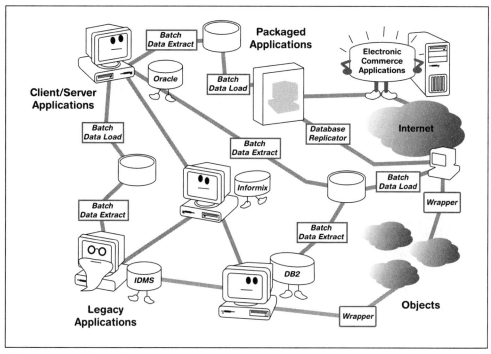

Figure 1.4   Enterprise chaos

Many enterprises that needed to integrate applications have implemented such integration architectures within their enterprises and continue to maintain them today.

While it is easy to criticize these enterprises, they have done the best they could, given the available technology. Unfortunately, even their best efforts have resulted in chaos.

The question is, If such chaos exists today, what can tomorrow hold?

The "order solution" to this chaos is twofold. First, the enterprise needs to understand the large-picture architecture. Understanding the processes and the data that exist within the enterprise and how each exists within the context of the other is the necessary first step in moving forward. Then, understanding the architecture, the enterprise can determine which applications and data stores need to share information, and why. With this basic requirement established, it is simply a matter of determining the correct architecture and enabling technology to solve the problem.

Sounds easy, doesn't it? It is—on paper. The truth of the matter is that enterprises are much more complex and difficult to contend with than one may think. Obstacles, such as interdepartmental turf battles and constantly changing business requirements, have little to do with technology but a lot to do with hindering solutions. Because a sound EAI solution often requires a change in organization, the psychological considerations of the workforce and the flow chart structures of the enterprise must be handled appropriately.

Second, new technology must be leveraged to solve the EAI problem. For example, point-to-point middleware, while providing value within the enterprise, does not—and cannot—provide the ultimate solution. **Message brokers** provide a vital "middle ground," offering real promise while other technologies are being created. These brokers are able to move messages from any type of system to any other type of system by changing the format of the messages so that they make sense to the target system. Message brokers also assure that messages are delivered in the correct sequence and in the correct context of the application. (See Figure 1.5.)

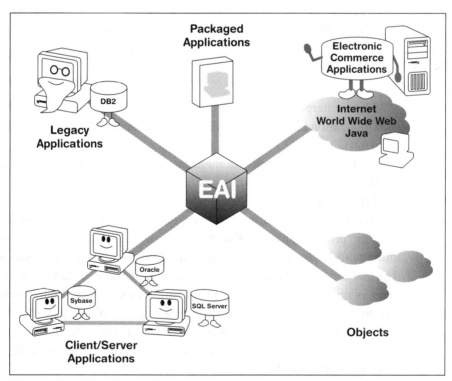

Figure 1.5   Using EAI technology to bring order to an enterprise

In addition to integrating messages and data, developers are learning to integrate processes as well. A new generation of application servers and distributed object technologies for solving the problem of integrating processes is appearing on the market. These technologies allow developers to build and reuse business processes within an enterprise—even between enterprises.

Evolution of Stovepipes

Within enterprises exist many stovepipe applications that address and solve very narrow problems within departments. (See Figure 1.6.) For example, the new SAP system implemented in accounting is a natural stovepipe application at the module level. Inventory control applications that exist within the sales organization and the resume-tracking system in human resources are also examples of stovepipe applications.

These applications came about when traditional mainframe systems failed to solve departmental problems or, more likely, did not solve them quickly enough. Because of this failure, a "departmentalized" solution ensued, and critical

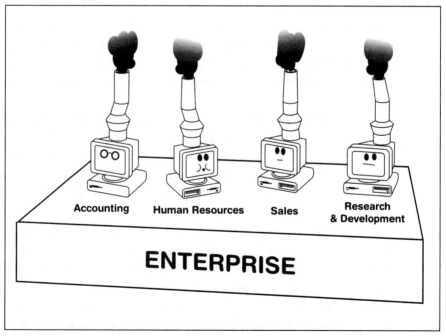

Figure 1.6   Many stovepipe applications exist in an enterprise.

departments implemented their own systems—systems that they owned, maintained, and *protected*.

While departments might have been protective toward their stovepipe systems, that did not mean that they, or the people who maintained them, did not want to share information; it just meant that data, and the audience for the system, typically existed within a single department. Inevitably, this reality demonstrated that the system was built without much thought having been given to the requirements for information sharing. As a result, there were no open application programming interfaces (APIs), open architectures, or other mechanisms that allowed for ready access to the processes and data that existed within these stovepipe systems.

The increased number of enterprise resource-planning applications and other packaged applications that are becoming commonplace in most enterprises represent the "mothers of all stovepipe systems." These systems do not provide effective methods for accessing data and processes within their own environments, and, while interfaces to these packaged applications are improving with time, integrating them within the enterprise represents a significant challenge.

Traditional Systems

Traditional systems (also known as "legacy systems") are stovepipe applications that may exist with many other stovepipe applications in a centralized environment. While mainframes continue to make up the majority of traditional systems, minicomputers and even large UNIX systems may also correctly be called traditional systems.

The characteristics that define the traditional system include centralized processing with terminal-based access. Features of the traditional system include both database and business processing existing together within the same environment. In addition, traditional systems typically support a large user and processing load. It is not unusual for these systems to support thousands of users concurrently accessing the same application.

The significance of this is that the much heralded death of traditional systems has proven to have been somewhat premature. Rather than becoming extinct, these systems not only continue to sell, but older applications leveraging traditional systems have demonstrated significantly more staying power than originally anticipated. The rise of EAI could be attributed, in part, to the need to maintain these older applications and integrate them within the new enterprise application infrastructure.

Microcomputer Systems

Microcomputer systems—personal computers—that exist within the enterprise today represent a significant challenge to those who seek to implement EAI within the corporation. This challenge is made clear by the fact that microcomputers exist on thousands of desktops within an organization, each microcomputer containing valuable information and processes. Complicating the situation is the fact that no two microcomputers are exactly alike. As a result, integrating the data and processes that may exist on these desktops within the enterprise could prove to be a nightmare.

Traditional microcomputer application development, such as those applications built during the rise of the PC, left far too many processes existing on the desktop and thus potentially impossible to access. Accessing both the processes and the data that exist on microcomputers may require rehosting, or moving the processes and data to a centralized server.

Distributed Systems

Simply stated, **distributed systems** are any number of workstation servers and hosts tied together by a network that supports any number of applications. This definition covers a broad spectrum of computing trends—client/server, Internet/intranet, and distributed object computing architectures.

Distributed computing implies that distribution provides clear benefits, including **scalability** and fault-tolerance. While these benefits do exist to a certain degree, distributed systems, though architecturally elegant, are difficult to implement. The majority of failed application development projects over the past decade resulted from overly complex distributed computing architectures. This does not mean that distributed computing is always a bad architecture. It does, however, urge caution and a broad perspective. Distributed computing, like any other powerful computing concept, must exist within context with other types of solutions.

Despite the complexities of distributed computing, there is a real advantage to this architecture when it is considered with EAI. Because the architecture is already distributed—riding on open systems with open, better-defined interfaces—it lends itself well to integration when compared to traditional, centralized computing architecture.

Packaged Applications

Packaged applications are any type of application that is purchased rather than developed. These applications contain reusable business processes that represent best-of-breed business models and don't require a full-scale development effort. The benefit to business is plain: Why develop a new inventory control system when the best inventory control system already exists?

While enterprise resource-planning applications are the leaders in the packaged applications market, many other types of packaged applications are finding their way into the enterprises. These include call center applications, sales automation applications, and inventory control applications.

While the question, "Why develop a new application when a packaged one exists?" is a valid one, the truth is that the popularity of packaged applications may very well be the driving force for EAI. Packaged applications are natural stovepipes. As we have seen, any stovepipe application is difficult to integrate with the rest of the enterprise.

EAI has been brought into play as a mechanism, not only to integrate existing enterprise applications, but also to integrate and free the information from the new generation of packaged applications. This was clear from the earliest days of EAI when most, if not all, integration efforts focused on bundling packaged applications.

Packaged applications mean so much within the context of EAI that we have dedicated several chapters of this book to discussing the details of the major enterprise resource-planning applications, including SAP and People-Soft.

Making the Business Case for EAI

We have already noted that the business environment no longer supports using technology for technology's sake. To justify its expense, a technology must demonstrate its usefulness. EAI is no exception.

While the business case for EAI is clear to most people versed in the technical aspects of this discussion, it might not be as clear to those who really need to understand its value. For example: will implementing EAI within an enterprise provide a return worthy of the investment? If so, how long before the return is realized? Is EAI a short-term or long-term proposition? And, perhaps most importantly, what are the methods that best measure success?

Before we make the business case for EAI, a number of things should be understood. First, implementing EAI requires that someone thoroughly understand the business processes in the enterprise. It is only by using this information that the degree of integration necessary to optimize those business processes can be determined. While there are methodologies and procedures that can be applied, most competent managers understand the degree of value when applying EAI without over-analyzing this information.

Not all organizations are equal. For this reason, some organizations will benefit more than others from EAI. While some organizations clearly demand an EAI initiative, others might find almost no value in implementing EAI within their enterprises. If a customer leverages a single, host-based computer system with few applications existing on that platform, only a few thousand users would have only limited benefit from EAI. When applications and data exist within the same environment, they are much easier to integrate. For years programmers have been successfully integrating homogeneous applications.

However, it is when applications and data do not exist within the same environment; when the organization has gone through mergers or acquisitions; when it has experienced uncontrolled architecture and unruly application development projects; or when it has a large, distributed system with a multitude of platforms and protocols that exist to support hundreds, or thousands of users, that the enterprise will realize a tremendous benefit from EAI.

While it may be possible to develop a "common sense" set of metrics to evaluate the success of EAI, the reality is that in most cases they must be significantly adjusted on a case-by-case basis to account for the many factors that exist in any given enterprise. Because of this, there is no easy way to create a broad-based way to define EAI success. It must be measured enterprise by enterprise.

In order to evaluate the value of EAI to your enterprise, you must establish a set of measures that define success for your organization. This can be accomplished by examining and measuring the current state of the enterprise. With this baseline, consider your goals and the amount of effort that will be required for you to realize them.

For example, if increasing sales is one of your goals, sharing inventory information with the sales order-processing system may allow sales to operate more effectively and thus help realize that goal. Even so, without a significant gain in user productivity or a reduction in error rate, the integration effort between two systems has minimal value. Therefore, in order to accurately assess EAI, you need to weigh both user productivity and error reduction, giving a measure to both. Only then can you determine the impact of EAI on your enterprise.

The Virtual System

The ultimate EAI scenario is the common virtual system. This allows any and all information required for all transactions to be immediately available no matter

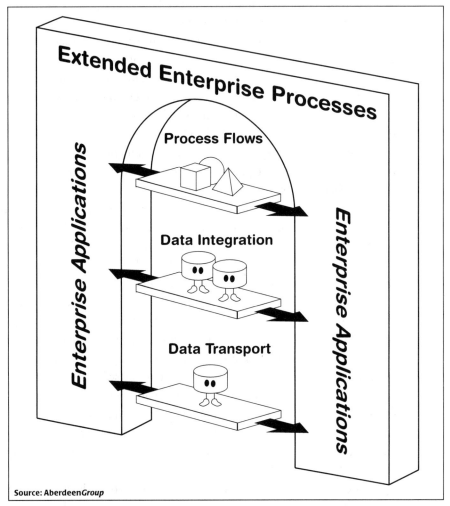

Figure 1.7   Extending the enterprise with EAI

where the information is located in the enterprise. Every application, database, transaction table, method, and other element of enterprise computing is accessible anytime, anywhere.

EAI is able to take many diverse systems and bundle them in such a way that they appear—and function—as a monolithic and unified application (see Figure 1.7). While this represents the nirvana of EAI—and as such is not achievable for most organizations in the near future—it represents what ultimately is the perfect integration of systems possible with EAI.

e-Business

e-Business (i.e., using electronic mechanisms to conduct business between your trading partners and your customers) is an ideally efficient method of commerce. e-Business comes in two "flavors": one, business-to-business inclusive of supply chain integration and, two, business-to-consumer, inclusive of Internet commerce or conducting commerce on the Web. While both "flavors" would benefit from EAI, it is a natural fit for business-to-business or supply chain integration in that one is able to serve the needs of the other.

The mechanism techniques and technology that make up EAI are also applicable to most supply chain integration scenarios, or Inter-Enterprise Application Integration. Because EAI is very good at integrating various applications and data stores, it is able to extend its reach outside the enterprise to include both trading partners and customers within the enterprise integration architecture. This enables any application or data store to share information with any other application or data store that exists within the supply chain scenario.

Using EAI mechanisms and technology allows you to link, for example, your SAP system to your supplier's Baan system and move information between them as needed to support the supply chain integration scenario. You may also include a "dealer" system in your supply chain by using EAI technology and techniques to first create the links and then the methods to share both data and business processes.

EAI is the "missing link" that has been absent in the quest for success in supply chain integration efforts of the past. There has always been the desire to have systems communicate seamlessly with suppliers' systems, but until now inexpensive solutions that could make it happen have not existed. The new generation of middleware that supports EAI concepts could make this a reality.

As in supply chain integration, business-to-consumer EAI is the process of exposing information within your enterprise to people or entities, known and unknown, that exist outside your enterprise. For example, if you want to expand your sales order entry system to allow unknown customers to link to your company Web site and purchase your products, you would have to expose that information using techniques and technology created by EAI.

Business-to-consumer e-business was slow to start, but its now explosive growth is becoming more and more evident every day—you need only consider amazon.com or barnsesandnoble.com to appreciate this.

Types of EAI

When contemplating EAI in your organization, you must first understand the sum and content of the business processes and data in your organization. IT also needs to understand how these business processes are automated (and sometimes not automated) and the importance of all business processes. Depending on your enterprise, this may demand a significant amount of time and energy. Many organizations seek new methodologies to assist them in this process and look closely at the best practices.

In brief, organizations must understand both business processes and data. They must select which processes and data elements require integration. This process can take on several dimensions, including:

- Data level
- Application interface level
- Method level
- User interface level

While this book includes chapters devoted to each type of EAI, a brief overview of the various types is provided here (see Figure 1.8).

Data-level EAI is the process—and the techniques and technology—of moving data between data stores. This can be described as extracting information from one database, perhaps processing that information as needed, and updating it in another database. While this sounds direct and straightforward, in a typical EAI-enabled enterprise, it might mean drawing from as many as one hundred databases and several thousands of tables. It may also include the transformation and application of business logic to the data that is being extracted and loaded.

The advantage of data-level EAI is the cost of using this approach. Because we are largely leaving the application alone, and not changing code, we don't need to incur the expense of changing, testing, and deploying the application. What's more, the technology that provides mechanisms to move data between databases, as well as reformats that information, is relatively inexpensive considering the other EAI levels and their applicable enabling technology.

The approach and enabling technology you leverage depends on the requirements of the problem domain.

Application interface–level EAI refers to the leveraging of interfaces exposed by custom or packaged applications. Developers leverage these inter-

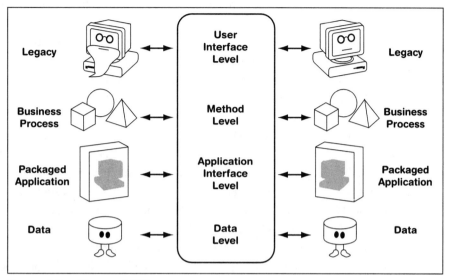

Figure 1.8   Types of EAI

faces to access both business processes and simple information. Using these interfaces, developers are able to bundle many applications together, allowing them to share business logic and information. The only limitations that developers face are the specific features and functions of the application interfaces.

This type of EAI is most applicable to packaged applications such as SAP, PeopleSoft, and Baan, which all expose interfaces into their processes and data, but do so in very different ways. In order to integrate those systems with others in the enterprise, we must use these interfaces to access both processes and data, extract the information, place it in a format understandable by the target application, and transmit the information. While many different types of technologies can do this, message brokers seem to be the preferred solution.

Method-level EAI is the sharing of the business logic that may exist within the enterprise. For example, the method for updating a customer record may be accessed from any number of applications, and applications may access each other's methods without having to rewrite each method within the respective application.

The mechanisms to share methods among applications are numerous, including distributed objects, application servers, TP (transaction processing) monitors, frameworks, and simply creating a new application that's the combination of two or more applications. There are two basic approaches: You may create a shared set of application servers that exist on a shared physical server, such as an application server, or you may share methods already existing inside of applications using distributed method-sharing technology such as distributed objects.

Method-level EAI is something we've been practicing for years as we sought to reuse application development efforts within the enterprises. We've not been largely successful due to both human and technological issues. Perhaps with EAI, we may get it right.

User interface–level EAI is a more primitive, but nonetheless necessary, approach. Using this scenario, architects and developers are able to bundle applications by using their user interfaces as a common point of integration (also known as screen scraping). For example, mainframe applications that do not provide database- or business process–level access may be accessed through the user interface of the application.

Although many consider leveraging the user interface as a point of integration to be an unstable and archaic approach, the fact is that we've been doing this for years and have worked out many of the issues, such as performance, reliability, and scalability. Although not preferred, it may be the only solution you have in many instances. Remember, EAI at its heart is the ability to leverage any existing system by finding a reliable point-of-integration. Existing 3270 interface middleware that is typically bundled with emulators is an enabling technology to serve user interface–level EAI .

Middleware and EAI

Much of the content of this book is devoted to middleware technology. While many texts describe the features and functions of middleware, in the world of EAI, middleware is used as a simple mechanism to move information and share business logic between applications. In short, middleware is the underlying technology of EAI.

As we have previously suggested, application integration has been going on for years, using a broad range of connection technology. In the past, this has been low-level play with developers working at the network protocol layer or just above, then moving to true middleware solutions such as RPCs, MOM, and **transactional middleware**. The next generation of middleware is here with new categories such as message brokers, application servers (this is actually an old category, but you wouldn't know it from the press), distributed objects, and intelligent agents. However, expect more middleware and middleware categories to emerge as more people become interested in EAI.

So, what's middleware? **Middleware** hides the complexities of the underlying operating system and network in order to facilitate the easy integration of various systems in the enterprise. Developers, generally speaking, deal with an API on each system, and the middleware handles the passing of information through the different systems on behalf of the application. These APIs are general purpose data movement or process invocation mechanisms. They typically don't know which applications and databases they are tying together. Developers have to create the links for the middleware; however, we are moving to a more plug-and-play solution set where the middleware is able to integrate applications intelligently with little or no programming.

Middleware provides developers with an easy way to integrate external resources using a common set of application services. External resources may include a database server, a queue, a 3270 terminal, Enterprise Resource Planning (ERP) applications, custom API, or access to real-time information. In the world of distributed computing, middleware usually is a means for connecting clients to servers, clients to clients, and servers to servers without having to navigate through many operating systems, networks, or resource server layers.

The advent of advanced middleware layers allowed distributed application development to take off. Middleware provided developers and application architects with the ability to bridge many different systems, bringing them together to form virtual systems. In fact, analyst groups such as Gartner have suggested that we are moving to a paradigm of the **Zero Latency Enterprise** where any application (or transaction) has access to any other application or data store instantaneously, without restriction.

It's certainly something worth aiming for.

CHAPTER TWO

Data-Level EAI

"You can use all the quantitative data you can get, but you still have to distrust it and use your own intelligence and judgment."

—Alvin Toffler

Most enterprises considering EAI look to data level EAI as their entry point, a decision that would allow moving data between data stores in order to share relevant business information among applications and, ultimately, stovepipes. An advantage of data level as an entry point for EAI is that a number of tools and techniques exist that allow the integration of information from database to database, adapting the information on the fly so it's represented correctly by the source and target applications. Further simplifying data-level EAI is the fact that accessing databases is a relatively easy task, which can be accomplished with few significant—if any—changes to the application logic or database structure.

However, the relative simplicity of data-level EAI should not give one the impression that it is simple. It is not. Migrating data from one database to another may sound simple and reasonable, but for data-level EAI to work, architects and developers need to understand the complex world of database technology as well as the way information flows throughout an enterprise (discussed in detail in Chapter 6).

In most enterprises, databases number in the thousands and represent a complex mosaic of various database technologies and models that provide data storage for applications. This reality makes integrating databases a difficult task, one that was virtually impossible before the introduction of powerful many-to-many EAI data movement and transformation tools and technologies.

Going for the Data

Accessing data in the context of EAI requires an "end run" around application logic and user interfaces in order to extract or load data directly into the database through an interface (see Figure 2.1). Fortunately, most applications built in the past two decades or so decouple the database from the application and interface, making this a relatively simple task. However, many databases are tightly coupled with the application logic. It is impossible to deal with the database without dealing with the application logic as well. This, of course, is a much more difficult proposition. It may be reason enough to employ method-level EAI along with data-level EAI, or even consider using method-level EAI exclusively.

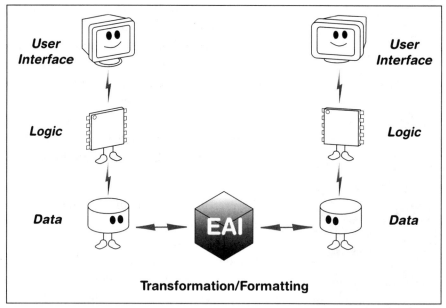

Figure 2.1   Within the context of EAI we sneak behind the application and extract or update data directly.

Coupling versus Cohesion

In looking at the applications and databases that make up the problem domain, it is necessary to consider the integration alternative. Generally speaking, it comes down to coupling versus cohesion.

In the dictionary, coupling might be described as the act of bringing or coming together. In terms of EAI, it's binding logic with data, logic with logic (e.g., a composite application), and/or data with data.

While coupling may seem like a good idea, it is really binding one application domain tightly to the next, and as such, it will require changing all coupled applications and databases in order to integrate them. What's more, as things evolve over time, a change to any source or target system means a change to the coupled systems as well. Coupling creates one application and database out of many, with each very dependent on the other. The downside to coupling is minor while the advantages are great, including tight integration with all source and target systems and the ability to better share and reuse application logic.

Cohesion, in contrast, is the "act or state of sticking together," or "the logical agreement." The applications and databases are independent, and thus changes to any source or target system should not affect the others. The advantage of cohesion is the ability to share information between databases and applications, without regard for application and database changes. Because the EAI solution is fundamentally cohesive rather than coupled, changes to a source or target system should not require that changes be made to the other systems in the EAI problem domain.

So, which is the best approach? It really depends. The cohesion approach provides the greatest flexibility as the EAI solution moves into the future. Systems can be added, changed, or removed from a cohesive EAI solution without requiring changes to the other systems. Generally, message brokers provide the technology infrastructure of cohesive EAI solutions, because they are able to "broker" the differences between the systems, accounting for the differences in the application semantics within a middle tier process. However, if common business processes are to be reused, then a coupled approach provides more value. Distributed objects, transaction processing monitors, and application servers provide a good technology solution for a coupled EAI solution.

Will XML Bring Standards to Data Movement Metadata?

While several standards bodies are seeking to define data movement and repository standards in support of EAI, the best option may already be available. The **Extensible Markup Language (XML)**, stolen from the world of the Web, may be just what the enterprise needs for a unified look at data.

Like **Hypertext Markup Language (HTML)**, XML is a subset of Standard Generalized Markup Language (SGML), a venerable standard for defining descriptions of structure and content in documents. However, where HTML is limited in that it can only provide a universal method to display information on a page (without context or dynamic behavior), XML addresses context and gives meaning to data. XML redefines some of SGML's internal values and parameters while simultaneously removing large numbers of little-used features that make SGML so complex. In addition, XML maintains SGML's structural capabilities, letting middleware users define their own document types. It also introduces a new type of document, one in which it is unnecessary to define a document type at all.

XML metadata can be any attribute able to be assigned to a piece of data. The metadata can represent more abstract concepts such as the industry associated with a particular document. XML can also be used to encode any number of existing metadata standards.

Because XML doesn't depend on any particular type of metadata format, there is little risk that a particular technology vendor will define its own set of metadata tags. In other words, XML cannot be made proprietary to a particular type of data.

XML is so important to EAI that we've included a chapter (Chapter 17) dedicated to leveraging XML for EAI.

Data-level EAI provides simplicity and speed-to-market. These advantages are the result of the fact that the business logic rarely has to be altered (a cohesive and not coupled approach). As a result, there is no need to endure the seemingly countless testing cycles, or the risk and expense of implementing newer versions of an application within any enterprise. Indeed, most users and applications will remain ignorant of the fact that data is being shared at the back-end.

The numerous database-oriented middleware products that allow architects and developers to access and move information between databases simplify data-level EAI. These tools and technologies allow for the integration of various database brands, such as Oracle and Sybase. They also allow for the integration of different database models, such as object-oriented and relational, models that we will discuss later in the chapter.

The advent of EAI-specific technology, such as message brokers, EAI management layers, and simple data movement engines gives the enterprise the ability to move data from one place to another—from anywhere to anywhere—without altering the target application source. What's more, this can now be done in real time, within online transaction-processing environments.

The technology for moving data between two or more data stores is a known quantity, well tested in real applications. Unfortunately, these gains do not exempt the architect or the developer from understanding the data that is being moved or from understanding the flow and business rules that must be applied to that data.

Data-Level EAI by Example

To better understand data-level EAI, it's helpful to work through a simple EAI problem. Let's say that a company that manufactures copper wiring would like to hook up the inventory control system, a client/server system using PowerBuilder and Oracle, and the **Enterprise Resource Planning (ERP)** system by using a proprietary application and the Informix relational database.

Primarily because the data movement requirements are light to moderate, and changing the proprietary ERP application to bind its logic with the inventory control system is not an option (because there is no access to the source code of the ERP application), the company would like to solve this EAI problem using data-level EAI.

In order to move data from the Oracle database to Informix, the EAI architect and developer first need to understand the metadata for each database in order to select the data that will move from one database to the next. In our example, let's assume that only sales data must move from one database to the other. For example, when a sale is recorded in the ERP system, creating an event, the new information is copied over to the inventory control system for order-fulfillment operations.

Another decision to be made involves frequency of the data movement. Let's say real time is a requirement for this problem domain. The event to be captured must also be defined in order to signal when the data needs to be copied, such as a specific increment for time (e.g., every 5 seconds) or when a state changes (e.g., an update to a table occurs).

There are many technologies and techniques for moving the data from one database to the next, including database replication software, message brokers, and custom-built utilities. Each comes with its own advantages and disadvantages, advantages and disadvantages that will become apparent later in this book. For our purposes here, we'll go with a database replication and integration solution, or piece of software that runs between the databases that's able to extract information out of one database, say the Informix database, reformat the data (changing content and schema) if needed, and updating the Oracle database. While this is a one-to-one scenario, one-to-many works the same way, as does many-to-many, albeit with more splitting, combining, and reformatting going on.

Once the middle-tier database replication software is in place, the information is extracted, reformatted, and updated from the Oracle database to the Informix database, and back again. The data is replicated between the two databases when an update occurs at either end to the corresponding sales table.

Using this simple approach, the application logic is bypassed, with the data moving between the databases at the data level. As a result, changes to the application logic at the source, or the target systems as in this case, provide an EAI solution when an application cannot be changed, such as is the case with most ERP applications.

There are more complex problem domains that also make sense for data-level EAI, such as moving data between traditional mainframe, file-oriented databases and more modern relational databases, relational databases to object databases, multidimensional databases to mainframe databases, or any combination of these. Once again, database replication and translation software and message brokers provide the best solutions, able to cohesively tie all source and target databases without requiring changes to the connected databases or application logic. This is the real value of nonintrusive approaches such as data-level EAI.

There are two basic approaches to data-level EAI and its accompanying enabling technology: database-to-database EAI and federated database EAI.

Database-to-Database EAI

Database-to-database EAI, like the point-to-point approach, is something we've been doing well for years. **Database-to-database EAI** means that we're simply sharing information at the database level and, by doing so, integrating applications.

Database-to-database EAI can exist in one-to-one, one-to-many, or many-to-many configurations. We approach database-to-database EAI with traditional **database middleware** and database replication software, such as replication features built into many databases (e.g., Sybase), or through database integration software. Message brokers also work with database-to-database EAI, but in the absence of sharing methods cohesively or needing to access complex systems, such as ERP applications, they tend to be overkill.

There are two types of solutions here. First, the basic replication solution moves information between databases that maintain the same basic schema information on all source and target databases. The second solution is replication and transformation. Using these types of products, it is possible to move information between many different types of databases, including various brands (e.g., Sybase, Oracle, and Informix) and models (relational, object-oriented, and multidimensional), by transforming the data on the fly so it's represented correctly to the target database or databases receiving the data. Such is the case in the inventory control system example described previously.

The advantage of this EAI approach is the simplicity of it all. By dealing with application information at the data level, there is no need to change the source or target applications, generally speaking. This reduces the risk and cost of implementing EAI. In many applications, the downside to this approach is the fact that the application logic is bound to the data, and it's difficult to manipulate the database without going through the application, or at least the application interface. This is certainly the case with SAP R/3, where, in order to avoid integrity problems, updating the database generally demands using the SAP R/3 interface.

Federated Database EAI

Federated database EAI also works at the database level, like database-to-database EAI. However, rather than simply replicating data across various databases, **federated database** software is leveraged to allow developers to access any number of databases, using various brands, models, and schemas, through a single "virtual" database model. This virtual database model exists only in software and is mapped to any number of connected physical databases. The developers use this virtual database as a single point of application integration, accessing data from any number of systems through the same single database interface.

The advantage of this approach is the reliance on middleware to share information between applications, and not a custom solution. Moreover, the middleware hides the differences in the integrated databases from the other applications that are using the integrated view of the databases. Unfortunately, this is really not a true integration approach; while there is a common view of many databases, a "unified model," there will still be the need to create the logic for integrating the applications with the databases.

Consider the Data Source

In order to implement data-level EAI, you first must consider the sources of the data and the database technology that houses the data. There is both good and bad news here for those looking to implement EAI within their organizations. The good news is that the majority of databases in existence today use the homogeneous relational database model, making it relatively simple to "mix and match" data from various databases. The bad news is that there are still many exceptions that form the "minority" heterogeneous models.

Relational databases make up the significant portion of the new application development that has occurred during the past 10 to 15 years. Unfortunately, traditional databases, such as those found on legacy systems, still hold the lion's share of enterprise data. Implementing EAI will mean confronting such old "friends" as IDMS, IMS, VSAM, ISAM, and even COBOL-driven flat files. Most of these will be defined later in the chapter.

When dealing with databases it is important to understand the following:

- The model that the database uses to store information
- The nature of the database itself, and how the differences between the databases existing within enterprises also provide an opportunity for integration

Relational Data

Relational databases are the reigning monarchs of the database world, and there is precious little sign of a palace coup occurring anytime soon. While many have questioned the enduring strength of relational databases, the simplicity of the model stands as the most compelling reason for their popularity. We seem to think in the relational model already. And, we continue to use databases primarily as storage mechanisms for data versus a location for application processing. Relational databases meet that need nicely.

Other factors that contribute to the popularity of relational databases include the availability of the technology, the fact that they are understandable, and that they pose the least amount of risk for systems. Using nonrelational

> ## Being All Things to All Data—Universal Databases
>
> While there might be no coup in sight, there is indeed palace intrigue afoot. There is a movement to retrofit existing relational databases to handle objects and other data types. These hybrid databases, known as **universal databases**, purport to be "all things to all data." The major players in the universal database market include Oracle, Informix, and Sybase.
>
> In mid-1996, Oracle announced the introduction of its universal database, Oracle's Universal Server, which integrated the existing Oracle database server with several special purpose services that included text, video, message, spatial data, and HTML by using an object-oriented or relational model. Informix took a different architectural approach. To support objects, Informix bought an object-oriented database company, Illustra. Informix is building the Illustra database into Informix's existing relational database technology. Rather than build object-oriented capabilities into its existing relational engine, Sybase looked to support objects through a partnering relationship with Persistence Software. Persistence provides a middleware solution that can map relational databases (such as Sybase's SQL Server) into objects on the fly. This strategy—layering a product on top of an existing relational database engine—will allow Sybase to handle objects before other database vendors.

products (e.g., object-oriented and multidimensional databases) adds risk to enterprise application development projects due to the lack of support from the mainstream development market. Still, nonrelational databases do serve niches and make sense, depending upon the application. This could change, of course, in the near future. Relational database vendors such as Oracle, Sybase, and Informix provide universal databases (see "Being All Things to All Data—Universal Databases" above) that can pretend to be object-oriented, multidimensional, Web-ready (intranet as well), and capable of storing binary information such as video.

Relational databases organize data in dimensional tables—and nothing but tables—that are tied together using common attributes (known as keys). Each table has rows and columns (see Figure 2.2).

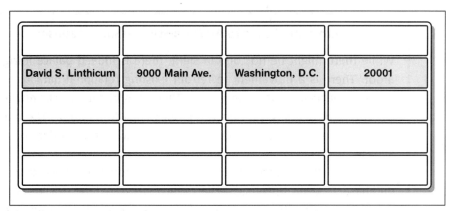

Figure 2.2   Relational table

Rows contain an instance of the data. For example, an address would be a row in a customer table in the database of a local power company (see Figure 2.2). Therefore, each row represents a record.

Columns are named placeholders for data, defining the type of data the column is set up to contain. For example, the columns for the customer table may include:

- Cust_Number
- Cust_First_Name
- Cust_Last_Name
- Cust_Address
- Cust_City
- Cust_Zip
- Cust_Birth_Day

While some columns may be set up to accept both text and numeric data, the Cust_Birth_Day column would be set up to accept only date-formatted information (e.g., 09/17/62), and the Cust_Number column would accept only numeric data.

As suggested previously, keys are columns common to two or more tables. Keys link rows to form groupings of data. Consider the previous example. While the customer table tracks information about power customers, there may be a billing table to track billing information. The columns in the billing table may include:

- Cust_Number
- Billing_Month
- Billing_Amount

In this example, the Cust_Number column is common to both tables and acts as a key to link the two databases. And, while there may be only one row in the customer table, the billing table may contain many rows.

Object-Oriented

Soon after it was articulated, the object-oriented model was considered a real threat to the dominance of the relational model. While object-oriented databases are certainly more prevalent than they were, they are a long way from toppling Sybase, Oracle, Informix, and IBM. Still, they have exerted their influence. Most relational vendors include object-oriented capabilities within their existing relational database technology—"universal databases," as we've noted previously. Perhaps more to the point, growing interest in the Web is renewing interest in the object-oriented model for content and Web-aware data storage.

It is still very much a "relational world," but many OODBMSs are making inroads into organizations that find the object-oriented database model a better fit for certain applications, including persistent XML. OODBMSs meet the information storage requirements for mission-critical systems having complex information storage needs, such as applications requiring storage of complex data (repositories) or applications using binary data (audio, video, and images). Fortunately, the choice today needn't be an "either-or" one. In addition to universal servers, there exists the middleware necessary to make relational databases appear as object-oriented.

Those with experience in object-oriented programming languages (such as C++ or Smalltalk) already understand how objects contain both data and the methods to access that data. OODBMSs are nothing more than systems that use this model as the basis for storing information and thus support the object-oriented concepts of encapsulation and inheritance.

Data management illustrates the fundamental differences between traditional relational database technology and object-oriented database technology. In traditional relational databases, developers separate the methods (programs that act upon the data) from the data. By contrast, object-oriented databases combine data and method. This synergy between data and method poses a significant challenge for EAI, because data-level EAI presumes and works best when data and application are separate. In order to address this challenge within object-oriented databases, data-level and method-level EAI must be combined.

Multidimensional

Multidimensional databases have evolved over the years and have been repackaged as databases that support online analytical processing (OLAP) or data mining—all wrapped up in a concept known as **data warehousing**. Currently, data warehousing is the focus of many MIS directors whose goal it is to turn thousands of gigabytes of company operational data into meaningful information for those who need it. Multidimensional databases are the tools that allow this goal to be realized.

Multidimensional databases manipulate data as if it resides in a giant cube. Each surface of the cube represents a dimension of the multidimensional database (see Figure 2.3). For example, while one side may represent sales, another may represent customers, and another, sales districts. The interior of the cube contains all the possible intersections of the dimensions, allowing the end user to examine every possible combination of the data by "slicing and dicing" his or her way through the cube with an OLAP tool that, for our purposes, must be understood to be joined "at the hip" with the multidimensional database.

OLAP products store data in one of two basic ways. The first is a true multidimensional database server, where the data is actually stored as a multidimensional

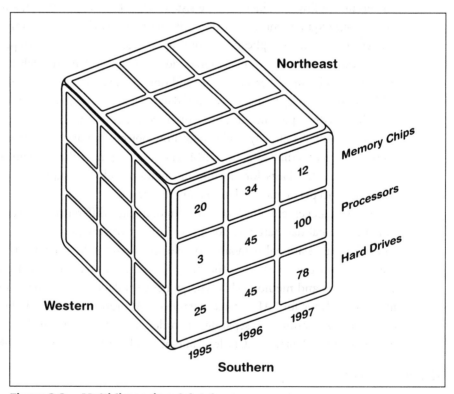

Figure 2.3   Multidimensional database

array or, a "real cube." A second, more convenient way to employ OLAP is to maintain the data in relational databases but map that data so it appears as multidimensional data—in other words, a "virtual cube" where the illusion of a "real cube" exists at the metadata layer.

The power of multidimensional databases and OLAP is that the technology provides a multidimensional view of the database that closely resembles the way the end user understands the business. OLAP offers a natural, "drill-down" interface that allows users to move through layer after layer of data abstraction until they find the information they require. Once found, the data is easily graphed, printed, or imported into documents and spreadsheets.

Other Data Storage Models

While the models previously described capture the primary models and methods of data storage, the reality is that many other technologies and models are out there. Within the problem domain of EAI, it is possible to encounter older, but certainly workable, methods such as hierarchical, indexed sequential access method (ISAM), virtual sequential access method (VSAM), Conference on Data Systems Languages (CODASYL), and Adabas. There may also be simple flat files and proprietary data storage techniques devised within the confines of the enterprise or by a now-defunct vendor.

One should keep in mind that the only surprise in EAI is no surprises.

Hierarchical

Databases subscribing to the **hierarchical database model** allow data representation in a set of one-to-many relationships. Each record in a hierarchy may have several offspring. IDMS, now part of Computer Associates, is an example of a hierarchical database model.

ISAM and VSAM

ISAM is a simple file organization providing sequential and direct access to records existing in a large file. ISAM is hardware dependent. VSAM is an updated version of ISAM and is also hardware dependent.

CODASYL

CODASYL is a standard created by an organization of database vendors to specify a method for data access for COBOL.

Adabas

Adabas, or the Adaptable Database, is able to support a variety of database models within a single database. It provides a high-performance database environment primarily for mainframe environments. Adabas provides a nested relational structure. It supports the relational database model to an extent, as well as document storage and retrieval.

Working with Data-Level EAI

The difficulty with data-level EAI is the large scope of integrating various databases within the enterprise. The initial desire and tendency is to solve all the integration woes of an enterprise at the same time by integrating all databases that need to communicate. However, given the complexity and difficulty in accomplishing this desired end, it is better to move forward in a clear, paced manner. Attempting to accomplish the entire process at one time is a massive undertaking and, for most enterprises, too much change to tolerate.

Enterprises should consider taking "baby steps" toward the goal of data-level EAI—and EAI in general. It would be wise to integrate two or three databases at first, allowing them to become successful, before moving forward to bigger problem domains. Not only does this ease the burden on the EAI architects pushing a new concept of EAI and shouldering a huge workload, it also eases the burden on the users who have to test the systems and work through problems as they become integrated.

CHAPTER THREE

Application Interface–Level EAI

"Computers are useless. They can only give you answers."

—Pablo Picasso

Those concerned with the EAI problem and solution define EAI at either the data model level or the business model level. They further break the business model level into three distinct types: the application interface level, the method level, and the user interface level. These distinctions result from the dynamic nature of application interfaces and the range of features and/or functions that each interface provides, as well as the design patterns they employ.

In addition to considering the two model levels, this chapter must also address the work that has been devoted to creating and using application interfaces. The simple fact is that lately, application interfaces have received a great deal of attention.

There was a time, not so very long ago, when applications were built as true monolithic stovepipes that addressed very narrow problem domains. Today, applications invariably are little more than a set of services and data that provide value to other applications. In other words, applications are no longer designed to stand alone, neither giving to nor taking from other applications.

It's about time.

The world of application interfaces is evolving rapidly. While application interfaces were once almost exclusively proprietary, APIs now use such standard mechanisms as Java's RMI (Remote Method Invocation), CORBA's (Common Object Request Broker Architecture) IIOP (Internet Inter-ORB Protocol), and Microsoft's DCOM (Distributed Component Object Model). This evolution presents today's developers with a tremendous advantage over their counterparts in the past. They can familiarize themselves with standard interfaces, no longer having to learn and implement interfaces that are not portable to other applications. Moreover, the language bindings exist from tool to tool.

Once standard interfaces are universal, integration will no longer pose such a difficult challenge for developers and architects. While development tools almost never communicate with an application using a proprietary interface, they may communicate with an application using a standard interface, making them better able to link with once-monolithic applications.

Application Interfaces

Simply put, application interfaces are interfaces that developers expose from a packaged or custom application to gain access to various levels or services of the application. Some interfaces are limited in scope while many are "feature rich." Sometimes these interfaces allow access to business processes; sometimes they allow access directly to the data. Sometimes they allow access to both.

Developers expose these interfaces for two reasons. The first is to provide access to business processes and data encapsulated within the applications they have created without forcing other developers to invoke the user interface (as outlined in Chapter 5) or to go directly to the database. Such interfaces allow external applications to access the services of these packaged or custom applications without actually making any changes to the packages or applications themselves. The second reason for exposing these types of interfaces is to provide a mechanism that allows encapsulated information to be shared. For example, if SAP data is required from Excel, SAP exposes the interfaces that allow the user to invoke a business process and/or gather common data. (SAP R/3 interfaces are dealt with in detail in Chapter 14.)

Application interfaces as a distinct type of EAI result from the fact that these scenarios are distinct from either method-level EAI or user interface–level EAI. (In the next chapter, we will discuss method-level EAI as the mechanism that allows the sharing of business logic among various applications.) While it is possible to distribute the methods that exist within enterprises among various applications, typically they are shared using a common business logic–processing mechanism, such as an application server or a distributed object. User interface–level EAI is similar to application interface–level EAI in that both make available business processes and data through an interface exposed by the packaged or custom application. However, the design pattern of the user interface–level scenario is contingent on user interaction. Traditional application interfaces, such as those provided by most popular applications, are true data- and method-sharing mechanisms utilizing traditional application interfaces. In other words, user interface–level EAI bypasses the lack of application interface by utilizing the existing user interface.

This difference in approach distinguishes application interface–level EAI from other types of EAI. The potential complexities of the application interfaces, as well as the dynamic nature of the interfaces themselves, add to the difference. Because interfaces vary widely in the number and quality of the features and functions they provide, it is nearly impossible to know what to expect when invoking an application interface. Packaged applications are "all over the board" when it comes to the types of interfaces exposed, as later chapters will make clear.

What's an API?

An understanding of **application programming interfaces (APIs)** is essential to understanding application interfaces. APIs are well-defined mechanisms that are built to connect to some sort of resource, such as an application server, middleware layer, or database (see Figure 3.1). APIs allow developers to invoke the services of these entities in order to obtain some value. For example, accessing customer information may require invoking the native middleware API for that database.

Programmers write APIs, so it should come as no surprise that they vary widely in the features and functions they provide as well as in the depth of their service offering. The best APIs can access real-time data such as information gathered from the floor of an industrial plant or draw information residing on mainframes—either by invoking a screen interaction interface, going directly to a resource, or going directly to the data.

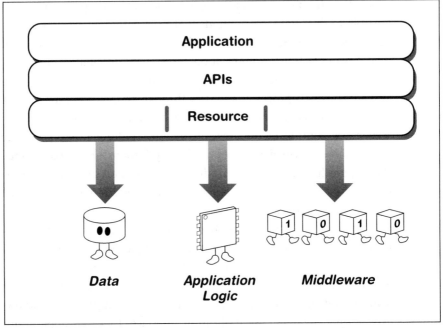

Figure 3.1   APIs are well-defined mechanisms that are built to connect to some sort of resource.

Interface by Example

The best way to understand how interfaces function in an EAI solution is to walk through an example. Let's say that a company maintains two systems: an ERP system that was just configured and installed and a custom COBOL system that has been functioning for years—a not atypical scenario. Each system exists on its own processor, connected by the corporate network.

Assume that the data-level EAI solution won't work due to the complexity of the databases and the binding of logic to the data. Thus, in order to integrate the old and new applications, the natural point of integration should be application interfaces.

Fortunately, the ERP vendor understands the need to integrate its business processes and data with the outside world and provides an API to access both. The API works within C++, C, and Java environments, with the libraries that drive the API downloadable from the company's Web site. For instance, from a C application with the appropriate API libraries existing, the function

```
GetInvoiceInformation("12345");
```

would produce:

```
<BOM>
John Smith
222 Main Street
Smalltown, VA 88888
Invoice Number: 12345
001        Red Bricks 1000      .50       500.00
<EOM>
```

The information returning from the API call is generated by invoking an API and passing in an invoice number as an argument. This information would have to be placed in an array or another location in memory (within the application program) for processing. From this point, we may place this information within a middleware layer, such as a message broker, for transmission to other systems. Understand that the database itself was not accessed directly, and the data is already bound to a business entity—namely an invoice. Using this same interface, we can also get at customer information:

```
GetCustomerInformation("cust_no");
```

or inventory information:

```
QuantityAvailable("product_no");
```

On the COBOL side, things are not quite so cut and dry. The developer and application architect who built the application did not build in an API to access the encapsulated business processes. Therefore, the application must be redesigned and rebuilt to expose an API in order that the processes of the application may be cohesively bound with the processes of the remote ERP application.

Due to the development and testing costs, building interfaces into existing applications is generally very expensive. Other options are to employ user interface–level EAI, where the user interface (screens) is the point of integration. These implementations generally don't require the redevelopment and redeployment of the application. (See Chapter 5.) Method-level EAI is an option as well. But, once again, we're going to have to redevelop the application to support that approach. Let's assume, for our example here, that application interface–level EAI is the best solution.

Once the interface is built into the COBOL application, it's really just a matter of selecting the right middleware to bind to the ERP API on one side and the custom application API on the other. This allows the EAI developer to extract business information (e.g., credit information) out of one and place it in another. Middleware that would work in this scenario might include message brokers, message queuing middleware, and **application servers**.

Note that the interfaces in this example, unlike data-level EAI, are able to provide access to both data and business processes. They are the reason we employ application interface—level API. However, the type of business information accessible is limited by the features and functions of the interface. That's the tradeoff with application interface—level EAI, as will become more evident as you continue through this chapter.

Approaching Application Interfaces

Packaged applications (which are most often present in a typical EAI problem domain) are only now beginning to open up their interfaces to allow for outside access and, consequently, integration. While each application determines exactly what these interfaces should be and what services they will provide, there is a "consensus" in providing access at the business model, data, and object levels.

In accessing the business model, or the innate business processes, a set of services are typically invoked through user interfaces. For example, credit information for a particular individual can be accessed through the user interface by driving the screens, menus, and/or windows. This same information can be accessed by invoking an API provided by the packaged application vendor, if one exists.

In the world of custom applications, anything is possible. With access to the source code, it is possible to define a particular interface or simply to open the application with standard interfaces such as CORBA, **COM**, or Java. For example, rather than accessing the user interface (scraping screens) in order to access an existing COBOL application residing on mainframes, it is possible to build an application programming interface for that application by simply exposing its services through an API. In most cases, this requires mapping the business processing, once accessible only through screens and menus, directly to the API.

The Interface Tradeoff

If the world were a perfect place, all the features and functions provided by packaged applications would also be accessible through their "well-defined" application programming interfaces. However, the world is not a perfect place, and the reality is a bit more sobering. (See our discussion of interface service levels in the section "Types of Services," later in this chapter.) While almost all packaged applications provide some interfaces, they are, as we have mentioned previously, uneven in their scope and quality. While some provide open interfaces based on open interface standards such as Java APIs (e.g., JavaBeans) or ORBs, many provide more proprietary APIs that are useful only in a limited set of programming languages (e.g., COBOL and C).

Most disturbing is that many packaged applications offer no interface whatsoever. With these applications, there is no opportunity for an application or middleware layer to access the services of that application cleanly. As a result, the business processes and data contained within the application remain "off limits." In these cases, half the cost must be dedicated to resorting to more traditional mechanisms, such as leveraging user interface–level or data-level EAI.

Packaged Applications

As we discussed in Chapter 1, packaged applications are natural stovepipes for the enterprise. As such, not only are packaged applications typically within the problem domain of most EAI projects, but they are often the most challenging to integrate. Enterprises need to access the information, and in many cases, they need to share the business logic locked up within packaged applications.

SAP, PeopleSoft, Oracle, and Baan dominate the many packaged applications on the market today. They offer certain advantages over their competitors. However, before taking advantage of what they offer, it is important to remember that, over the years, hundreds of packaged applications have entered the enterprise. Many of these no longer enjoy the support of their vendors, or, just as likely, the vendors are out of business. These represent special challenges for EAI.

Packaged applications come in all shapes and sizes. The majority of large packaged applications that exist within the enterprise are "business critical". SAP, for example, provides modules for accounting, inventory, human resources, manufacturing, and many other vital functions. PeopleSoft and Baan provide many of the same types of services and modules.

Vendors, such as Lawson Software, JD Edwards, and others, some with less than a dozen installations, offer packaged applications. There are packaged applications such as Scopus, a call-center management application, which are limited to highly selected and specialized applications. Siebel, a sales-force automation package, is designed to allow sales organizations to function more effectively.

Packaged Application Technology Architecture

Packaged applications found in enterprises today tend to use one of three distinct architectures: centralized, two-tier, and three-tier.

Centralized architecture is most traditional and, as such, is easiest to follow. Centralized architecture places both data application logic and user interfaces within the same machine, generally a mainframe or large minicomputer that houses a packaged application accessible by dumb terminals (see Figure 3.2).

There are a number of advantages to centralized architecture. First, because the data, process logic, and user interface all exist together on the same processor, maintenance is much easier than in traditional distributed environments. Second, integration is more easily accomplished within one machine than among several. In an EAI scenario, encapsulated services and data that reside on a central computer can be accessed by a single gateway.

Even while acknowledging these advantages, the industry is moving away from the centralized structure and toward the distributed model. Although this model doesn't possess all of the advantages of centralized architecture, it does bring some real strengths to the table. The distributed model has the ability to tailor equipment, databases, and operating systems to the specifications of the enterprise. Moreover, the graphical user interface, now a staple in the world of computing, is innate to traditional distributed type architectures.

The evolution toward the distributed model can be measured by the evolution of SAP. The previous generation of SAP, SAP R/2, leveraged this centralized

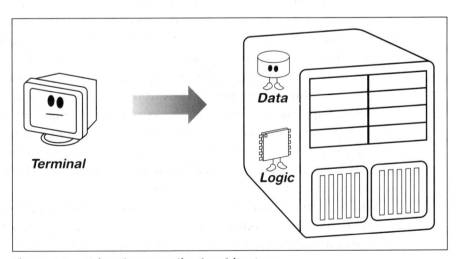

Figure 3.2   Using the centralized architecture

architecture and was found on traditional mainframe-type environments. The latest SAP generation, SAP R/3, uses a three-tier distributed model.

Two-tier architecture (see Figure 3.3) is drawn from the traditional, two-tier client/server model where the application is separated into three distinct "pieces" or layers: the user interface layer, the business logic layer, and the data layer. (This is also the case in three-tier architecture, the difference being in the distribution of the layers). Despite being divided into three logical pieces, two-tier architecture is physically and logically separated onto just two layers (tiers), the client and the server. These two tiers are connected by a network. The client always contains the user interface, but it may or may not also contain the business logic. Obversely, the database always contains the data, but it may or may not contain business logic.

Placing the business logic on the client means having a "fat" client. Placing the business logic on the database (or a middle tier, as in the three-tier architecture) means having a "thin" client. Most client/server systems opt for the "fat" client approach.

It's important to note that with the two-tier approach, the difference is not necessarily the physical distribution of the application, between the client and the server, but the fact that the logic is bound to the user interface.

The **three-tier architecture** is, as we have noted, very similar to the two-tier architecture. The significant difference is the placement of an application server

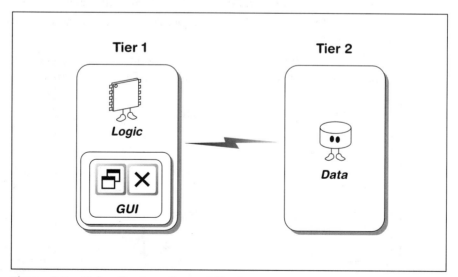

Figure 3.3   Using the two-tier architecture

between the client and the database to provide a location for the business logic (see Figure 3.4). Thus, in the three-tier system, the client only deals with the interactions with the user, while the database only deals with the processing of the data. The middle tier, or application server, provides almost all application logic–processing services. The client, while interacting with the user, is able to invoke application services on the application server; the application server, in turn, is able to access information residing on a database on behalf of the client.

For good reason, the three-tier architecture is the most popular architecture among packaged applications. The three-tier structure provides a clean separation between the user interface, the business logic, and the data. It also provides enhanced scalability. The number of database connections increase in direct proportion to the increase in the number of clients. With a finite number of connections available to the database, two-tier architecture is self-limiting vis-à-vis scalability, because there is a one-client/one-database connection limitation. Three-tier architecture circumvents this restriction because the application server is able to multiplex the database connections. This process is known as **database funneling** or connection pooling. Rather than the direct proportionality of the two-tier architecture, 100 clients in three-tier architecture might require only ten connections to the back-end database.

While most of the major packaged applications today use the three-tier architecture, the enabling technology they use to implement the architecture varies considerably from vendor to vendor. Where SAP uses a proprietary application server to process its business logic, PeopleSoft leverages the Tuxedo TP monitor from BEA.

What does architecture have to do with interfaces? The long and short answer is, *everything*. When invoking application interfaces, it is extremely helpful to

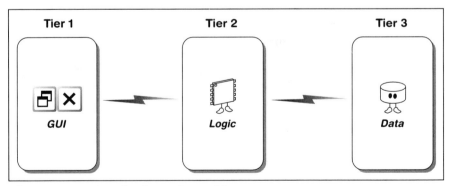

Figure 3.4   Using the three-tier architecture

understand which portions of the packaged applications are being accessed. Interfaces allow access to the user interface and application as well as to the data (many allow access only to one or two tiers). Many packaged applications allow direct access to the database with the caveat, based on the fact that the business logic controls the database integrity, that the user do so only by using a business logic or application layer. To do otherwise could damage database integrity and thus produce erroneous results.

Understanding the architecture as well as the enabling technology also presents opportunities for integration. Many packaged applications use open technologies such as message-oriented middleware, application servers, and TP monitors. In certain instances, it may make sense to go directly to those layers, bypassing the interfaces provided by the packaged application vendors (see Figure 3.5). In PeopleSoft, invoking the Tuxedo interface allows access to its business logic. Just as Tuxedo is a major middleware technology, other third-party tools may be available that allow the same result.

Packaged Application APIs

As we've noted, some, but not all, packaged applications expose interfaces or APIs that allow other applications to access encapsulated services and data. While

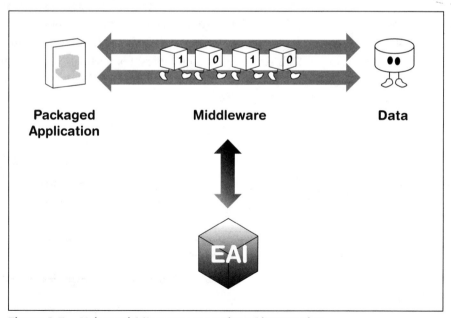

Figure 3.5   Using middleware as a point of integration

these interfaces vary widely in features and function, categorizing some types may clarify what is available. There are three types of services available to these interfaces—business service, data service, and objects.

Types of Services

Business services, as the name implies, include interfaces to any piece of business logic that may exist within the packaged application (see Figure 3.6). For example, if the user wants to use the packaged application interface to update the customer database with a new customer from another application, it would be possible to invoke the customer update business service from the API and pass along the new information. The interface would invoke that particular business service as if a user was invoking the same business service through the user interface of the packaged application.

There may exist as many as 10,000 business services available within a single packaged application. Each business service, when invoked by the application interface or user interface, carries out preprogrammed functions. The EAI architect must understand what each of these business services does, what the required information for each service is, and what the expected outcome is.

In addition to providing access to business logic, business services provide a virtual gateway to the data that resides within packaged applications. As such, the business services stand as sentry to the data by providing integrity controls. For example, adding a sales transaction to the database directly could circumvent integrity controls set up by the developers. For this reason, the application will almost always require going through the business logic in order to access the data.

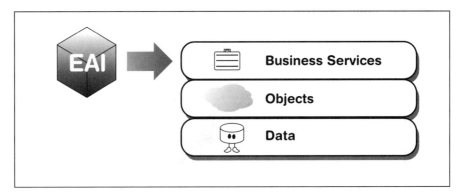

Figure 3.6   Invoking the business services layer

Packaged Applications Becoming Shared Services

Packaged applications are monolithic beasts that dwell within many enterprises today. Vendors are moving quickly toward allowing these "beasts" to share services among other applications within the enterprise. In one sense, these packaged applications are becoming elaborate distributed objects with preprogrammed functions that provide thousands of methods and database tables, accessible to anyone within an enterprise that understands the interface.

The applications for this are numerous. Packaged application information will be accessed directly from any tool that communicates using DCOM (e.g., Word for Windows, PowerPoint, Excel, and so on). This places the packaged application squarely on "Main Street," simplifying both the mechanism and the process for accessing the encapsulated methods and data. The difficulty in moving all packaged applications to the "neighborhood" is not in concept but in architecture.

Packaged applications are trying to function like distributed object solutions while not truly being distributed objects. In order to accomplish this, the vendors are forced to wrap their packaged application logic and data using some type of standard interface—CORBA, COM, or Java. When the problem is solved, the packaged application will appear as a true distributed object to other applications that exist within the enterprise—a clear benefit to those who seek to integrate other applications with these packaged applications (see Figure 3.7) at any EAI level.

Accessible by application interfaces, **data services** are direct routes to the logical or physical database, sometimes both (see Figure 3.8). These interfaces are not unlike traditional data-level access tools; however, the ERP vendor provides them as a verified mechanism to access the ERP data. Of course, each vendor varies greatly in features provided.

As we have noted, use of this interface is generally for extraction only. However, some data service interfaces offer database update services as well, either with or without integrity checks.

While most application interfaces provide data services, the EAI architect has the option of going directly to the database by utilizing database-oriented middleware. (However, doing so means bypassing all the integrity controls that

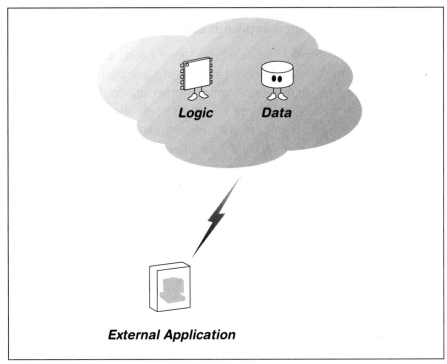

Figure 3.7   Using packaged applications as distributed objects

the packaged application may have put in place.) In the case of Oracle, this is simply a matter of accessing the Oracle database using native middleware from Oracle or other solutions such as JDBC, **ODBC (Open Database Connectivity)**, or OLE DB (Object Linking and Embedding Database). We will discuss the details of database-oriented middleware later in the book.

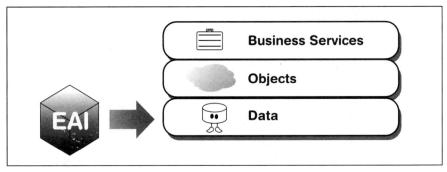

Figure 3.8   Accessing the data services layer

Watch Out for the Packaged Applications Schemas!

Sure, it looks good. It looks easy. Too easy. EAI architects and developers need to be aware of the complexities involved in doing an "end run" around the packaged application and going directly to the database. The database schemas for most packaged applications were never set up for third-party access. Thus, they have a tendency to be very complex. For example, SAP has thousands of tables within its database, which require a fairly large and detailed "road map" to get at the desired information.

While the "times they are a-changin'" and packaged application vendors are becoming more aware of the need to simplify their schemas or to provide easy-to-understand abstraction layers on top of their schemas, the complexity still exists. Add to that the fact that most EAI projects involve packaged applications that have been in place for several years or more, and the result is an emphatic "proceed with caution."

Objects are simply data and business services bound as objects. Just as in the world of object-oriented development, the object inside packaged applications is the encapsulation of both data and methods that act upon the data (see Figure 3.9).

The advantage of objects rests in the fact that there is never a concern regarding bypassing the integrity checks set up by the packaged applications, because data cannot be accessed without invoking the method. However, these objects are not typically standard distributed objects. They are proprietary objects defined by the packaged application vendor that, therefore, might not fit directly into every development or reporting environment.

Many packaged application vendors are recognizing the need to expose these objects using a standard interface such as CORBA or Java. SAP, PeopleSoft, Oracle, and Baan all have initiatives to provide standard object interfaces to existing packaged applications. The difficulty rests in the fact that many packaged applications were never designed to be distributed objects.

Types of Interfaces

Knowing the types of services available through an interface, it is now useful to explore the various types of interfaces themselves that exist within packaged applications. As in other contexts, there is a broad spectrum of possibilities that

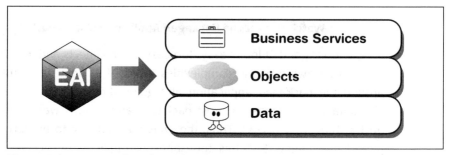

Figure 3.9   Leveraging the object layer

can be grouped into three convenient types: full-service, limited-service, and controlled.

Full-service interfaces, as the name implies, afford a wide range of benefits. They provide access to the business services level, the data services level, and the object level (see Figure 3.10). While most packaged applications promote their interfaces as being full-service interfaces, the reality is often a bit less promising. For the most part, interfaces in packaged applications were an afterthought. As such, they tend to be somewhat limited. For example, within the SAP interface infrastructure, many types of interfaces need to be invoked in order to access information and services. The same is true for PeopleSoft and Oracle.

Limited-service interfaces are the most common interfaces, typically allowing access to only one level (e.g., business services level, data services level, or object level—see Figure 3.11). In addition to being "access limited," these interfaces generally provide only a limited set of services at those levels.

As application interfaces become the "next, greatest" thing for packaged applications, they will expand to include more levels and features and functions

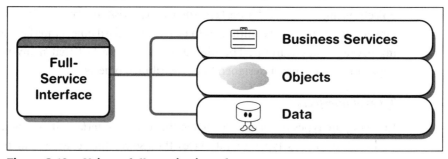

Figure 3.10   Using a full-service interface

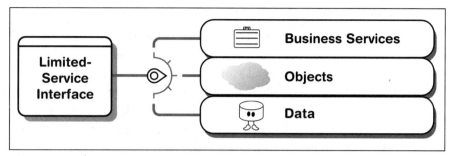

Figure 3.11   Using a limited-service interface

within those levels, and, perhaps in an effort to live up to their promotional billing, they will provide genuine full-service interfaces in the near future.

Controlled interfaces provide only a bare minimum of features and functions (see Figure 3.12). These are limited not because of the limitations of technology but, rather, because of the marketing and/or economic decisions of the vendor. Controlled interfaces are very proprietary and closed, providing controlled access to business logic and data.

Other Interfaces

While packaged application APIs represent the lion's share of application interfaces that an organization will confront, other standard application interfaces should be recognized. These exist for the same purpose as packaged application interfaces—to provide access to information that may be required from other remote applications.

There are thousands of application interface types, many more than we can discuss here. We will confine our review to major categories, including vertical market application interfaces and application interfaces built into custom applications.

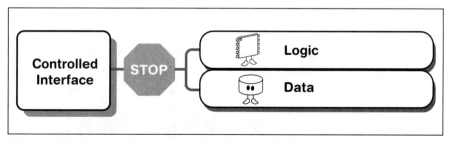

Figure 3.12   Leveraging a controlled interface

Vertical Market Application Interfaces

Vertical market application interfaces provide access to industry-specific applications—industrial, health care, and finance, to mention just three. Vertical market application interfaces take into account the specific needs of a particular type of vertical. This may include the manner in which the information is formatted, processed, or moved from application to application. For example, in the banking industry, security is paramount. Therefore, interfaces that are used within banking applications place security high on their priority list.

SWIFT

SWIFT (Society for Worldwide Interbank Financial Telecommunications) is really a messaging standard and a cooperative organized under Belgian law. It began operations in 1977 and is owned by member banks, including the central banks of most countries. SWIFT provides communication services to the international banking industry, which include payment and common administrative tasks. It also supports security settlements. Most message brokers that support the financial community, including NEON, SAGA Software, and Active Software, also support SWIFT. An integral part of the international financial community, SWIFT provides a rapid, cost-effective, secure, and reliable transmission service. In addition to message processing, the worldwide network, and the availability of an increasing number of message standards to support new financial instruments, this technology provides a variety of specialized financial services as well as software network–compatible interfaces.

Organizations in the financial community will likely deal with SWIFT. In 1977, over 6,153 institutions used SWIFT to communicate with one another in a 7x24 environment. Today, SWIFT operates in 174 countries and processes more than 800 million messages each year. A typical SWIFT message load is 1.6 million messages daily.

FIX

SWIFT is obviously not the only application interface supporting the world of finance. The **Financial Information Exchange (FIX)** protocol is a messaging standard developed specifically for the real-time electronic exchange of securities transactions. FIX is a public domain specification maintained by the FIX organization, a cooperative effort of principal asset management and brokerage firms in the United States and Europe.

The Elusive Enterprise API

Because the EAI problem is not a new one, there have been attempts at solving it for years. One of the most popular solutions is the notion of the all-enterprise API, or a single, well-defined API that is able to access every piece of information and every process that exists within an enterprise (see Figure 3.13).

While the all-enterprise API might seem like a wonderful idea "on paper," the difficulties in actually creating such a creature are immense. The first step—and arguably the *easiest* one—would be to get every organization in the enterprise to agree that such an API would be a good idea. Then, a layer of abstraction must be created between the API and all the enabling technologies that exist within the environment.

The reality is that either of these tasks is nearly impossible in today's technology milieu. In addition, for most enterprises, such an API would be so complex as to be unusable. Worse still, such an API would be a proprietary, two-year enterprise-only API, meaning that it would have to be maintained and enhanced for it to function.

The elusive enterprise API is the holy grail of EAI. It is, simply put, the ability to get any information or any business process at any time for any reason using a common interface. This is, of course, the notion behind the Gartner Group's Zero Latency Enterprise, or what most would agree is the ultimate goal of EAI. Some might suggest that such a level of enlightened possibility is a religious state and not a technical possibility—it's something to put on paper but cannot be implemented in the real world. At least not yet.

The advantages to FIX include shorter settlement dates, providing a straight-through processing package for the financial community. The FIX protocol specifications are maintained by the FIX Technical Committee. Information regarding FIX can be obtained by visiting its Web site located at www.fixprotocol.org.

The technical aspect of FIX is quite straightforward. FIX uses a flexible tag value message format, which imposes no structural constraints on a message. This forces all validation to occur at the application level, a problem that FIX is

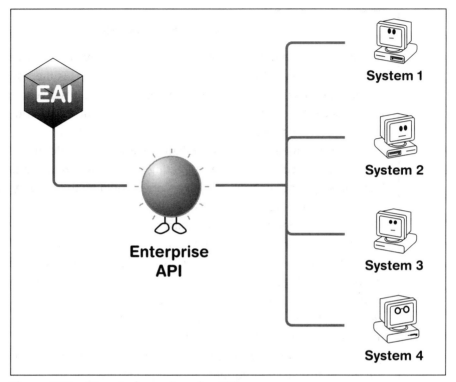

Figure 3.13   The elusive enterprise API

addressing by evolving FIX into FIXML—a structured, validated XML-derived grammar that is encapsulated within the standard FIX message. FIX, along with many other interfaces, is discovering that XML has the potential to provide a "least common denominator" approach. It certainly has proven successful for metadata.

HL7

HL7, or Health Level 7, is a standard for electronic data exchange in a health care environment. HL7 emphasizes inpatient, acute care facilities such as hospitals. A committee of health care providers, vendors, and consultants established in March 1987 are responsible for the creation of HL7.

While HL7 is primarily limited to hospitals and clinics (it is most useful when moving information in and out of MUMPs environments), it also exists within the pharmaceutical and biomedical industries.

Custom Applications

That there exist application interfaces that have been standardized by committees or vendors is useful. But what about creating interfaces for custom applications? As we saw in our preceding examples, while interfaces may exist for many packaged applications and technologies, custom applications are yet another challenge.

Rolling Your Own API

Truth be told, few build a custom application with the goal of providing an application interface for other applications. Why not? Because most applications were considered monolithic beasts or were created as stovepipes to serve a single purpose within the enterprise, not to share information.

It has become obvious that the underlying assumptions here—that *anything* in an enterprise could, or should, exist in such a proprietary manner—were terribly incorrect.

One might believe that building application interfaces for custom applications is a difficult proposition. However, if thought through correctly, the task is not nearly as difficult as it might first appear. First, no one needs to reinvent the wheel. Building an application interface to a custom application basically means exposing business processes that already exist within the application through another mechanism, namely an API (see Figure 3.14). Access to those business processes is already being exposed through the user interface. This is simply another mechanism to obtain the same service.

While some organizations consider building application interfaces an expensive proposition, a luxury item beyond their reach, the fact is that applications are going to be changed in order to provide an application interface, and any change can range from very minor to very major. What's more, as we've mentioned, applications that are not designed from the ground up to utilize an application interface may need a new architecture in any case. In these situations, it may make more sense to rebuild the application from the first line of code. The prospect of rebuilding from the first line of code up is a prospect most organizations shy away from. It is the reason they integrate applications using other, less sophisticated approaches such as user interface–level and data-level EAI mechanisms.

Application Wrapping

An even more sophisticated option is **application wrapping**. This is the process of changing an existing application so that it appears as a distributed object

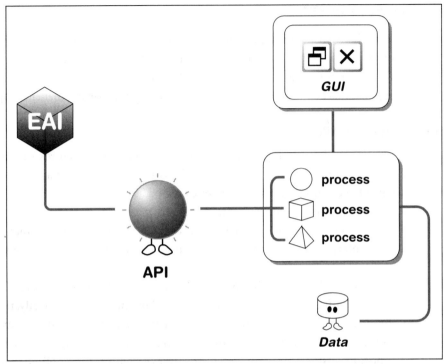

Figure 3.14   Exposing an API

to other, external applications (see Figure 3.15). Put another way, application wrapping requires going through the entire application and exposing its business processes as methods within a distributed object standard such as CORBA or COM.

There are many advantages to application wrapping. First, because it requires leveraging a standard distributed object infrastructure, the application can be exposed to many more types of applications than if a proprietary application interface was built. Many of these applications don't need to change in order to use the remote application services, because they are wrapped using an available distributed object standard. Second, because the process for taking an existing application and rebuilding it as a distributed object is well defined, there are many tools, techniques, and technologies available that support application wrapping.

The downside to application wrapping is time. It takes many man-months to wrap an existing application, and man-months inevitably translate into money,

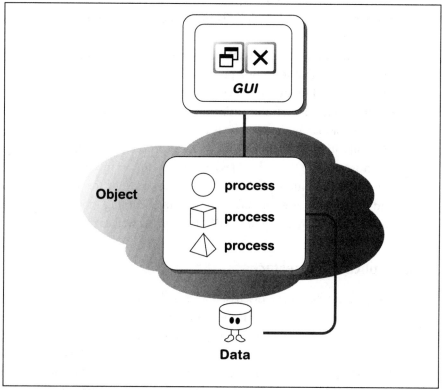

Figure 3.15   Application wrapping

money that an organization might be unwilling to spend on an existing solution. Moreover, many applications have to be rebuilt from the ground up and may need a new application architecture. For these reasons, application wrapping should not be considered as a "stop gap" measure but rather as a mechanism that significantly extends the life of existing applications and supports the integration of those applications within the infrastructure of the enterprise.

There are many ways to wrap existing applications, but COM and CORBA are the most popular. Arguing the viability of either of these distributed object standards is beyond our scope here. However, the following are some general guidelines to consider.

CORBA is the better fit for applications that have to exist in a heterogeneous environment. If the enterprise supports UNIX, NT, mainframes, and a variety of other platforms, CORBA is probably the best choice because CORBA solutions exist on a wide variety of platforms. What's more, there are many proven CORBA applications in existence along with the tools and technology that contributed to its success.

Of the two standards, COM is the more Windows platform–centric, which is not to suggest that it is not a powerful ORB. It is. COM is supported by most of the Microsoft line of tools, development environments, and office automation solutions. Therefore, for organizations looking to expose an application interface to most popular applications, it is the path of least resistance. Wrapping an existing application and exposing its business processes through a COM ORB infrastructure allows those business processes to be invoked by any number of common office automation products, such as Word for Windows, PowerPoint, and Excel. COM is even making strides in becoming more heterogeneous, with support for the majority of UNIX platforms as well as the mainframe platforms.

Using Application Interfaces

So, given all that we've discussed in this chapter, the question begs to be asked, "What's the future of application interfaces?" Answering the question depends on the way change will be wrought in a particular enterprise—by evolution or by revolution. For most packaged or custom applications, interfaces to both methods and data encapsulated within those applications are little more than an afterthought. As a result, supporting interfaces requires retrofitting existing applications. Although this represents a step in the right direction, it is the first step in that proverbial "journey of a thousand miles." Make no mistake, it is going to be a long, slow journey. These applications typically support business-critical functions within the enterprise. Making significant changes to these applications to support interfaces for the purpose of integration may not excite the sensibilities in the boardroom. However, the EAI problem has raised the profile of application interfaces, making them a priority for those who sell and maintain both packaged and custom applications.

Taking into account the information we've presented in this chapter, we see two possibilities for the future. One, application interfaces will be standard equipment for most packaged applications. (Even more to the point, many custom applications will obtain application interfaces in future enhancements and upgrades.) Two, more applications will use standard interfaces such as CORBA and COM to enable remote applications to access both the data and services of these applications as standard object request brokers. Either outcome will add value to the EAI story.

CHAPTER FOUR

Method-Level EAI

"A complex system that works is invariably found to have evolved from a simple system that worked."
—John Gall

Method-level EAI allows the enterprise to be integrated through the sharing of common business logic, or methods. This is accomplished either by defining methods that can be shared, and therefore integrated, by a number of applications or by providing the infrastructure for such method sharing. Methods may be shared either by hosting them on a central server or by accessing them between applications (e.g., distributed objects).

There is really nothing new here. Attempts to share common processes have a long history, starting more than ten years ago with the distributed object movement and multitiered client/server—a set of shared services on a common server that provided the enterprise with the infrastructure for reuse, and now, for integration. "Reuse" is an important concept in this context. By defining a common set of methods, we're able to reuse those methods among enterprise applications. As a result, the need for redundant methods, and/or applications, is significantly reduced.

Absolute reuse has yet to be achieved on the enterprise level. The reasons for this failure range from internal politics to the inability to select a consistent technology set. In most cases, the limit on reuse is the lack of enterprise architecture and central control. The question presents itself, "What does this failure of reuse have to do with EAI?" The short and long answer is: everything.

Composite Applications—The Goal of Method-Level EAI

In the world of EAI, you'll also hear a lot about **composite applications**. Composite applications are nothing more than applications bound together by business logic or methods. This, of course, has been the ultimate goal of distributed objects and transactional technology for years and is certainly a goal of method-level EAI. So, make no mistake, we are walking down the same alley here.

Using the tools and techniques of EAI to integrate an enterprise creates not only the opportunity to learn how to share common methods, but the infrastructure to make such sharing a reality as well. We are integrating applications so that information can be shared, as well as providing the infrastructure for the reuse of business logic. While this might sound like the perfect EAI solution, the downside is that it also represents the most invasive level of EAI. Unlike data-level, user interface–level, and application interface–level EAI, which do not typically require changes to either the source or target applications, method-level EAI requires that many, if not all, enterprise applications be changed in order to take advantage of the paradigm.

Changing the applications, as we noted in Chapter 1, is a very expensive proposition. In addition to changing application logic, there is the need to test, integrate, and redeploy the application within the enterprise—a process that often causes costs to spiral upwards (see Figure 4.1).

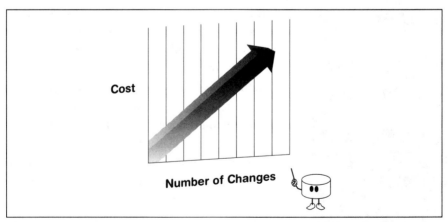

Figure 4.1   As the number of changes to source or target applications increases, so do the costs.

Considering the invasiveness and expense of method-level EAI, enterprises must clearly understand both its opportunities and its risks in assessing its value. Being able to share business logic that is common to many applications, and so integrate those applications, is a tremendous opportunity. However, it comes with the risk that the expense to implement method-level EAI will outpace its value.

Method-Level Example

An example of method-level EAI is the simple binding of two or more applications, at the method level, in order to integrate both business processes and data. Let's say two applications exist within an enterprise. One application is a C++-based application running on a Linux machine. The other is a NT-based client/server application written in Java on the front-end, with Sybase serving as the back-end database.

It is the intention of the EAI architect to create a composite application using method-level EAI techniques and technology. For example, the applications need to be tightly coupled in order to share common business logic, as well as to expose the business logic of both applications to other applications for future use.

Unlike other EAI levels, there is little choice here other than to rebuild the applications so that they support method-level EAI. To accomplish this, we have two options with method-level EAI. First, we can move much of the business logic to a shared server, such as an application server. Second, we can rebuild each application using a method-sharing mechanism, such as distributed object technology, to create a tightly coupled application that allows easy cross-access of methods.

If we decide that the second option is the most attractive, we will have to "wrap" the application logic encapsulated inside of both applications using a distributed object technology, such as CORBA or COM, so that there is a common mechanism to share methods remotely. This means rewriting the applications and then testing them. Fortunately, there are tools for each environment to wrap each application, recreating the applications as truly distributed systems able to share both methods and data.

In spite of available tools, the process is laborious. For example, if both applications need to add a new customer to their systems, they may invoke different methods. For example:

```
Add_Cust();
```

on the Linux/C++ system, and

```
AddNewCustomer();
```

on the NT/Java system.

Within the context of method-level EAI, we could expose each method using either a distributed object standard or a custom programming solution. As a result, we could bind the methods or invoke one or the other. Once the methods are bound, the applications move to a coupled state where methods and data are shared easily within both domains, solving the EAI problem.

What's a Process?

The goal of method-level EAI is to share processes; thus it's helpful to discuss the attributes of a process. For the purposes of EAI, a business process is any rule or piece of logic that exists within the enterprise that has an effect on how information is processed—for example, logic tied to a taxation system within the organization or a method within a C++ application that updates customer information.

Thousands of business processes reside in the applications of most organizations. The difficulty is not the definition or identification, but the fact that these processes depend on a chaotic mix of enabling technologies. For example, the taxation logic referred to previously may be contained within a two-tiered client/server application where the logic resides on the client, while the logic in the second example may reside within a shared C++ application. Difficulties arise because these two enabling technologies do not easily communicate with one another or, at least, don't without a lot of rework.

Scenarios

In order to implement method-level EAI, it is necessary to understand all the processes that exist within the enterprise. Confronted with such a monumental task, the question is, "How best to proceed?" The first step should be to break the processes down into their scenarios, or types. For the purposes of EAI, these types are rules, logic, data, and objects.

Rules

A **rule** is a set of conditions that have been agreed upon. For example, a rule may state that employees may not fly first class on flights of less than 5,000 miles or

---

> ## Rule Servers
>
> Because rules must be distributed, some corporations are setting up special servers, known as **logic** or **rule servers**. These servers are accessible by a number of applications and provide the infrastructure for centralized rule processing. With a rule server in place, changing a rule—for example, one governing travel policy—would simply require changing the appropriate rule on the logic server rather than in each and every application that uses that rule.

that all transactions over one million dollars must be reported to the government. The rules that exist within a given enterprise are built into the applications in order to control the flow of information.

Normally, rules exist in stovepipes—in a single application and accessible to a single department. EAI must provide the infrastructure that allows for the sharing of these rules, making them accessible to many applications where they currently exist or by moving them to a central location.

Within the world of EAI, rules need to be understood because they affect every aspect of the manipulation of data—identifying, processing, and transforming it. In fact, rules processing at the middleware level—for example, through message brokers or process automation tools—will become the first generation of EAI.

Logic

Logic differs from rules in that logic is simply a sequence of instructions in a program—for example, **if** this button is pushed **then** the screen pops up—while rules define business restraints. The difficulty with addressing logic comes from the reality that any ten programmers, given a set of specifications, may come up with ten slightly different program logics that all function perfectly well.

There are three classes of logic: sequential processing, selection, and iteration. **Sequential processing** is the series of steps in the actual data processing. Input, output, calculation, and move (copy) are instructions used in sequential processing. **Selection** is the decision-making within the program, performed by comparing two sets of data and, depending on the results, branching to different parts of the program. **Iteration** is a repetition of a series of steps. It is accomplished with DO-LOOPS and FOR-LOOPS in high-level languages.

Data

In this context, **data** is nothing more than sharing information between enterprise applications and computers or humans. Reporting systems, enterprise accounting systems, and human resource systems all share data. Because methods act on data, how information is shared at the method level needs to be understood in order for method-level EAI to be successful.

Objects

Objects, as defined in Chapter 3, are bundles of data encapsulated inside an object and surrounded by methods that act upon that data. Objects are so important to method-level EAI that much of this chapter will be dedicated to the discussion of the object model and its use within the EAI problem domain.

Objects in systems generally use object-oriented technology such as C++ or Java. Despite the fact that most objects are service-level objects (that is, objects that *do something* when an interface is invoked—more on these later in this chapter), the object "mix" may also include distributed objects.

Identifying objects within the enterprise is a more complex endeavor than identifying business processes. It requires an understanding of the object models used to construct the applications—if they exist or if they were ever created. In the absence of the object model, the applications must be re-engineered from the existing code base. (Fortunately, a good set of tools and technologies exists to aid in this re-engineering. Without such tools, the task would demand reading each line of code and creating the object models from scratch.)

Method Warehousing

Method warehousing finds an analogy in data warehousing in that methods that exist within many applications are being moved to a centralized entity. The concept of method warehousing, the process of aggregating all business processes within an organization and then hosting them on a centralized server (the method warehouse), is a concept that grows directly from the concept of method-level EAI (see Figure 4.2). The value of such a process should be clear. If all the methods existing within the enterprise are located on a centralized server, then the method-level EAI, or integration of all these processes, becomes simply a matter of remotely invoking these processes, or methods, for any application.

The advantages of method warehousing rest both with the power to integrate all enterprise applications through the sharing of methods (e.g., composite

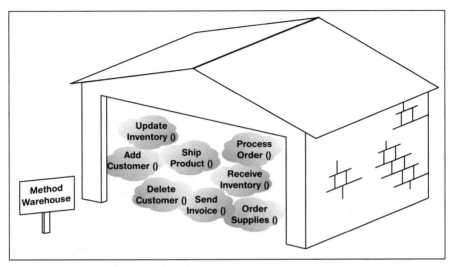

Figure 4.2   Method warehousing

applications) and the ability to maintain and reuse application logic from a centralized server. For example, if the tax law changes, it would be unnecessary to locate all applications within the enterprise that use tax law in order to incorporate the changes. The changes would automatically propagate to all link applications simply by a change in the logic, or rules, within the method warehouse.

The downside to method warehousing lies in its expense. As we noted at the start of this chapter, method warehousing requires the conversion of the significant methods of every source and target application into a common enabling technology, one that all enterprise applications will be able to access. For example, if the decision is made to implement a method warehouse project using an application server, or a distributed object technology infrastructure, then, in addition to creating the method warehouse itself, all applications will have to be rewritten in order to invoke these methods remotely.

Leveraging Frameworks for EAI

The notion, and use, of frameworks can be helpful in integrating an enterprise at the method level. A fundamental difficulty with frameworks has been the many definitions of the term. In the context of EAI, the most useful definition can be found in the *Computer Glossary* (Freedman, 1993): "[Frameworks] consist of abstract classes and their object collaboration as well as concrete classes. While object-oriented programming supports software reuse, frameworks support design reuse" (p. 242).

Frameworks are fully debugged and tested software subsystems, centrally located and accessible by many applications (see Figure 4.3). They fit in well with method-level EAI where, in many instances, shared objects, processes, and/or methods are being identified for the purpose of integration. Although frameworks may work at the application or enterprise level, in the world of EAI, frameworks are an enterprise play. They provide the infrastructure for sharing methods—providing objects that are accessible by a number of applications. As such, they allow for the construction of a "library" of enterprise objects for use by many applications. While this concept is the basis of frameworks in general, it is particularly valuable when applied to EAI.

EAI architects are able to leverage frameworks to integrate applications.

The process of decoupling frameworks from the object-oriented development model is a reaction to the success of using component-enabled and procedural frameworks. While the object-oriented, component-based, and procedural

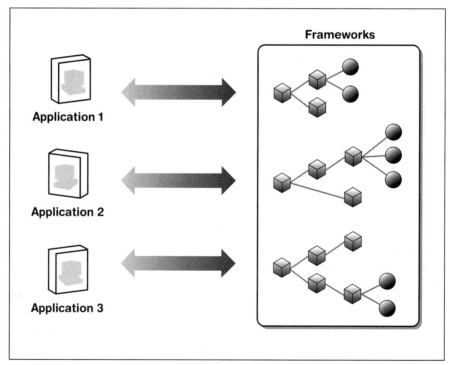

Figure 4.3   Applying frameworks to method-level EAI

approaches hold very different views of frameworks, the goal of reuse is consistent throughout and provides a commonality that is beneficial from all perspectives. We focus here on object frameworks because they dominate the number of frameworks in use today, and because many method-level EAI projects will leverage object-oriented frameworks if they leverage frameworks at all.

The Value of Frameworks

The concept of object frameworks is well known, but many development organizations remain confused regarding their value to EAI. While there are many benefits, nearly every one comes with a note of caution. The most obvious benefit of frameworks is the ability to reuse existing code. Because frameworks contain pre-built objects, those objects can be shared among many applications. As such, they represent a natural point of integration. Frameworks provide more than reuse within an organization; they provide reuse throughout an industry—such as shipping or logistics business—where many of the processes are the same and reusable frameworks make sense. Well-designed frameworks represent a billion dollar, third-party industry.

Frameworks also provide a standard set of predesigned and pretested application architectures. These architectures provide a common infrastructure for all enterprise applications. Frameworks hide all the "dirty little details" from the developer, allowing him or her to concentrate on the functionality of the application and to remain architecture independent.

There are many benefits to frameworks, but there are also downsides. First, design is an essential part of application development. It allows the EAI and application architect to derive the most benefit from using a framework. In short, knowing how the application and framework fit together is essential for success. Second, because there has been such dissension in determining a common language, or binary object standard, frameworks are typically bound to a technology. As a result, C++ frameworks are incompatible with a PowerBuilder application, Delphi frameworks are incompatible with Smalltalk, and so on. To be successful, there needs to be a commitment to a common set of enabling technologies—something next to impossible to achieve in many organizations. Finally, the frameworks themselves must undergo a very costly design, architecture, development, and testing process. Poorly designed frameworks lead to bad applications—no matter how well the application itself was designed and developed. The cost of quality assurance in building frameworks is too high for many organizations.

Framework Functionality

Frameworks work by allowing EAI architects to take advantage of prebuilt subsystems, application architecture, and code that already exists in the enterprise. Because frameworks largely define the architecture for an application, developers and application architects must build and leverage only those frameworks that are extensible and flexible. For example, when using object frameworks, developers can change as much of the existing functionality as required to meet the needs of the application—inheriting what is useful and overriding what needs changing. Interface frameworks are the best example of this. Developers can leverage the custom buttons in a data window while overriding the default fonts in favor of new ones. Frameworks can be customized by adding sets of classes, or frameworks may change themselves to take advantage of changes in hardware and software as new revisions are released.

Components don't provide the same degree of customization as object-oriented frameworks (see Figure 4.4). For example, most components do not come with the source code. However, they typically provide mechanisms (or

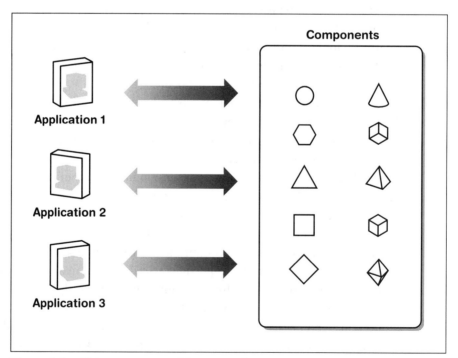

Figure 4.4   Using component frameworks

interfaces) that allow developers to change their look, feel, and behavior by altering their properties. ActiveX controls are a prime example.

Object frameworks also work with other frameworks, allowing developers to "mix and match" features from each framework (see Figure 4.5). For example, C++ applications leverage GUI frameworks for interface development, database access frameworks for communicating with databases, and system-level frameworks for interacting with native operating systems. Many of these "combined" frameworks are now bundled with object-oriented development tools.

Typically, object frameworks provide access to their services through APIs, which are simply abstractions of the framework services. A framework approach to APIs differs from the traditional procedural world in that most of the code runs inside the frameworks, calling the code when a particular state is reached. While applications rarely invoke frameworks, developers may choose to leverage APIs to access the services of other frameworks.

The critical factor to successfully building frameworks is the ability to provide a complete framework that supports the features required by the client and the client's application—for example, providing concrete derivation for the

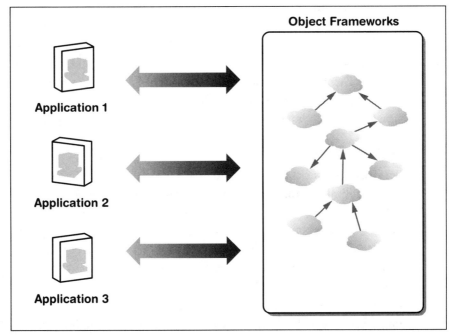

Figure 4.5   Using object frameworks

abstract classes and default member function implementation, making them easier to understand. Frameworks must allow a client to add and modify the functionality of the framework. Finally, frameworks should be well documented and understandable to all users.

Framework Types

Object frameworks are a part of most application development. However, the prominence of component service and procedural frameworks is gaining quickly. As near parity is reached, it becomes useful to distinguish between these different types of frameworks and their use within an EAI context.

Object frameworks are made up of both abstract and concrete classes. They provide application services through the inheritance mechanisms that most object-oriented languages and tools provide. This means that developers get a copy of the framework source code and have an opportunity to customize the framework. In addition, by using an open source approach and the object-oriented mechanism of inheritance, developers have the ability to make changes to meet the requirements of the application. These changes are made using features of the object-oriented programming language such as encapsulation, polymorphism, inheritance, and abstraction. The resulting object frameworks, or "white box" frameworks, allow developers to look inside and modify them where needed.

Object frameworks are language and tool dependent. While most object frameworks are created using C++, there are object frameworks for Power-Builder, Delphi, and most Smalltalk tools. Most client/server and intranet-enabled development tools come bundled with some type of framework to provide common interface development and database access services.

Service Frameworks

Service frameworks, in contrast to object frameworks, don't provide functionality to applications through inheritance. They provide services and, as such, are the best fit from the perspective of most EAI problem domains. Distributed object frameworks are the best example of service frameworks in that they allow applications to invoke methods that are encapsulated in a centrally located distributed object. In addition, service frameworks generally don't provide access to the source code for the distributed objects, making it difficult—though not impossible—(depending on the tool or language) to modify or extend the behavior of distributed objects and service frameworks for an application.

Distributed objects, such as those created around CORBA and COM, offer a common approach to being created and deployed. CORBA-compliant distributed objects are sold through a number of third-party vendors, while DCOM comes with the infrastructure of the Windows operating systems. The idea is to create a set of distributed objects, using either technology, then access those objects either locally or remotely through a well-defined interface from the application that needs a service. For example, distributed objects are built into service frameworks to provide access to accounting functions, financial trading functions, database access functions, and so on.

Distributed objects also provide the "plumbing" for easy access to objects residing on network-connected computers.

Distributed objects represent one of the best hopes for frameworks because they offer tool- and language-independent frameworks for applications. C++, PowerBuilder, Delphi, and Smalltalk applications can all access distributed object services. Object frameworks, as we have noted, are tool and language dependent.

Procedural Frameworks

Procedural frameworks provide a good approach to method-level EAI. They also represent a "black box" perspective on frameworks because they do not allow developers to extend or modify their basic set of services. Consequently, if a functionality required for a particular application in a procedural language is missing . . . tough luck. The procedural framework itself will have to be modified to add the functionality, or the function will have to be coded directly into the application without the use of a framework.

Enabling technology, which supports procedural frameworks, includes **TP monitors** (such as Microsoft Transaction Server—MTS, BEA's Tuxedo, and IBM's CICS). TP monitors typically exist on a remote server. Any number of applications create transaction services within the TP monitor environment. They also provide database access services and are thus the concept behind three-tier client/server computing in which clients invoke the transaction service on the TP monitor, which carries out the transaction for the client. Access to data can be included in that transaction. Application servers, such as Netscape Application Server, are really the next generation of TP monitors, providing many of the same features, but are easier to use. We'll discuss the details of TP monitors, application servers, and other types of transactional middleware in Chapter 7.

The worlds of TP monitors and distributed objects could, in the near future, merge. COM- and CORBA-compliant distributed objects that provide TP monitor services are now on the market. Tuxedo and MTS are just two examples of this trend. Procedural frameworks provide heterogeneous services using a CORBA-defined interface, allowing the gradual transition to objects from the existing set of legacy systems (since wrapping the TP monitor services makes the services appear "object-like").

Component Frameworks

Of all types of frameworks, **component frameworks** are the fastest growing. Driven by the Web, and the rise of component-enabling technologies such as ActiveX and Enterprise JavaBeans (EJB), it is now possible to begin to understand the value of sharing entire components beyond their discrete functionality. Component-based frameworks differ from traditional object frameworks in a number of ways. Developers reuse objects by embedding them inside an application with application development tools that, through a well-defined interface, know how to use a type of component (e.g., ActiveX). Developers, either through the process of aggregation or the use of the host tool, can modify the look, feel, and behavior of the component by setting the properties of the component. (The component developer—and the enabling technology—limit the developer's ability to change the component to the exact need of the application.) The developer generally does not have access to the source code. Components deal with the interface on the client, where application services and procedural frameworks provide basic application services on the back-end. In addition, component frameworks don't provide the reuse granularity of true object-framework development. Instead, they provide reusable features that eliminate the need-to-know component implementation details.

The ability to mix and match components allows EAI architects to purchase expertise they may not already possess. For example, vertical market component vendors from petroleum, financial, and retail industries offer developers specialized functionality that requires little or no custom coding.

In contrast to object frameworks, component frameworks usually contain fewer features and functions than applications, but they provide more services than a simple program function or object. In a number of respects, components are "retro" in that they adhere more to the modular program model of the past than they do to object-oriented development.

Framework Categories

Putting aside for now the different types of frameworks that exist, we can examine the three categories of frameworks based on the types of features they offer: application service, domain, and support. *Any* of these frameworks could be object, service, procedural, or component enabled.

Application Service Frameworks

Application service frameworks encapsulate enterprise application functionality. They are created to provide horizontal functionality across many EAI problem domains. Most frameworks today are examples of application service frameworks. These include the GUI interface frameworks that come with C++ development tools such as Microsoft's Foundation Classes (MFC).

Domain Frameworks

Domain frameworks encapsulate expertise for certain problem domains and provide vertical functionality for certain areas of the enterprise (e.g., accounting, marketing, or logistics). The idea here is to build common application architectures into a common framework shared across applications.

Support Frameworks

Support frameworks offer native system-level services such as network support, device access, or file access. These frameworks are typically platform dependent.

Enabling Technology

Armed with a knowledge of the various approaches to method-level EAI, we can turn our attention to the enabling technology that makes method-level EAI possible. The best technology for this is represented by those software services that allow remote applications to invoke a set of application services, or methods maintained at a central server. With this criterion in mind, the enabling technologies for method-level EAI include application or transaction servers, distributed objects, and message brokers. (In addition to the brief discussions that follow, these technologies are covered in detail in Chapter 7.)

Application or Transaction Servers

TP (transaction processing) monitors are industrial-strength middleware products that provide many features that make large-scale distributed transaction-oriented development possible. TP monitors provide the only option for high-volume, high-use distributed systems. A holdover from the world of the mainframe, TP monitors allow developers to make distributed systems scale to an enterprise-level system (1,000 client/server users or more) through a sound architectural solution.

In addition to such well-known TP monitors as BEA's Tuxedo, Microsoft's Transaction Server (MTS), and IBM's CICS, there is a "new kid on the block"—a new breed of middleware known as **application servers**. Like TP monitors, application servers support the concept of a transactional system. Products like WebLogic, iPlanet, and WebSphere are among this new breed. In addition, many traditional development tool vendors and object database vendors are moving toward application servers as well.

Message Brokers

A message broker is a technology that acts as a broker between one or more target entities (such as network, middleware, applications, and systems), allowing them to share information with less difficulty than would be the case with other methods, such as traditional middleware. In other words, message brokers are the "middleware for middleware." Using a variety of enabling technologies and points of integration, they allow developers to bring many systems together.

While message brokers are the best solution for data-level and application interface–level EAI, they are of limited value at the method level of the EAI problem domain. This limitation results from the basic design of message brokers. They are good at moving and translating information between many applications but are poor places to host centralized business processes. Their rules engines are designed for message routing and transformation, not application logic. Even so, that benefit alone justifies their mention in the context of method-level EAI.

Distributed Objects

When it comes to distributed objects, there are only two choices: Distributed Component Object Model (DCOM) and Common Object Request Broker Architecture (CORBA). While it may be a stretch to refer to distributed objects as middleware, as they become more functional they will be able to provide many of the same features as MOM, message brokers, and TP monitors—including sharing data and application logic and providing a central clearinghouse for enterprise information.

Sharing Methods to Bind Your Enterprise

The road to method-level EAI is not an easy one to travel, but it may yet prove to be the best path to a solution, or to the integration of all applications through the reuse of common methods. Most organizations requiring EAI will likely opt for data-level and application interface–level EAI before attempting method-level EAI. The former are easier to deploy and carry less risk. However, "no guts, no glory." Method level, for all its difficulties, has much more value for the EAI solution, depending on the requirements of the problem domain.

CHAPTER FIVE

User Interface–Level EAI

> "I think there is a world market for maybe five computers."
> —Thomas John Watson, Sr. (1874–1956),
> President, IBM

User interface–level EAI, the most primitive of all EAI levels, is also the most necessary. Other EAI levels might be more technologically appealing and more efficient, but the simple reality is that, in many applications, the user is the only available mechanism for accessing logic and data. In spite of its inefficiency in "getting into" an application, the user interface has an advantage in that it does not require any changes to the source or target application.

In the context of user interface–level EAI, the user interface *is* the EAI interface. In a process known as "screen scraping," or accessing screen information through a programmatic mechanism, middleware drives a user interface (e.g., 3270 user interface) in order to access both processes and data. So, why does such a simple topic need an entire chapter? Simply put, many application integration projects will have no other choice but to leverage user interfaces to access application data and processes. But few are willing to admit it. Moreover, user interface–level EAI is very different from application interface– and method-level EAI, which are generally much more complex.

Leveraging User Interface–Level EAI

There really isn't much to user interface–level EAI. It is just one of many techniques and technologies that can be used to access, or place, information in an application. The technology has been around for a number of years. As a consequence, there is very little risk using it. There are, however, problems that need to be overcome. In user interface–level EAI, a user interface that was never designed to serve up data is being used for precisely that purpose. It should go without saying that the data-gathering performance of user screens leaves a lot to be desired. In addition, this type of solution can't scale, so it is unable to handle more than a few screen interfaces at any given time. Finally, if these mechanisms are not set up carefully by the EAI architect and developer, they may prove unstable. Controller and server bouncing are common problems.

There are, of course, a number of tricks for sidestepping these limitations, but they bring additional risk to the project. Still, with so many closed and proprietary applications out there, the EAI architect has little choice. The name of the game is accessing information—by any means possible. Ultimately, going directly to the user interface to get at the data is like many other types of technology—not necessarily pretty, but it gets the job done.

Going to the User Interface

For the reasons noted previously, user interface–level EAI should be the "last ditch effort" for accessing information residing in ordered systems. It should be turned to only when there is no well-defined application interface (e.g., BAPI), such as those provided by many ERP applications, or when it doesn't make sense to leverage data-level EAI. Having said that, we can also state that user interface–level EAI needn't be avoided. In most cases, it will prove to be successful in extracting information from existing applications and as a mechanism to invoke application logic. Moreover, if performed correctly, there will be virtually no difference between using the user interface or a true application interface.

As in other levels of EAI, the architect or the developer has the responsibility to understand the application, the application architecture, and the database information in great detail. At the user-level interface, this may prove difficult. Remember, the decision to leverage user interface–level EAI was made specifically to bypass the restrictions of closed proprietary systems, or because it

CASE STUDY: Using User Interface–Level EAI

An existing mainframe application created using DB2 and COBOL needs to share processes and data with a custom distributed object system running on Linux, and PeopleSoft running on NT. The mainframe application is older and does not have an application interface, nor do the skills exist within the company to create one.

Instead of creating an application interface, or moving information at the data level, the EAI architect opts to leverage user interface–level EAI. Using this approach the EAI architect is able to extract both application data and business information from the COBOL/DB2 system exposed by the user interface. The EAI architect may leverage this approach, perhaps to save money and lower the risk of the EAI project, or due to the simple fact that this may be the only solution considering the state of the technology (the most popular reason).

The process of extracting information using the user interface (as we'll see in this chapter), is really a matter of defining how to get to the appropriate screens, locating the correct information on the screens, reading the information from the screens, and finally processing the information. You're creating an automated program that simulates an actual user, navigating through screens, emulating keystrokes, and reading screens into memory where the information is parsed, reformatted, and transported to any number of middleware layers where it's sent ultimately to the target system, to the PeopleSoft system, for instance. You also need to check for errors and be able to handle and recover from the inevitable problems such as system and network failures.

You need to consider the business case. In this instance it may not make good business sense to create a new interface into the older mainframe-based system, and it may not make sense to integrate the applications at the data level (e.g., if we need to extract calculated information, versus just raw data). By creating a new interface, the existing mainframe system will typically have to undergo a small-to-medium re-architecture effort, redevelopment to add the application interface, and redeployment and testing of the application before it's placed into production. This is a long and drawn out process, and perhaps it's not needed, considering what we can do these days with user-level EAI. Is it the best solution? It's another tradeoff.

just makes good business sense not to augment an existing system to create an interface, or because other EAI levels are not applicable. In spite of the difficulty, this information is necessary for two reasons: one, the need to understand all the information that an application is producing, and two, to understand how all the data and methods residing within an application relate to all the data and methods existing within the enterprise. In short, it is necessary to know how the application data and methods fit within the enterprise metadata model and the enterprise object models, and map the source system into this logical and physical layer. Using the user interface as a point of integration does not free us from this requirement.

Understanding the Application

In order to implement user interface–level EAI, it is necessary to understand the application. This requires understanding the underlying data storage schema, much of the application logic, and, most importantly, how the information is presented to the user interface. In order to understand how the data elements are represented on the screen, it is necessary to understand how they exist within the application. Unlike other interface levels, information presented to a user interface may not map back to a database. Most of the data elements on the screen, such as calculated fields (e.g., an order total), are created by the application logic and do not come directly from the database. This being the case, it is evident that an understanding of the application logic is also desirable. This requires reading the documentation so that the mechanisms of the application—as well as the logic—can be understood. Unfortunately, as in other contexts, the applications are not always well documented. If this proves to be the case, the source code itself will have to be read. Ultimately, regardless of how it is achieved, the goal is to be able to trace all data that appears on the screen to the application logic and database schema information.

Reaching this goal will often require "breaking the data out" from its representation on the screen, a task accomplished with simple, mathematical formulas. There are times when it will be necessary to break out six separate data elements from a single number presented on the user interface. This, in and of itself, is a strong statement for the EAI architect or developer to understand the application logic in detail. There are many cases of user interface EAI projects where a failure to understand the application has led to a misreading of the user interfaces and, consequently, erroneous data being fed into target applications.

> ### Creating Special Interfaces for User-Level EAI
>
> The ability to "scrape" information from existing user interfaces doesn't suggest that user screens have to be relied on exclusively. Many EAI architects and developers have discovered a way to free information from more recalcitrant systems by creating special screens, screens with the sole purpose of supporting the extraction of information from the source, or target applications. For example, it may be possible to access customer and accounts receivable information contained within certain mainframe-based systems by extracting data from as many as ten user screens. A developer may choose to combine all information relevant to customers and accounts receivable on a single screen as a mechanism to extract all the required information by invoking only that one screen.
>
> Other screens can be created for the same purpose. The advantage of these screens is performance. They reduce the dependence on user screens that frequently change, as do most of the programs developed to extract information from them. However, depending on the system, you're going to have to change code to create these screens that expose so much information. If you do that, perhaps it's better to just go the extra mile and create a well-defined API.

Creating the Screen Catalog

Once the database schema and application logic contained within the source or target application is understood, a catalog of all the information that appears on the user interfaces must be created. This task requires capturing each screen image and then cataloging each data element that appears on each screen. For example, a data element that appears next to the "Accounts Receivable" label would have to be cataloged by screen, label, and description. In addition to simply cataloging these data elements, the logic that creates them (e.g., mathematical equations, on the fly from user input) would also have to be documented, preferably from the application documentation, or source code.

Screens are typically cataloged by screen name, data element, description, database reference, and any applicable business logic (see Figure 5.1). This format allows for the efficient location of appropriate information from any source or target system that exists in the screen catalog. In addition, this information will facilitate an update of the enterprise metadata model.

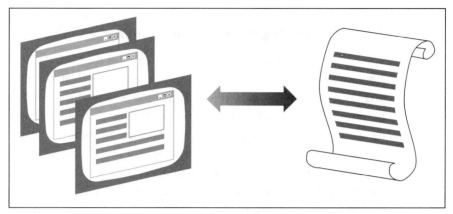

Figure 5.1   Example screen catalog

Mapping Screens

In addition to the creation of a screen catalog of the information found in the user interface, it is necessary to map the positions of that same information. This process—**screen mapping**—determines the location of each data element on each screen, the number of positions it holds, and any other relevant information. This will better enable screen access technology to locate the appropriate information. For example, in order to find accounts receivable information, it would be necessary to know both its exact position on the screen where it appears, and how to process that information according to the information contained in the screen catalog.

The same piece of information can often be found at several locations in the application screens. For example, customer information may appear on every screen pertaining to updating a customer account. In screen mapping, the place that a particular data element is accessed is not important, but consistency is.

Finding the Information

Having said all that, we should be quick to point out that extracting information from screens is not as straightforward as it may seem at first glance. There are two basic techniques to extract information from screens: static and dynamic. Each has advantages and limitations. Knowing how each works can optimize user interface EAI.

Static Extraction

Static screen extraction means that, whichever technology is being used, the information is being accessed from a static point on the screen (e.g., Column 10,

Row 12, Position 10). Consequently, there is no need to search the screen or employ a conditional logic to find the information.

The advantage of static extraction lies in its simplicity. Without the need to create a logic for each screen extraction, acquiring the required information simply means going to the predetermined location and grabbing the information. Simple. But the downside is profound. If the application interface changes for any reason (e.g., by adding more information), then the position where the data element once resided may not continue to be the position where it resides. As a result, the EAI screen extraction process may extract *no* information, or worse, the wrong information. Clearly, this method of extraction should only be used for applications that never, or rarely, change.

Dynamic Extraction

Dynamic extraction is a more sophisticated process than static extraction. It gives EAI architects and developers the ability to look at a screen using conditional logic. For example, rather than going directly to a fixed position when looking for accounts receivable information, this technique would *search* for the "accounts receivable" label and would use *that* as a reference point.

The obvious advantage to dynamic extraction is the ability to automatically adapt to changes within an application and react to changes in the structure of the screen. Another advantage of dynamic extraction is the ability to place specific logic sequences in the extraction process, such as a logic to flag errors if a particular label is not found, or one that determines if a data element does not make sense.

Error Processing

Both the dynamic and the static extraction techniques must go through a rudimentary error-checking routine in order to ensure that only valid data is extracted. This routine takes place after the data has been extracted from the screen. It looks for easy-to-spot problems, such as character information in a numeric data element.

The goal of error processing is to alert the appropriate person to a problem, so that it can be corrected before bad data is extracted. Error-processing routines are vital to user interface–level EAI.

Approaches

There are two approaches for getting information from application interfaces: using screens as raw data and using screens as objects. Both extract the information by using the interface as if the program was an actual user, and reading the information to the virtual interface. Naturally, it is impossible to get all necessary information from a single user interface. Most user interface–level EAI efforts will require as many as a thousand instances of a user interface in order to obtain the correct information in the correct volume (see Figure 5.2).

Screens-as-Data

The **screen-as-data** scenario involves looking at a screen as a simple stream of text. The information is extracted and then incorporated into the program as a string of text. Once there, the information is parsed, identified, converted, and processed within the program that is responsible for processing the user interface information (e.g., the message broker itself, or an adapter).

The advantage to screens-as-data is simplicity. Information never really changes states and therefore remains easy to comprehend. In addition, the screen information is never tied directly to methods. Unfortunately, the very advantage of this method—its simplicity—is also its disadvantage. Because only information is being tracked—and not the methods that act upon that information—only half the story is being told. The other half requires the screens-as-objects scenario.

Screens-as-Objects

The **screens-as-objects** scenario is much more sophisticated than the screens-as-data scenario. It may even be too sophisticated for most user interface–level EAI

Figure 5.2　**Using user interface–level EAI may require running hundreds of instances of the source, or target application's, user interface.**

projects. Using screens-as-objects requires translating the information gathered from a user interface into an application object, either a Java object, a CORBA, or a COM ORB. Translating the information into objects requires adding the methods needed to interact on the data (see Figure 5.3).

The advantage of using screen objects is the ease with which they can be placed into other environments that support objects, among them application servers and message brokers. These environments can act on the screen objects like any other application object. Moreover, developers can extend the capabilities of the objects to meet the exact requirements of the EAI problem domain or application.

Enabling Technology

Examples of enabling technology that supports user interface–level EAI include terminal emulation software, middleware, and software development kits (SDK).

Screen Access Tricks

Most user interface–level EAI projects will leverage 3270 (used by most IBM-type mainframe users) or 5250 (used by most AS/400 users) terminal emulation software as a mechanism to access user interface information. Either product generally comes with two components: the emulator and the SDK to automate screen access operations, including extraction.

There are three technical approaches to extracting information from user interfaces: 3270/5250 user interface access using HLLAPI (High Level Language Application Program Interface), accessing ASCII terminals such as VT100s, accessing Windows-based GUIs using OLE automation, and converting screens into objects. While a detailed discussion of each approach is beyond the scope of this book, it's helpful to look briefly at each.

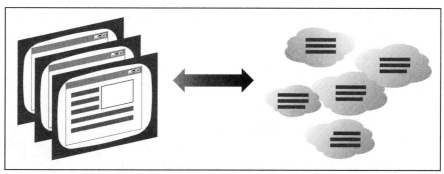

Figure 5.3   Using screens as objects

HLLAPI

HLLAPI is an IBM programming interface allowing PC applications to communicate with a mainframe application through 3270 emulation. The HLLAPI interface is able to read and write to 3270 and 5250 screens as well as process errors and manage the connection. HLLAPI is shipped with most PC-based 3270 emulators on the market today; programming HLLAPI is something that's been going on for well over ten years, and we're pretty good at it. This is the most popular screen extraction mechanism for user interface–level EAI, and many EAI solutions, such as message brokers and application servers, use 3270 adapters (using HLLAPI) to read and write information from and to 3270 and 5250.

ASCII or ANSI

ASCII or ANSI terminals, such as VT100 and VT220, support simple screen scraping as well, but instead of a 3270 data stream, they leverage an ASCII data stream used by these terminals that are connected to host-based UNIX systems and DEC minicomputers. The extraction mechanism is an API that works with the VT emulator software (e.g., TELNET) to locate and extract screen information.

OLE Automation

Of course, while 3270 and VT100 terminals were the preferred user interface several years ago, Windows has long since taken over. Extracting information from applications that run within the Windows Win32 environment is a necessity from time to time. This is done, generally, through **OLE automation**. OLE automation enables a client application to communicate with a server application, allowing it to exchange information between applications easily. Thus, it's a simple matter of creating an application that's able to read the application information (exposed by OLE automation) from the Windows application that we're interested in. We implement OLE automation through any number of programming tools that support it, including Visual Basic and Visual C++. We'll discuss the use of OLE automation and Microsoft's COM (Component Object Model) in more detail in Chapter 10. OLE automation and COM also lend themselves well to method-level EAI.

Screens as Objects

Screens as objects use any one of the user interface communications mechanisms explained previously but go a step further by encapsulating the data and the methods that act upon that data into a binary or program object. This may be a CORBA object, a COM object, a C++ object, or a Java object depending on what you're interacting with. The advantage of this approach is that the screen information is transformed into a set of objects. These objects are easily queried by other applications as true objects and not as a simple stream of data. This approach is much more sophisticated and is the future of user interface–level EAI; it binds user interface–level EAI to method-level EAI, which makes use of objects as a mechanism to share methods.

CHAPTER SIX

The EAI Process— Methodology or Madness?

"I do not fear computers. I fear lack of them."
—Isaac Asimov

This chapter builds on a working knowledge of method-level, data-level, application interface–level, and user interface–level EAI to suggest a high-level process, or methodology, that can be applied to most enterprise application integration projects. Naturally, we cannot present all possible answers here. Our goal is to provide a workable checklist of the issues that need to be considered within the context of any given EAI project. That said, we must add that every problem domain is unique and that the methodology approaches will vary greatly from project to project. For example, EAI projects that work exclusively at the data level must consider data-level activities such as data cataloging and enterprise metadata modeling, while projects working at the object model level will require composite applications. Still others may use both types of EAI, and therefore, the associated activities needed to get them there. Ultimately, the successful approach is the one that matches the processes or steps in a particular problem domain. The best way to achieve that success is to understand all the details of a problem domain, leaving no proverbial stone unturned.

Applying a Procedure/Methodology

By the time this book has gone to press, most professional service organizations will have instituted some form of EAI methodology that, they will claim, will assure ultimate EAI success. These methodologies are most often found in a series of binders (each at least six inches thick) and outline as many as a thousands steps before reaching EAI nirvana. That's all fine and good but a bit on the overkill side for most organizations. Most organizations don't need that kind of rigor to be successful with EAI. What they do need are some good architectural skills and a base of knowledge pertaining to state-of-the-art technology solutions.

The following activities should be considered when approaching EAI (which is not to say that these are the *only* steps in an EAI project). Our strategy relies on a practical approach to EAI. We reuse some of the activities we've learned with traditional database design, application design, and development. Many times, we use the same design patterns to bind applications together as we did to build them. After all, there is no need to reinvent the wheel if the result will only confuse an already complex process.

This pragmatic approach relies on familiar concepts and terms such as metadata, schemas, object-oriented modeling, object-oriented analysis and design (OOA/OOD), patterns, and "good old" requirements-gathering techniques. Our suggestion for integrating applications relies on a simple set of techniques, our own "12-step program":

1. Understanding the enterprise and problem domain
2. Making sense of the data
3. Making sense of the processes
4. Identifying any application interfaces
5. Identifying the business events
6. Identifying the data transformation scenarios
7. Mapping information movement
8. Applying technology
9. Testing, testing, testing
10. Considering performance
11. Defining the value
12. Creating maintenance procedures

In this chapter, we concentrate on steps 2 and 3 because it is at those steps where we begin to define the models that will serve as the basis for our EAI solution. These steps are also unique to our approach and to this book. The remaining steps will be discussed briefly as concepts. If you require more detailed information about the remaining steps, we suggest the tremendous amount of information available in other books and articles, some of which you'll find listed in the Bibliography.

Step 1: Understanding the Enterprise and Problem Domain

Sounds simple, huh? Too bad this is the most complex and time-consuming part of the entire process. However, it is unavoidable. At some point, the problem domain must be studied, both freestanding and in the context of the enterprise. Understanding the problem domain requires working with many organization heads in order to get a handle on the structure and content of the various information systems, as well as the business requirements of each organization—how they do business, what's important, and, perhaps more importantly, what's not.

This process is a basic requirements-gathering problem. It requires interfacing with paper, people, and systems to determine the information that will allow the EAI problem to be defined correctly so that it can be analyzed, modeled, and refined. Only then can the appropriate solution set be employed.

The quality of the information gathering at this step leads directly to, and impacts the success of steps 2 and 3.

Step 2: Making Sense of the Data

We begin with the data for a couple of reasons. First, most EAI projects exist only at the data level. This reality alone justifies the quest to understand what exists in the databases scattered throughout an enterprise. Second, even if the EAI project works at the method, application interface, and user interface levels, it is still necessary to understand the databases. Face it. There's no getting around this step.

Ultimately, the implementation of data-level EAI comes down to understanding *where* the data exists, gathering information *about* the data (e.g., schema information), and applying business principles to determine *which* data flows *where*, and *why*.

There are three basic steps that must be followed to prepare for implementing data-level EAI:

1. *Identifying* the data
2. *Cataloging* the data
3. Building the *enterprise metadata* model, which will be used as a master guide for integrating the various data stores that exist within the enterprise (see Figure 6.1)

In short, implementing an EAI solution demands more than the movement of data between databases and/or applications. A successful solution requires that the enterprise also define both *how* that information flows through it, and how it does business.

Identifying the Data

Unfortunately, there are no shortcuts to identifying data within an enterprise. All too often, information about the data, both business and technical, is scattered throughout the enterprise and of a quality that ranges from "somewhat useful" to "you've got to be kidding me!"

The first step in identifying and locating information about the data is to create a list of candidate systems. This list will make it possible to determine which databases exist in support of those candidate systems. The next step will require determining who owns the databases and where they are physically located, and it will include relevant design information and such basic information as brand, model, and revisions of the database technology.

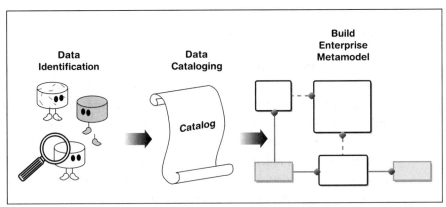

Figure 6.1   Implementing data-level EAI

Data Identification: A Thankless Process

There is no fairy godmother who will cast her wand to simplify data identification. It is a fortunate enterprise that has a functional architect capable of addressing the task. Data identification demands a lot of hard work and a deep reservoir of patience. As the architect moves forward, he or she will discover that the concept of EAI itself—integrating information between departments—is not only technically difficult but it is very often threatening to database administrators (DBAs). Welcome to the world of institutional warfare! Turf battles are unfortunate but real. Considered alone, the EAI technology is terribly complex. When the psychological obstacles that will have to be overcome are added into the mix, the EAI architect might quickly wish that the world could be reduced to binomial realities. It can't—at least, not yet.

As with any enterprise-wide evolution, a successful EAI effort must be fully supported from the top. The value of EAI *must* be understood by the enterprise's decision-makers. If the architect has limited "people skills," it would be a good idea to develop them before embarking on the task. Making friends and being sensitive to the defensiveness of the various departmental users will go a long way toward simplifying the overall task.

Any technology that is able to reverse-engineer existing physical and logical database schemas will prove helpful in identifying data within the problem domains. However, while the schema and database model may give insight into the structure of the database or databases, they cannot determine how that information is used within the context of the application.

The Data Dictionary

Detailed information can be culled by examining the data dictionaries (if they exist) linked to the data stores being analyzed. Such an examination may illuminate such important information as

- The reason for the existence of particular data elements
- Ownership
- Format

- Security parameters
- The role within both the logical and physical data structure

While the concept of the data dictionary is fairly constant from database to database, the dictionaries themselves may vary widely in form and content. Some contain more information than others do. Some are open. Most are proprietary. Some don't even exist—which is often the case with less sophisticated software.

Integrity Issues

When analyzing databases for data-level EAI, integrity issues constantly crop up. In order to address these issues, it is important to understand the rules and regulations that were applied to the construction of the database. For example, will the application allow updating customer information in a customer table without first updating demographics information in the demographics table?

Most middleware fails to take into account the structure or rules built into the databases being connected. As a result, there exists the very real threat of damage to the integrity of target databases. While some databases do come with built-in integrity controls, such as stored procedures or triggers, most rely on the application logic to handle integrity issues on behalf of the database. Unfortunately, the faith implicit in this reliance is not always well placed. Indeed, all too often it is painfully naive.

The lack of integrity controls at the data level (or, in the case of existing integrity controls, bypassing the application logic to access the database directly) could result in profound problems. EAI architects and developers need to approach this danger cautiously, making sure not to compromise the databases' integrity in their zeal to achieve integration. Perhaps this is where a decision to use another EAI level as primary point-of-integration might be considered.

Data Latency

Data latency, the characteristic of the data that defines how current the information needs to be, is another property of the data that needs to be determined for the purposes of EAI. Such information will allow EAI architects to determine when the information should be copied, or moved, to another enterprise system and how fast.

> ### What's Real Time Anyway?
>
> Although real time typically means updating a screen, memory segment, or database with current, up-to-the-minute information, there is no consensus on exactly what real time means. Purists contend that **real time** means updating with a frequency approaching **zero latency**. For them, anything less is not real time. Others take a much more lenient view.
>
> For the purposes of EAI, the purists' view is closer to the one that should be embraced. Real-time data in EAI is current, up-to-the-second data.

While an argument can be made to support a number of different categories of data latency, for the purpose of EAI within the enterprise there are really only three:

- Real time
- Near time
- One time

Real-time data is precisely what it sounds like it would be—information that is placed in the database as it occurs, with little or no latency. Monitoring stock price information through a real-time feed from Wall Street is an example of real-time data. Real-time data is updated as it enters the database, and that information is available immediately to anyone, or any application, requiring it for processing.

While zero latency real time is clearly the goal of EAI, achieving it represents a huge challenge. In order to achieve zero latency, EAI implementation requires constant returns to the database, application, or other resource to retrieve new and/or updated information. In the context of real-time updates, database performance also has to be considered—simultaneous to one process updating the database as quickly as possible, another process must be extracting the updated information.

The successful implementation of zero latency presents architects and developers with the opportunity to create such innovative solutions as method-level EAI, where business processes are integrated within the EAI solution. In many cases method-level EAI makes better sense than data level–only EAI solutions because it allows data and common business processes to be shared at the same

---

EAI Brings Real-Time Data to the Data Warehouse

Unlike EAI, which can support real-time data movement, data warehousing provides adequate business information but without up-to-the-minute access of information. In many cases, the data is weeks, even months old, and the data mart or data warehouse is updated through antiquated batch, extract-aggregate-and-load processes.

EAI, and the technology that comes with it, provides data warehouse architects and developers with the ability to move information—no matter where it comes from or where it is going—as quickly as they want it to move. As a result, it is not unheard of to have all participating databases in an EAI solution receiving new data constantly, thus providing more value to those using the source and target systems—including those using them as a data warehouse or data mart. Therefore, the rise of EAI will also lead to the rise of real-time data warehouse solutions, with many users able to leverage up-to-the-minute information to make better business decisions.

---

time. The downside to method-level EAI is that it is also the most expensive to implement.

Near-time data refers to information that is updated at set intervals rather than instantaneously. Stock quotes posted on the Web are a good example of near-time data. They are typically delayed 20 minutes or more, because the Web sites distributing the quotes are generally unable to process real-time data. Near-time data can be thought of as "good-enough" latency data. In other words, data only as timely as needed.

Although near-time data is not updated constantly, providing it still means facing many of the same challenges encountered when providing real-time data, including overcoming performance and management issues.

One-time data is typically updated only once. Customer addresses or account numbers are examples of one-time information. Within the context of EAI, the intervals of data copy, or data movement, do not require the kind of aggressiveness needed to accomplish real-time or near-time data exchange.

The notion of data typing goes well beyond the classification of the data as real-time, near-time, or one-time. It is really a complex process of determining the properties of the data, including updates and edit increments, as well as the behavior of the data over time. What do the applications use the particular data for? How often do they use it? What happens with the data over time? These are questions that must be addressed in order to create the most effective EAI solution.

Data Formats

Another identifying component of data is **data format**. How information is structured, including the properties of the data elements existing within that structure, can be gleaned from knowledge of the data format. Likewise, length, data type (character or numeric), name of the data element, and what type of information stored (binary, text, spatial, and so on) are additional characteristics of the data that may be determined by its format.

Resolution of data format conflicts must be accomplished within such EAI technologies as message brokers and/or application servers. Different structures and schemas existing within the enterprise must be transformed as information is moved from one system to another. The need to resolve these conflicts in structure and schema makes knowing the structure of the data at both the source and target systems vital. (Our discussion of message broker technology in Chapter 18 will deal with how message brokers are able to adapt to differences in data formats found in different databases that exist within the enterprise. For now, it is enough to note that message brokers are able to transform a message or database schema from one format to another so that it makes sense both contextually and semantically to the application receiving the information—see Figure 6.2). This often needs to be accomplished without changing the source or target applications, or the database schemas. Message broker technology allows two systems with different data formats to communicate successfully.)

Data Cataloging

Once the logical and physical characteristics of the databases to be integrated are understood, it is time to do the "grunge" work—data cataloging. In the world of EAI, **data cataloging** is the process of gathering metadata and other data throughout the problem domain. Once accomplished, it is possible to create an enterprise-wide catalog of all data elements that may exist within the enterprise. The resulting catalog then becomes the basis of the understanding needed to create the enterprise metadata model—the foundation of data-level EAI.

For most medium- to large-sized enterprises, the creation of this data catalog is a massive undertaking. In essence, it demands the creation of the "mother

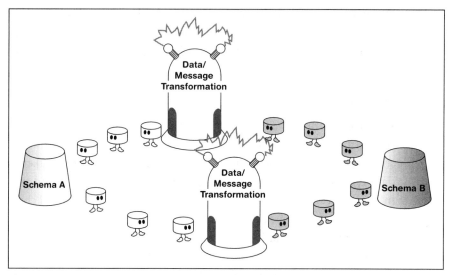

**Figure 6.2   Message brokers are able to transform schemas and content,
accounting for the differences in application semantics and
database structure between applications and databases.**

of all data dictionaries," a data dictionary that includes not only the traditional
data dictionary information, but also all the information that is of interest to
EAI—system information, security information, ownership, connected processes,
communications mechanisms, and integrity issues, along with such traditional
metadata as format, name of attribute, description, and so on.

While there is no standard for cataloging data within EAI projects, the guid-
ing principle is clear: the more information, the better. The catalog will become
both the repository for the EAI engine to be built and the foundation to discover
new business flows. It will also become a way to automate existing business flows
within the enterprise.

While data catalogs can be made using index cards or paper, electronic
spreadsheets (e.g., Microsoft Excel) or PC-based databases (e.g., Microsoft
Access) provide more attractive alternatives. Remember that a data catalog is not
the enterprise metadata. It is the foundation of the metadata. Therefore, there is
no need to expand the data catalog into a full-blown metadata repository until it
is completely populated.

It is an understatement to suggest that this catalog will be huge. Most enterprises will find tens of thousands of data elements to identify and catalog even
while reducing redundancies among some of the data elements. In addition to

being huge, the data catalog will be a dynamic structure. In a very real sense, it will never be complete. A person, or persons, will have to be assigned to maintain the data catalog over time, assuring that the information in the catalog remains correct and timely, and that the architects and developers have access to the catalog in order to create the EAI solution.

Building the Enterprise Metadata Model

Once all the information about all the data in the enterprise is contained in the data catalog, it is time to focus on the enterprise metadata model. The difference between the two is sometimes subtle. It is best to think of the data catalog as the list of potential solutions to your EAI problem and to think of the metadata model as the data-level EAI solution. The **metadata model** defines not only all the data structures existing in the enterprise but also how those data structures will interact within the EAI solution domain.

Once constructed, the enterprise metadata model is the enterprise's database repository of sorts, the master directory for the EAI solution. In many cases, the repository will be hooked on to the messaging system (e.g., message brokers) and used as a reference point for locating not only the data but also the rules and logic that apply to that data. However, the repository is more than simply the storage of metadata information. It is the heart of the ultimate EAI solution, containing both data and business model information.

The metadata repository built using the process outlined in this chapter will not only solve the data-level EAI problem but will provide the basis for other types of EAI as well (e.g., method level, user interface level, application interface level). As in the world of client/server and data warehousing, the process builds up from the data to the application and from the application to the interface, if necessary. This "hierarchical" flow identifies data-level EAI as the foundation for the larger EAI solution.

Logical Model

Just as with traditional database design methods, the enterprise metadata model used for data-level EAI can be broken into two components: the logical and the physical. And, just as with the former, the same techniques apply to the latter. Creating the logical model is the process of creating an architecture for all data

> No matter which levels of EAI are to be implemented within a given enterprise, they must begin with the data level.

stores that are independent of a physical database model, development tool, or particular DBMS (e.g., Oracle, Sybase, Informix).

A **logical model** is a sound approach to an EAI project in that it will allow architects and developers the opportunity to make objective data-level EAI decisions, moving from high-level requirements to implementation details. The logical data model is an integrated view of business data throughout the application domain or of data pertinent to the EAI solution under construction. The primary difference between using a logical data model for EAI versus traditional database development is the information source. While traditional development, generally speaking, defines new databases based on business requirements, a logical data model arising from an EAI project is based on existing databases.

At the heart of the logical model is the **Entity Relationship Diagram (ERD)**. An ERD is a graphical representation of data entities, attributes, and relationships between entities (see Figure 6.3) for all databases existing in the enterprise.

CASE (Computer Aided Software Engineering) technology is but one of the many tools to automate the logical database-modeling process. Not only do these tools provide an easy way to create logical database models, but they are also able to build logical database models into physical database models. They also create the physical schema on the target database(s) through standard middleware.

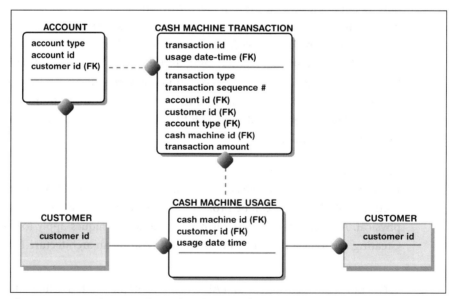

Figure 6.3   Entity Relationship Diagram (ERD)

Physical Model

The myriad of database types in any given enterprise minimizes the importance of the physical enterprise model because, with so many database types, the physical model will rarely be used. The reason is clear—there is simply no clear way to create a physical model that maps down to object-oriented, multidimensional, hierarchical, flat files, and relational databases all at the same time. However, if those databases are to be integrated, some common physical representation must be selected. Only then can the model be transformed as required. (The necessity of the physical model is only for those times when it is possible to map the logical to the physical—that is, those times when an enterprise uses a homogeneous database approach, usually all relational. The input for the physical model is both the logical model and the data catalog. When accessing this information, consider the data dictionary, business rules, and other user-processing requirements.)

Normalizing the Enterprise

Before the logical, and sometimes physical, database is completed, it is desirable to normalize the model. This is a process of decomposing complex data structures into simple relations using a series of dependency rules. **Normalization** means reducing the amount of redundant data that will exist in the database or, in the case of EAI, in the enterprise. It is a good idea to do this in both the logical and physical database design, or the EAI redesign.

When considered within the context of EAI, the normalization process is very complex and risky. Because there can be no control over most of the databases that are being integrated, normalizing the logical enterprise metadata model often results in a new version of the model that has no chance of being implemented physically. This result violates an essential credo of EAI: Whenever possible, it is best to leave the applications and databases alone. Changes to databases inevitably translate into expense and risk. Furthermore, most enterprises employ a chaotic mosaic of database technology, making it technically unfeasible to accomplish such changes without rehosting the data. This is almost always completely out of the question.

The question remains, however, "Are changes to be made to source and target databases or not?" Generally, it is wise to normalize the logical enterprise metadata model to discover areas within the enterprise that may benefit from changes in their data structures. Changes to databases may allow the enterprise to reduce the amount of redundant data and thus increase the reliability of the integrated data. Remember, the notion of data-level EAI is to perceive all the databases within the enterprise as a single database and, in turn, to make that huge enterprise database as efficient as possible through processes such as normalization.

Step 3: Making Sense of the Processes

Once the enterprise data is understood, and baseline information such as the enterprise metadata model has been created, the decision must be made as to how to approach the enterprise business model. This decision will depend on how the particular EAI problem domain is addressed. This is a view of the enterprise at the process, or method level, understanding and documenting all business processes and how they relate to each other, as well as to the enterprise metadata model.

As with the database analysis procedures outlined previously, it is desirable to use traditional process-modeling techniques, such as object modeling (e.g., the Unified Modeling Language [UML]) to create business processes. What's more, instead of creating the business processes from a set of application requirements, it is preferable to document existing business processes and methods, to better understand what they do and, therefore, how to integrate them at the method level through a composite application.

Process Integration

We have already stated that identifying processes that exist within an enterprise is a difficult task, requiring the analysis of all the applications in the enterprise that exist in the EAI problem domain. The task is made even more difficult due to the possibility that many entities embrace numerous types of applications over a number of generations of technology.

Once the applications in the problem domain have been analyzed, the enabling technology employed by each application within the problem must be identified. With applications in the enterprise dating from as long ago as 30 years, this step will uncover everything from traditional centralized computing to the best-distributed computing solutions. Once this identification has been made, the next step is to determine ownership of the processes and, subsequently, develop insight into those processes—for example, why information is being processed in one manner versus another, or why multiple arrays are used to carry out a particular operation. In most cases, ownership will rest with the application manager who determines when the application is to be changed and for what reason(s).

Finally, the documentation for the application will need to be found. In a small number of instances, applications are not only well documented but have been updated as they have matured. The vast majority of the time, applications are poorly documented, or the documentation has not been updated to keep up with the maturation of the application. Proper documentation has a profound impact on method-level EAI. Therefore, even if documentation is nonexistent, it is imperative that baseline documentation be created as the EAI solution is put into place. This is an area of significant expense as applications are opened in order to be understood and their features documented.

Process identification is important to the method-level EAI project lifecycle. Without understanding the processes, moving forward is a lot like a guessing game or like playing blind man's bluff. There can never be real certainty that the enterprise is being accurately integrated. While data is relatively easy to identify and define, processes are much more complex and difficult.

Process Cataloging

In the same way that data-level EAI requires a data-level catalog, method-level EAI requires a "process catalog"—a list of all business processes that exist within an enterprise or, at least, within the problem domain. For example, if an EAI architect needs to understand all the processes that exist within an inventory application, he or she will read either the documentation or the code to determine which processes are present. Then, the architect will not only enter the business processes into the catalog but will also determine the purpose of the process, who owns it, what exactly it does, and the technology it employs (e.g., Java, C++). In addition, the architect will need to know which database a particular business process interacts with as well as its links to the metadata model. The catalog will require other information as well, such as pseudocode, data flow diagrams, and state diagrams, which are able to define the logic flow for the particular process. In the world of traditional, structured programming, this would mean a flowchart, or pseudocode. However, in the world of object-oriented development, this refers to the object model. Thus, it is important not only to identify each process but also to understand how the logic flows within that process.

Other information may be maintained in the catalog as well, information which may include variables used within the processes, object schemas, security requirements, and/or performance characteristics. Each process catalog must maintain its own set of properties, custom built for each specific EAI problem domain (see Figure 6.4).

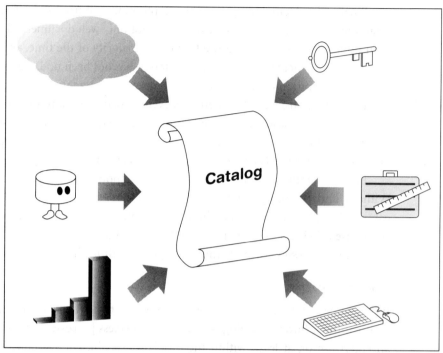

Figure 6.4   Building a process catalog requires input from many different sources.

The Common Business Model

If the enterprise metadata model is the end state for data-level EAI analysis, then the common business model is the end state for method-level EAI. Simply put, the **common business model** is the aggregation and high-level model of all objects, methods, properties, procedural logic, batch processing, and everything else in the enterprise that processes information.

The common business model is assigned this name (and not the "object model") for one reason: In order for it to document and account for such a wide array of techniques and technologies, the model must remain, at least at first, an independent paradigm. Many of the applications written in the last ten years use the object-oriented paradigm for both programming and design. However, most traditional applications (those older than ten years) use a structured application-programming paradigm, as well as structured design. The common business model must remain independent of both (see Figure 6.5).

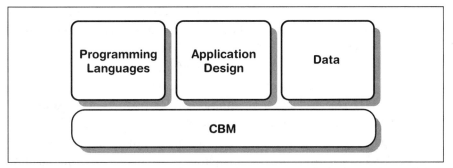

Figure 6.5   The common business model must remain independent of all programming paradigms in order to succeed with method-level EAI.

Having an independent paradigm results in a simplification of the business processes in the enterprise or the EAI problem domain. The common business model does not map out a complex, detail-oriented model, but rather a high-level understanding of the processes in the enterprise along with their functions and features—all with an eye toward those that may be combined or reused.

Business modeling is important for another reason as well. The ultimate goal of EAI is to move beyond the simple integration of applications to the much more complex integration of business process flow analysis and design. Thus, the business model provides the basis of understanding that allows for the creation of a proper business process flow necessary within the enterprise. To accomplish this, the current state and the desired state—along with a plan to get from one to the next—must be documented.

Are the Common Business Model and Object Model Necessarily Wedded?

The common business model possesses some object-oriented characteristics (because it is best represented using object-oriented modeling techniques). This should not suggest that the object-oriented model is the only one available for method-level EAI, only that object-oriented analysis and design notation seem to be most compatible with method-level EAI. This is due to the fact that method-level EAI is largely the sharing or reusing of methods within an enterprise, tasks easily accomplished within an object-oriented model.

For the sake of clarity, EAI architects should use the Unified Modeling Language (UML) to define the common business model. Using UML affords EAI architects a twofold benefit. First, an abundance of tools is available to create and maintain UML. Second, a deep pool of information exists regarding leveraging UML for a variety of purposes (see Figure 6.6).

The real challenge to creating a common business model is scope. The temptation—and thus, the trap—to re-architect and redesign each source and target application is very real. However, creating a business model is *not* an application *development* problem. It is an application *integration* problem. The EAI architect must recognize that the purpose of the common business model is to document existing processes, not to change the source and target applications. While it is certainly possible to rewrite everything from scratch in order to integrate the enterprise, such an endeavor would largely outweigh the value of EAI.

Leveraging Patterns for Method-Level EAI

Patterns are always interesting. More than interesting, they are useful in the context of method-level EAI. They enable the EAI architect to identify common business processes among the many business processes that already exist within the enterprise. Or they may be used to identify new processes in need of integration. Using patterns in this way is simply borrowing them from the world of

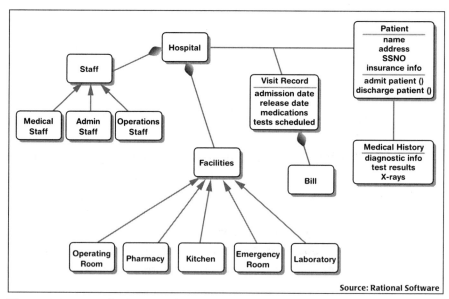

Figure 6.6   UML is the best fit for the common business model.

application architecture, and applying them to the world of enterprise architecture—a perfect fit.

Patterns arise over and over during considerations of EAI architecture. Patterns formalize and streamline the idea of EAI—to build once at the application level and then reuse throughout the solution domain. Patterns describe recurring design problems that appear in certain design contexts. They describe generic schemes for the solution of the problems, solution schemes created by defining their components, responsibilities, and relationships.

A three-part schema is part of every pattern: context, problem, and solution. **Context** describes the circumstances of the situation where the problem arises or which have to be true for the pattern to be valid. For example, an object uses data from an external system. The **problem** is what is addressed by the pattern—and that which arises over and over in the context. The challenge for the architect or designer is to capture the essence of the problem or what design issues define the problem. For example, changing the state of the object means that the object and the external data are inconsistent. As a result, there is a need to synchronize the external data and the object. The resulting **solution** is the well-proven and consistent resolution of the problem.

Types of Patterns

All patterns are not created equal. There are types, or categories, of patterns to be used in specific situations in the EAI problem domain. For example, some patterns assist EAI architects in structuring a system into subsystems, while others allow the architect to refine the subsystems and applications and the ways in which they interact. Some patterns assist EAI architects in determining design aspects using pseudocode or a true programming language such as C++. Some address domain-independent subsystems or components or domain-dependent issues such as business logic. Clearly, the range of patterns makes it difficult to define neat categories for them. However, there are three useful, and generally accepted, categories: architectural patterns, design patterns, and idioms.

Architectural patterns are complex patterns that tend to link to particular domains. They provide EAI architects with the basic system structure—subsystems, behavior, and relationships. It would not be unfair to consider these architectural patterns as templates for EAI architecture, defining macro system structure properties. **Design patterns** are not as complex as architectural patterns. They tend to be problem domain independent. These patterns provide application architects with a means of refining the subsystems and components, and the relationships between them. The goal in using these patterns is to find a common structure that solves a particular problem. An **idiom** is a low-level pattern coupled with a specific programming language. It describes how to code the object at a low level.

Pattern descriptions, or micro-methods, provide specifications for deploying the pattern. They give application architects problem-independent analysis and design methods that are found in traditional, object-oriented analysis and design methodologies such as UML.

Application to EAI

Patterns, as recurring phenomena, provide EAI architects with a methodology for defining and solving recurring problems. They allow application architects to create reusable solutions that can then be applied to multiple applications (see Figure 6.7). The ensuing information is too often kept "in the architect's head" where it is either forgotten or simply unavailable when the problem arises again. Unfortunately, EAI architects, even the good ones, tend to be poor documentation generators.

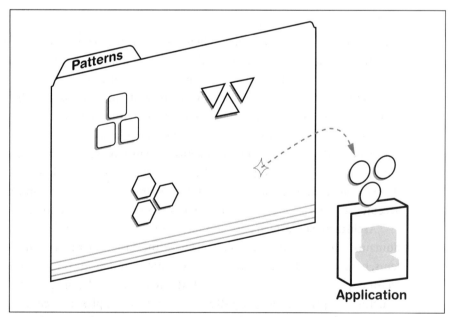

Figure 6.7   Patterns provide EAI architects with a methodology for defining and solving recurring problems.

Extending the previous concept, it becomes clear that patterns do a good job of recording design experience across a development group. They "level the playing field," providing every team member with access to this valuable information. EAI and application architects may create a database of architecture patterns—with search features and links to code and models. Patterns also provide a standard vocabulary and a base set of concepts for EAI and application architecture. For this reason, terms used to represent concepts should be chosen carefully. Thoughtful terminology results in greater efficiency because terms and concepts no longer have to be explained over and over. When endowed with a common terminology, patterns provide a natural mechanism for documenting application architectures. The vocabulary should be consistent across many projects. If this consistency is adhered to—and the patterns are accessible and understandable to all members of the application development teams—then patterns can be employed with striking success.

Patterns allow EAI and application architects to build complex architectures around predefined and proven solutions because they provide predefined components, relationships, and responsibilities. While patterns don't provide all the design detail necessary to solve a problem at hand, they do define a starting point. Moreover, they provide EAI architects with the skeleton of functionality.

Using patterns, EAI architects can manage software complexity because all patterns provide predefined methods to solve a problem. For example, if the problem is integrating an enterprise, there is no need to "reinvent the wheel." The task is simply to find the pattern that describes the problem and then to implement the solution. (This assumes that only sound patterns with working solutions are captured.)

The Value of Patterns

Patterns add value to the EAI architecture and the software development life cycle. They have the potential to increase the quality of most system development and to provide effective integration without increasing cost. However, they are not necessarily the panacea for "all that ails" the system. Patterns should not be assumed to be a mechanism for replacing a sound methodology, or a sound process. Patterns are able to become part of each, and in many instances, some pattern-oriented enterprise architecture is already taking place. Patterns simply formalize the process, filling in the gaps and providing a consistent approach.

There are those who describe patterns as the "second coming" of enterprise architecture. As comforting as that assertion might be, there is no evidence to validate it. Patterns are, simply, another available tool to be used. What is more, patterns are valuable only if they are practiced *consistently* for all applications in the enterprise. Capturing patterns for a single application is hardly worth the effort. EAI architects need to establish the infrastructure for patterns, creating standard mechanisms to capture and maintain the patterns over the long haul, refining them when necessary.

Finally, patterns only provide an *opportunity* for reuse within the EAI problem domain. They are not a guarantee of success. Object-oriented analysis and design methodologies formalize the way reusable elements (objects) are implemented. Patterns define architectural and design solutions that can be reused. There is a difference. Patterns need not be linked to object-oriented analysis, design, or implementation languages. Nor do they need rigorous notation, a rigid process, or expensive tools. Patterns can be captured easily on 3x5 index cards or a word processor. The ideal way to capture patterns in the context of EAI is within the process catalog described previously. Doing so allows both process information and pattern information to be gathered at the same time.

Again, the concept of patterns is a very simple one. However, patterns, as described by the pattern community, are too often difficult to understand and use. The depth and range of academic double-speak regarding patterns has "spooked" many application architects. Hopefully, as with other technologies based on complex theory, patterns can be freed of the shackles of academia and be made available to the "masses" so that they can become a primary tool for integration at the method level.

Step 4: Identifying Application Interfaces

In addition to seeking common methods and data to integrate, it is important as well to take note of the available application interfaces in support of application interface–level EAI, or integration with application interfaces and other EAI levels.

Interfaces are quirky. They differ greatly from application to application. What's more, many interfaces, despite what the application vendors or developers may claim, are not really interfaces at all. It is important to devote time validating assumptions about interfaces.

The best place to begin with interfaces is with the creation of an application interface directory. As with other directories, this is a repository for gathered information about available interfaces, along with the documentation for each interface. This directory is used, along with the common business model and the enterprise metadata model, to understand the points of integration within all systems of the EAI problem domain.

Application Interface Directory

The **application interface directory** can be thought of as a list of business processes that are available from an application—packaged or custom made. It must, however, be a true application (database, business processes, or user interface) and not a database or simple middleware service. The application interface directory expands on the enterprise metadata model, tracking both data and methods that act on the data.

Application Semantics

The first portion of the application interface directory is a list of application semantics. These establish the way and form in which the particular application refers to properties of the business process. For example, the very same customer number for one application may have a completely different value and meaning in another application. Understanding the semantics of an application guarantees that there will be no contradictory information when the application is integrated with other applications. Achieving consistent application semantics requires an EAI "Rosetta stone" and, as such, represents one of the major challenges to the EAI solution.

The first step in creating this "Rosetta stone" is to understand which terms mean what in which applications. Once that step is accomplished, that first very difficult step has been taken toward success.

Business Processes

Business processes are listings of functions or methods provided by the application. In some applications, such a listing is easy to determine because the business processes are well documented and easily found by invoking the user interface. However, in other applications, determining these processes requires a search through the source code to discover and understand the various methods and functions available.

As with application semantics, it is critical to understand all business processes that are available within a particular application. Once understood and documented in the application interface directory, it is possible to determine the particular combination of processes to invoke in order to carry out a specific integration requirement. For example, in an application that contains as many as 30 business processes for updating customer information, it is vital to know which process wants to invoke what and why.

Step 5: Identifying the Business Events

The next step is the identification of all relevant business events that occur within an enterprise. This means when something happens—an event —then there is a resulting reaction. For example, a customer signing up for credit on an online Web store represents an "event." It may be desirable to capture this event and make something else happen, such as running an automatic credit check to assure that the customer is credit worthy. That consequence, of course, may kick off a chain of events at the credit bureau and return the credit status of the customer, which typically fires off still other events, such as notifying the customer through e-mail if the credit application is accepted or denied. These events are generally asynchronous in nature but can be synchronous in some instances.

This should make clear that in attempting to understand an EAI problem domain, a real attempt should be made to capture the business events that may take place within the domain. It is important to understand *what* invoked a business event, *what* takes place during the event, and any other events that may be invoked as a consequence of the initial event. The end result is a web of interrelated events, each dependent on the other. Currently, this web exists through automatic or manual processes. In the EAI solution set, all these events will be automated across systems, eliminating the manual processing entirely.

Step 6: Identifying the Schema and Content Transformation Scenarios

With an existing understanding of the data and application semantics that exist within an EAI problem domain, it is good to get an idea about how schema and content of the data moving between systems will be transformed. This is necessary for a couple of reasons. First, data existing in one system won't make sense to another until the data schema and content is reformatted to make sense to the target system. Second, it will assure the maintenance of consistent application semantics from system to system. (This subject will be discussed in more detail when we discuss message brokers in Chapter 18.)

Step 7: Mapping Information Movement

Once the preceding steps have revealed all the information available, it is time to map the information movement from system to system—what data element or interface the information is moving from, and to where that information will ultimately move.

For example, the customer number from the sales databases needs to move to the credit-reporting system, ultimately residing in the customer table maintained by the credit system. This knowledge enables us to map the movement from the source systems, the sales system, to the credit system, or the target system. It should be noted where the information is physically located, what security may be present, what enabling technology exists (e.g., relational table), and how the information is extracted on one side to be placed on the other.

It is also necessary to note the event that's bound to the information movement. Or if no event is required, what other condition (such as time of data, real time, or state changes) causes the movement of information from the source to the target. (This process is typically more relevant to cohesive systems rather than coupled systems, because coupled systems are usually bound at the method level, which is where the data is shared rather than replicated. Mappings need to be adapted to the EAI level that is being used to integrate the systems.)

Step 8: Applying Technology

Now, finally, the "fun" part (not to mention the reason for the rest of the book): selecting the proper enabling technology to solve the EAI problem. Many technologies are available, including application servers, distributed objects, and message brokers. The choice of technology will likely be a mix of products and vendors that, together, meet the needs of the EAI solution. It is very rare for a single vendor to be able to solve all problems—not that that reality has ever kept vendors from making the claim that they can.

Technology selection is a difficult process, which requires a great deal of time and effort. Creating the criteria for technology and products, understanding available solutions, and then matching the criteria to those products is hardly a piece of cake. To be successful, this "marriage" of criteria and products often requires a pilot project to prove that the technology will work. The time it takes to select the right technologies could be as long as the actual development of the EAI solution. While this might seem daunting, consider the alternative—picking the wrong technology for the problem domain. A bad choice practically assures the failure of the EAI project.

Step 9: Testing, Testing, Testing

Testing is expensive and time consuming. To make testing an even more "attractive" endeavor, it is also thankless. Still, if an EAI solution is not tested properly, then disaster looms large. For example, important data can be overwritten (and thus lost). Perhaps worse, erroneous information could appear within applications. Even without these dire eventualities, it is necessary to ensure that the solution will scale and handle the other rigors of day-to-day usage.

To insure proper testing, a test plan will have to be put in place. While a detailed discussion of a test plan is beyond the scope of this book, it is really just a step-by-step procedure detailing how the EAI solution will be tested when completed. A test plan is particularly important because of the difficulty in testing an EAI solution. Most source and target systems are business critical and therefore cannot be taken offline. As a result, testing these systems can be a bit tricky.

Step 10: Considering Performance

Performance is too often ignored until it's too late. A word of advice: Don't ignore performance! EAI systems that don't perform well are destined to fail. For example, if processing a credit report for a telephone customer takes 20 minutes during peak hours, then the EAI solution does not have business value.

While most EAI solutions won't provide zero latency with today's technology, the movement of information from system to system, or the invocation of common business processes, should provide response times under a second. What's more, the EAI solution should provide that same response time under an ever-increasing user and processing load. In short, the EAI solution will scale.

So, how do you build performance into a system? By designing for performance and by testing performance before going live. Remember, performance is something that can't be fixed once the EAI solution has been deployed. Performance must be designed "from the ground up." This means the architecture of the EAI solution needs to provide the infrastructure for performance, as well as the selected enabling technology. It is possible to make some adjustments before the solution is deployed using traditional performance models, such as those developed over the years within the world of distributed computing.

Finally, it is necessary to run some performance tests to ensure that the system performs well under a variety of conditions. For example, how well does it perform at 100 users, 500 users, 1,000 users, and even 10,000 users? What about processing load? What happens to performance as you extend the EAI solution over time?

Step 11: Defining the Value

With the hard part out of the way, it's time to define the value of the EAI solution, to determine the business value of integrating systems. In this scenario, the method of determining value is generally evaluating the dollars that will be saved by a successful EAI solution. Two things should be considered here: the soft and hard dollar savings. Hard dollars, simply put, represent the value of the EAI solution easily defined by the ability for the solution to eliminate costly processes, such as automating manual processes, reducing error rates, or processing customer orders more quickly. In contrast, soft dollar savings are more difficult to define. These savings include increased productivity over time, retention rate increase due to the ability to make systems work together for the users, and customer satisfaction (based on ease of use) with an organization with integrated systems.

Of course, defining value in a particular system can be based on any criteria and will differ from problem domain to problem domain, and from business to business.

Step 12: Creating Maintenance Procedures

Last but not least, it is necessary to consider how an EAI solution will be maintained over time. Who will administer the message broker server? Who will manage security? Who will monitor system performance and solve problems?

In addressing the need for ongoing maintenance, a good idea is to document all of the maintenance activities that need to occur—and assign people to carry them out. Remember, an EAI solution represents the heart of an enterprise, moving vital information between mission-critical systems. As such, it is also a point of failure that could bring the entire enterprise to its knees.

With that happy thought in mind, this might also be a good time to consider disaster recovery issues, such as redundant servers and networks, as well as relocating the EAI solution should a disaster occur.

Method or Madness?

As we noted at the outset of this chapter, we have not (and could not) define everything that you must do in order to create a successful EAI project. Our goal here has been to outline the activities that may be necessary for your EAI project. Unlike traditional application development, where the database and application are designed, EAI solutions are as unique as snowflakes. When all is said and done, no two will be alike. However, as time goes on, common patterns emerge that allow us to share best practices in creating an EAI solution. We still need to travel further down the road before we can see the entire picture. But we're getting there. We're getting there.

CHAPTER SEVEN

An Introduction to EAI and Middleware

"All programmers are playwrights and all computers are lousy actors."

    —Anonymous

The first six chapters have been devoted to EAI approaches and implementation. In the following chapters, we will concentrate on the technology that makes EAI possible: middleware. This chapter provides an overview of middleware, setting the stage for the next several chapters that will describe several types of middleware technologies that may assist us in solving the EAI problem.

The evolution of middleware has created the opportunity to orchestrate an enterprise through the conduit of middleware, making it the primary enabling technology that can make EAI work.[*]

Middleware: The Engine of EAI

Middleware is not a magic bullet. It provides, quite simply, a mechanism that allows one entity (application or database) to communicate with another entity or entities. The notion that a middleware product can be installed within an enterprise, and information can suddenly—magically—be shared, is simply not based on reality. Even with a good middleware product, there remains a lot of work to be done, including the effort already outlined in Chapters 1 through 6.

---

[*]Middleware information is being discussed in the context of EAI and not as general-purpose technology.

Middleware is just another tool, nothing more. So, why use it? The answer is simple: because it really is the best and only solution that allows applications to communicate with one another. Middleware is able to hide the complexities of the source and target systems, thereby freeing developers from focusing on low-level APIs and network protocols and allowing them to concentrate on sharing information. For example, the same middleware API may be used across many different types of application development products, as well as many different platforms. This use of a common API hides the complexities of both the entities being connected and the platforms they reside on. That's the idea behind middleware.

Middleware is the best hope for moving information between applications and databases. Unfortunately, traditional middleware as it exists today does very little to solve the classic EAI problem. Point-to-point middleware, such as remote procedure calls (RPCs) and message-oriented middleware (MOM), can provide connections between applications, but in order to facilitate the use of the middleware, changes to the source and target applications must be made. What's more, as we demonstrated in Chapter 1, creating many point-to-point connections between many source and target systems quickly becomes unmanageable and inflexible. Thus, new types of middleware have come into play, including application servers and message brokers; however, we are bound to have even better solutions as EAI technology progresses over time.

What's Middleware?

Although there are many definitions of middleware, middleware is basically any type of software that facilitates communications between two or more software systems. Granted, this is a broad definition, but it is certainly applicable as long as you bear in mind that middleware may be as simple as a raw communications pipe running between applications, such as Java's RMI (Remote Method Invocation) or as sophisticated as information-sharing and logic execution mechanisms, such as TP (Transaction Processing) monitors.

Types of Middleware

The evolution of middleware is bringing about a change in many of the identifying features that made categorizing middleware an easier task. As a result, placing middleware in categories is becoming ever more difficult. For example, many message queuing products now do publish and subscribe, provide transactional features, and host application logic. The challenge of categorizing such a product should be plainly evident.

Is Middleware Becoming a Commodity?

Middleware is evolving into more of a commodity product. Many of the mechanisms considered unique just a few years ago are being pushed down in the operating system and bundled. This is certainly the case with RPCs and MOM, and perhaps with application servers and TP monitors as well.

In this context, as in many others, Microsoft is a driving force. Microsoft's strategy includes bundling what used to be high-end middleware products with their operating systems. This is the case with MSMQ (Microsoft Message Queue) and MTS (Microsoft Transaction Server).

Even so, several types of middleware solve particular types of problems. For the purposes of our EAI discussion, we will describe RPCs, MOM, distributed objects, database-oriented middleware, transactional middleware (including TP monitors and application servers), and message brokers (see Figure 7.1).

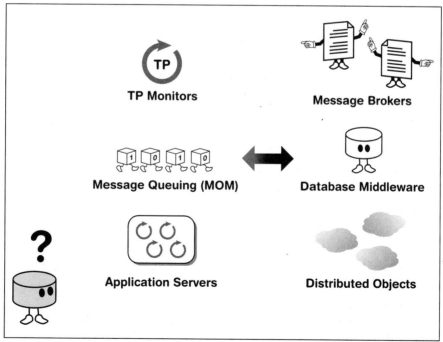

Figure 7.1   **There are many types of middleware, each solving its own set of problems.**

RPCs

RPCs are the oldest type of middleware. They are also the easiest to understand and use. Basically, RPCs provide developers with the ability to invoke a function within one program and have that function actually execute within another program on another remote machine (see Figure 7.2). The fact that the function is actually being carried out on a remote computer is hidden. To the developer, the function is executing locally.

RPCs are synchronous (see the discussion of synchronous function in "Synchronous versus Asynchronous" later in this chapter). They stop the execution of the program in order to carry out a remote procedure call. Because of this, RPCs are known as blocking middleware. Because carrying out a remote procedure call requires so much "overhead," RPCs require more bandwidth than other types of middleware products.

RPCs have also become a commodity product. Most UNIX systems, for example, ship RPC development libraries and tools as part of the base operating system. While particular vendors, such as NobleNet, sell RPCs, the best known type of RPC is the **Distributed Computing Environment (DCE)** from the Open Software Foundation (OSF).

DCE provides a very sophisticated distributed RPC mechanism with many layers of services (such as security services, directory services, and the ability to maintain integrity between applications). Although DCE is a component of many other types of middleware products (such as COM and many application servers), it has been pretty much a failure due to the performance overhead of the product. In fact, most RPCs are not well-performing middleware products. Their advantage is their simplicity.

The major downside with RPCs is their requirement for a lot more processing power. In addition, many exchanges must take place across a network to carry

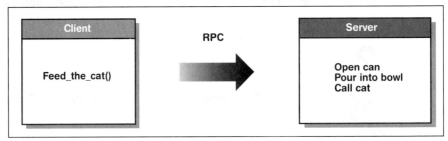

Figure 7.2   RPCs allow local function calls to execute on remote computers.

out the request. As a result, they suck the life out of a network or a computer system. For example, a typical RPC call may require 24 distinct steps in completing the requests—that's in addition to several calls across the network. This kind of performance limits the advisability of making RPC calls across slower networks, such as the Internet.

RPCs require 10,000 to 15,000 instructions in order to process a remote request. That's several hundred times the cost of a local procedure call (a simple function call). As is the case with DCE, one of the most famous (or infamous) RPCs around, the RPC software also has to make requests to security services in order to control access to remote applications. There may be calls to naming services and translation services as well. All of this adds to the overhead of RPCs.

As we've noted, the advantages of RPCs are the sheer simplicity of the mechanism and the ease of programming. Again, these advantages must be weighed against RPCs' huge performance cost and their inability to scale well, unless combined with other middleware mechanisms, such as a TP monitor or message-queuing middleware.

Unfortunately, it is difficult to know when RPCs are in use because they are bundled into so many products and technologies. For example, CORBA-compliant distributed objects are simply another layer on top of an RPC. They thus rely on synchronous connections to communicate object to object (although they are now deploying messaging and transaction services as part of the standard). This additional layer translates to additional overhead when processing a request between two or more distributed objects. Ultimately, this is the reason why distributed objects, while architecturally elegant, typically don't scale or provide good performance. Given the benefits of RPCs, the **Object Management Group (OMG),** who is the consortium of vendors who created CORBA, and CORBA vendors are working to solve the performance problem.

Message-Oriented

MOM was created to address some shortcomings of RPCs through the use of messaging. Although any middleware product that uses messages can correctly be considered MOM, we've placed message brokers in their own category because they provide a different set of services than traditional MOM, and also because of their importance to the new world of EAI. Traditional MOM is typically queuing software, using messages as a mechanism to move information from point to point.

Because MOM uses the notion of messages to communicate between applications, direct coupling with the middleware mechanism and the application is not required. MOM products use an asynchronous paradigm. Decoupled from the application, they allow the application to function independently.

The asynchronous model allows the application to continue processing after making a middleware service request. The message is dispatched to a queue manager, which makes sure that the message is delivered to its final destination. Messages returning to the calling application are handled when the calling application finds the time (see Figure 7.3).

The asynchronous paradigm is much more convenient for developers and users because it does not block the application from processing, although the model is a bit more complex than the synchronous model. Moreover, MOM is able to ensure delivery of a message from one application to the next through several sophisticated mechanisms, such as message persistence.

The use of messages is an advantage as well. Because messages are little, byte-sized units of information that move between applications, developers find them easier to manage. Messages have a structure (a schema) and content (data). In a

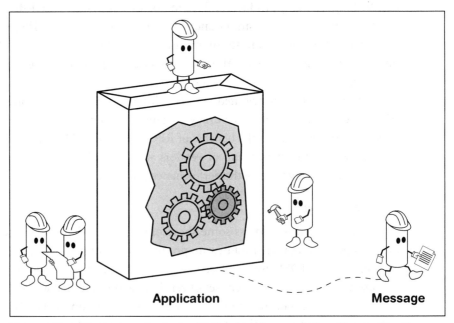

Application   **Message**

Figure 7.3   **Message-oriented middleware does not stop the application from processing.**

sense, they are little, one-record databases that move between applications through message-passing mechanisms.

While MOM is one of the newest players in the middleware world, it already possesses a mature technology with some performance and usability advantages over traditional RPCs. There are two models supported by MOM: point-to-point and **message queuing** (**MQ**)—the latter being our primary focus here.

MQ has several performance advantages over standard RPC. First, MQ lets each participating program proceed at its own pace without interruption from the middleware layer. Therefore, the calling program can post a message to a queue and then "get on with its life." If a response is required, it can get it from the queue later. Another benefit to MQ is that the program can broadcast the same message to many remote programs without waiting for the remote programs to be up and running.

Because the MQ software (e.g., IBM's MQSeries or Microsoft's MSMQ) manages the distribution of the message from one program to the next, the queue manager can take steps to optimize performance. Many performance enhancements come with these products, including prioritization, load balancing, and thread pooling.

There is little reason to be concerned that some messages may be lost during network or system failure. As mentioned previously, most MQ software lets the message be declared as persistent or stored to disk during a commit at certain intervals. This allows for recovery from such situations.

Distributed Objects

Distributed objects are also considered middleware because they facilitate inter-application communications. However, they are also mechanisms for application development (therein lies an example of the middleware paradox), providing enabling technology for enterprise-wide method sharing.

Distributed objects are really small application programs that use standard interfaces and protocols to communicate with one another (see Figure 7.4). For example, developers may create a CORBA-compliant distributed object that runs on a UNIX server and another CORBA-compliant distributed object that runs on an NT server. Because both objects are created using a standard (in this case, CORBA), and both objects use a standard communications protocol (in this case, Internet Inter-ORB Protocol—IIOP), then the objects should be able to exchange information and carry out application functions by invoking each other's methods.

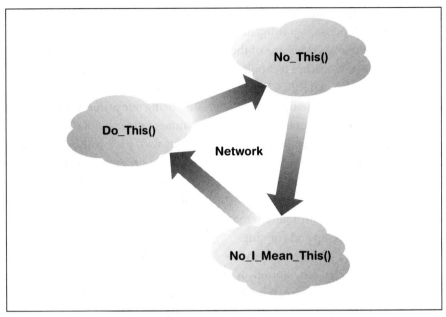

Figure 7.4   Using distributed objects

Two types of distributed objects are on the market today: CORBA and COM. CORBA, created by the OMG in 1991, is really more of a standard than a technology. It provides specifications outlining the rules that developers should follow when creating a CORBA-compliant distributed object. CORBA is heterogeneous, with CORBA-compliant distributed objects available on most platforms.

COM is a distributed object standard promoted by Microsoft. Like CORBA, COM provides "the rules of the road" for developers when creating COM-enabled distributed objects. These rules include interface standards and communications protocols. While there are COM-enabled objects on non-Windows platforms, COM is really more native to the Windows operating environments and therefore more homogeneous in nature.

Database-Oriented

Database-oriented middleware is any middleware that facilitates communications with a database, whether from an application or between databases. Developers typically use database-oriented middleware as a mechanism to extract information from either local or remote databases. For example, to get information residing within an Oracle database, the developer may invoke database-oriented middleware to log onto the database, request information, and process the information that has been extracted from the database (see Figure 7.5).

Database-oriented middleware works with two basic database types: call-level interfaces (CLIs) and at-native database middleware.

While CLIs provide access to any number of databases through a well-defined common interface and are common APIs that span several types of database, they work most typically with relational databases. Such is the case with Microsoft's Open Database Connectivity (ODBC). ODBC exposes a single interface in order to facilitate access to a database and then uses drivers to allow for the differences between the databases. ODBC also provides simultaneous, multiple database access to the same interface—in the ODBC architecture, a driver manager can load and unload drivers to facilitate communications between the different databases (e.g., Oracle, Informix, and DB2).

Another example of a CLI is JavaSoft's JDBC. JDBC is an interface standard that uses a single set of Java methods to facilitate access to multiple databases. JDBC is very much like ODBC, providing access to any number of databases from most Java applets or servlets.

OLE DB from Microsoft is the future of Microsoft database middleware. OLE DB provides a standard mechanism to access any number of resources, including databases, as standard objects (e.g., COM objects, see Figure 7.6). OLE DB also provides access to resources other than databases, such as Excel spreadsheets and flat files. Again, this information is accessed as COM objects.

Native database middleware does not make use of a single, multidatabase API. Instead, it accesses the features and functions of a particular database, using only native mechanisms. The ability to communicate with only one type of database is the primary disadvantage of using native database middleware. The advantages of native database middleware include improved performance and access to all of the low features of a particular type of database.

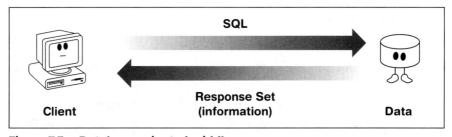

Figure 7.5   Database-oriented middleware

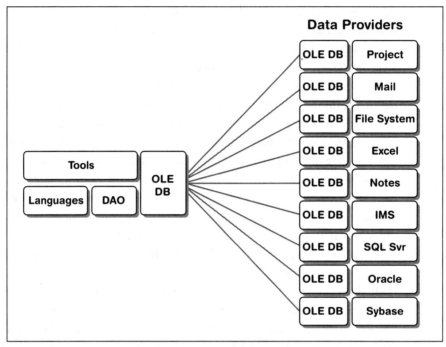

Figure 7.6   Microsoft's OLE DB

Transaction-Oriented

Transactional middleware, such as TP monitors and application servers, do a pretty good job at coordinating information movement and method sharing between many different resources. However, while the transactional paradigm they employ provides an excellent mechanism for method sharing, it is not as effective when it comes to simple information sharing, the real goal of EAI. For instance, transactional middleware typically creates a tightly coupled EAI solution, where messaging solutions are more cohesive in nature. In addition, the source in target applications will have to be changed to take advantage of transactional middleware.

TP Monitors

TP monitors are, in fact, first-generation application servers and a transactional middleware product. They provide a location for application logic in addition to a mechanism to facilitate the communications between two or more applications (see Figure 7.7). Examples of TP monitors include Tuxedo from BEA Systems, MTS from Microsoft, and CICS from IBM. These products have been around for some time now and are successfully processing billions of transaction a day.

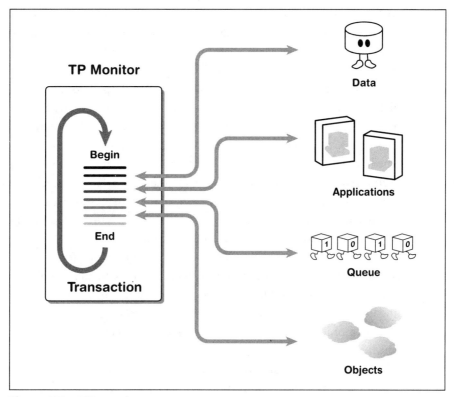

Figure 7.7   TP monitors

TP monitors (and application servers for that matter) are based on the premise of a transaction. A **transaction** is a unit of work with a beginning and an end. The reasoning is that if application logic is encapsulated within a transaction, then the transaction either completes, or is rolled back completely. If the transaction has been updating remote resources, such as databases and queues, then they too will be rolled back if a problem occurs.

An advantage of using transactions is the ability to break an application into smaller portions and then invoke those transactions to carry out the bidding of the user or another connected system. Because transactions are small units of work, they are easy to manage and process within the TP monitor environment. By sharing the processing of these transactions among other, connected TP monitors, TP monitors provide enhanced scalability by relying on transactions. They can also perform scalability "tricks" such as thread and database connection pooling.

TP monitors provide connectors that allow them to connect to resources such as databases, other applications, and queues. These are typically low-level connectors that require some sophisticated application development in order to connect to these various resources. The resources are integrated into the transactions and leveraged as part of the transaction. As mentioned previously, they are also able to recover if a transaction fails.

TP monitors are unequaled when it comes to support for many clients and a high transaction-processing load. They perform such tricks as using queued input buffers to protect against peaks in the workload. If the load increases, the engine is able to press on without a loss in response time. TP monitors can also use priority scheduling to prioritize messages and support server threads, thus saving on the overhead of heavyweight processes. Finally, the load-balancing mechanisms of TP monitors guarantee that no single process takes on an excessive load.

When an application takes advantage of these features, it is able to provide performance as well as availability and scalability.

TP monitors provide queuing, routing, and messaging features, all of which enable distributed application developers to bypass the TP monitor's transactional features. As a result, priorities can be assigned to classes of messages, letting the higher priority messages receive server resources first.

TP monitors' real performance value is in their load-balancing feature, which allows them to respond gracefully to a barrage of transactions. A perfect example of this advantage is end-of-the-month processing. As demand increases, the transaction manager launches more server processes to handle the load and kills processes that are no longer required. In addition, the manager can spread the processing load among the processes as the transaction requests occur.

Application Servers

Application servers are really nothing new (certainly TP monitors should be considered application servers, and they share many common features). However, the fastest growing segment of the middleware marketplace is defined by the many new products calling themselves application servers. Most application servers are employed as Web-enabled middleware, processing transactions from Web-enabled applications. What's more, they employ modern languages such as Java, instead of traditional procedural languages such as C and COBOL (common with TP monitors).

Put simply, application servers are servers that not only provide for the sharing and processing of application logic, they also provide connections to back-end resources (see Figure 7.8). These resources include databases, ERP applications, and even traditional mainframe applications. Application servers also provide user interface development mechanisms. Additionally, they usually provide mechanisms to deploy the application to the platform of the Web. Examples of application servers include Netscape's Netscape Application Server (NAS) and Inprise's Application Server.

With vendors repositioning their application server products as a technology that solves EAI problems (some without the benefit of a technology that works), application servers, as well as TP monitors, will play a major role in the EAI domain. Many vendors are going so far as to incorporate features such as messaging, transformation, and intelligent routing, services currently native to message brokers. This area of middleware is one that will undergo something closer to a revolution than an evolution.

Message Brokers

Message brokers represent the nirvana of EAI-enabled middleware, as you'll see in Chapter 18. At least, the *potential* of message brokers represents that nirvana. Message brokers can facilitate information movement between two or more resources (source or target applications) and can account for the differences in application semantics and platforms. As such, they are a perfect match for EAI.

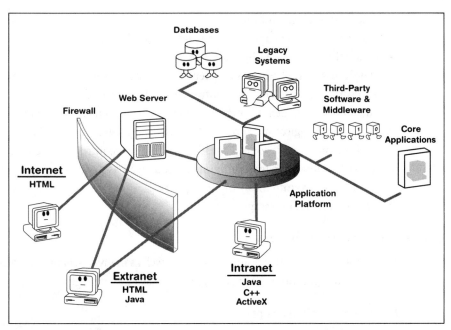

Figure 7.8   The architecture of a typical application server

Message brokers can also join many applications using common rules and routing engines. They can transform the schema and content of the information as it flows between various applications and databases. However, they can't quite "do it all." Message brokers are not perfect . . . yet. Message brokers need to evolve some more before they are able to solve most of the problems in the EAI problem domain.

Message brokers, as we already discussed in the previous chapters, are servers that broker messages between two or more source or target applications. In addition to brokering messages, they transform message schemas and alter the content of the messages (see Figure 7.9). Message brokers are so important to EAI that we have dedicated Chapter 18 to a discussion of the technology.

The importance of message brokers is a function of their place within the enterprise. In general, message brokers are not an application development–enabling technology. Rather, they are a technology that allows many applications to communicate with one another and can do so without the applications actually understanding anything about the applications they are sharing information with. In short, they "broker" information.

Middleware Models

It is useful to understand the general characteristics of each type of middleware in order to evaluate each technology and vendor. There are two types of middleware models: logical and physical.

The **logical** middleware model depicts how the information moves throughout the enterprise conceptually. In contrast, the **physical** middleware model depicts how the information *actually* moves and the technology it employs. This contrast is analogous to the logical and physical database designs presented in Chapter 6.

A discussion of the logical middleware model requires a discussion of one-to-one and many-to-many configurations, as well as synchronous versus asynchronous. An examination of the physical middleware model requires a discussion of several messaging models.

One-to-One versus Many-to-Many

Middleware can work in a point-to-point, as well as many-to-many (including one-to-many) configurations. Each configuration has its advantages and disadvantages.

Point-to-Point Middleware

Point-to-point middleware is middleware that allows one application to link to one other application—application A links to application B by using a simple

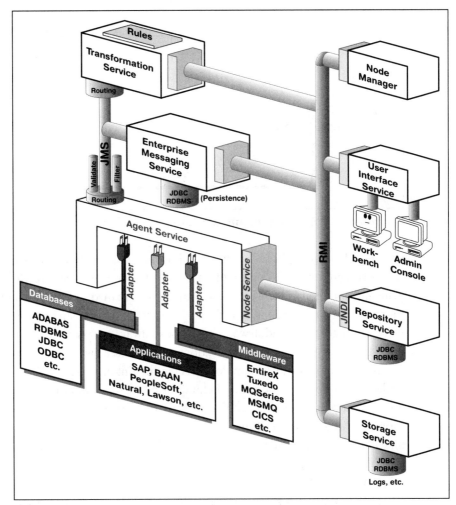

Figure 7.9   Architecture of an advanced Java-enabled message broker

pipe. When application A desires to communicate with application B, they simply "shout down" the pipe using a procedure call or message (see Figure 7.10).

What limits point-to-point middleware compared to other types of middleware is its inability to properly bind together more than two applications. It also lacks any facility for middle-tier processing, such as the ability to house application logic or the ability to change messages as they flow over the pipe.

There are many examples of point-to-point middleware, including MOM products (such as MQSeries) and RPCs (such as DCE). The purpose of these products is to provide point-to-point solutions, primarily involving only a

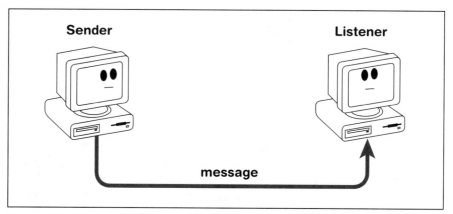

Figure 7.10   Point-to-point middleware

source and target application. Although it is now possible to link together more than two applications using traditional point-to-point middleware, doing so is generally not a good idea. Too many complexities are involved when dealing with more than two applications. In order to link together more than two applications using point-to-point middleware, it is almost always necessary to run point-to-point links between *all* of the applications involved (see Figure 7.11).

Because most EAI problem domains require linking many applications, this understanding of the general idea behind the point-to-point model should make it clear that point-to-point middleware does not represent an effective solution. Moreover, in order to share information in this scenario, applications have to be linked, and information has to be brokered through a shared, centralized server. In other words, sharing information requires a message broker or transactional middleware.

However, as with all things, there are both disadvantages and advantages. The great advantage of point-to-point middleware is its simplicity. Linking only one application to another frees the EAI architect and developer from dealing with the complexities of adapting to the differences between many source and target applications.

Many-to-Many Middleware

As its name implies, many-to-many middleware links many applications to many other applications. As such, it is the best fit for EAI. This is the trend in the middleware world. It is also the most powerful logical middleware model in that it provides both flexibility and applicability to the EAI problem domain.

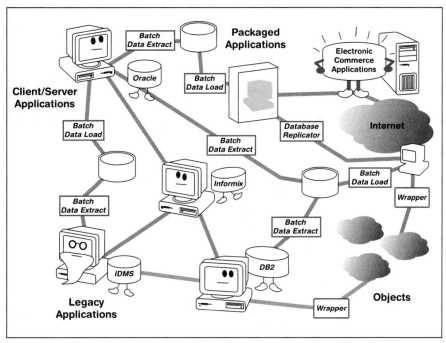

Figure 7.11   Point-to-point middleware does not work well with many applications.

There are many examples of many-to-many middleware, including message brokers, transactional middleware (application servers and TP monitors), and even distributed objects. Basically, any type of middleware that can deal with more than two source or target applications at a time is able to support this model (see Figure 7.12).

Just as the advantage to the point-to-point model is its simplicity, the disadvantage to the many-to-many model is the complexity of linking together so many systems. Although the current generation of middleware products are becoming better at handling many external resources, much work remains to be done. After all, struggling with this complexity falls primarily on the shoulders of the developer.

Synchronous versus Asynchronous

As noted previously, middleware employs two types of communication mechanisms: asynchronous and synchronous.

Asynchronous middleware is middleware that moves information between one or many applications in an asynchronous mode—that is, the middleware

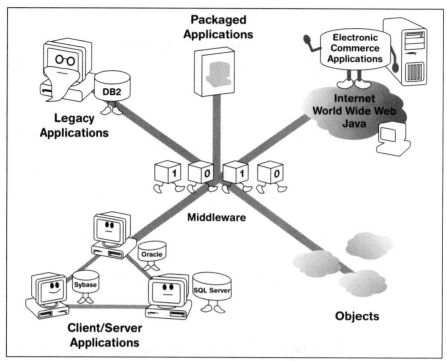

Figure 7.12   The many-to-many middleware model

software is able to decouple itself from the source or target applications, and the applications are not dependent on the other connected applications for processing. The process that allows this to occur has the application(s) placing a message in a queue and then going about their business, waiting for the responses at some later time from the other application(s).

The primary advantage of the asynchronous model is that the middleware will not block the application for processing. Moreover, because the middleware is decoupled from the application, the application can always continue processing, regardless of the state of the other applications.

In contrast, **synchronous** middleware is tightly coupled to applications. In turn, the applications are dependent on the middleware to process one or more function calls at a remote application. As a result, the calling application must halt processing in order to wait for the remote application to respond. We refer to this middleware as a "blocking" type of middleware.

The disadvantage of the synchronous model rests with the coupling of the application to the middleware and the remote application. Because the application is dependent on the middleware, problems with middleware, such as network or remote server problems, stop the application from processing. In addition, synchronous middleware eats up bandwidth due to the fact that several calls must be made across the network in order to support a synchronous function call. This disadvantage and its implications make it clear that the asynchronous model is the better EAI solution.

Connection-Oriented and Connectionless

Connection-oriented communications means that two parties connect, exchange messages, and then disconnect. Typically this is a synchronous process, but it can also be asynchronous. **Connectionless communications** means that the calling program does *not* enter into a connection with the target process. The receiving application simply acts on the request, responding if required.

Direct Communications

In **direct communications**, the middleware layer accepts the message from the calling program and passes it directly to the remote program. While either direct or queued communications are used with synchronous processing, direct is usually synchronous in nature, and queued is usually asynchronous. Most RPC-enabled middleware uses the direct communications model.

Queued Communications

Queued communications generally require a queue manager to place a message in a queue. The remote application then retrieves the message either shortly after it has been sent or at any time in the future (barring time-out restrictions). If the calling application requires a response (such as a verification message or data), the information flows back through the queuing mechanism. Most MOM products use queued communications.

The queuing communication model's advantage over direct communications rests with the fact that the remote program does not need to be active for the calling program to send a message to it. What's more, queuing communications middleware typically does not block either the calling or the remote programs from proceeding with processing.

Publish/Subscribe

Publish/subscribe (pub/sub) frees an application from the need to understand anything about the target application. All it has to do is send the information it desires to share to a destination contained within the pub/sub engine, or broker. The broker then redistributes the information to any interested applications. For example, if a financial application wishes to make all accounts receivable information available to other applications who want to see it, it would inform the pub/sub engine. The engine would then make it known that this information was available, and any application could subscribe to that topic in order to begin receiving accounts receivable information.

In this scenario, the publisher is the provider of the information. Publishers supply information about a topic, without needing to understand anything about the applications that are interested in the information (see Figure 7.13). The subscriber is the recipient, or consumer, of the information. The publisher specifies a topic when it publishes the information. The subscriber specifies a topic that it's interested in. As a result, the subscriber receives only the information it's interested in.

Request Response

The **request response** model does exactly what its name implies. A request is made to an application using request response middleware, and it responds to the request. Examples of request and response middleware include any middleware that can facilitate a response from a request between applications, such as message brokers or application servers.

Fire and Forget

The **fire and forget** model allows the middleware user to "fire off" a message and then "forget" about it, without worrying about who receives it, or even if the

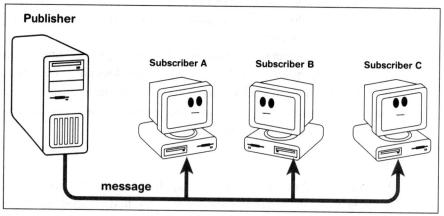

Figure 7.13   The publish and subscribe model

message is ever received. This is another asynchronous approach. The purpose of fire and forget is to allow a source or target application to broadcast specific types of messages to multiple recipients, bypassing auditing and response features. It also allows central servers to fire off messages.

Conversational-Mode

A primary advantage of conversational-mode middleware is its ability to host complex business logic in order to maintain state and negotiate transactions with the application. This middleware mode is particularly critical when integrating with transactional systems. Often the data elements required for brokering are deeply nested within subtransactions and can only be obtained by engaging in a "conversation" with the transactional system.

Tough Choices

Ah, wouldn't life be wonderful if there were only one perfect middleware layer that provided all the features we need, coupled with unexcelled performance? Well, unfortunately, life may be wonderful, but it's almost never that easy. Before hooking your application to a middleware technology, you need to examine all the technologies and carefully weigh their advantages and disadvantages to *your particular situation*.

Although RPCs are slow, their blocking nature provides the best data integrity control. For example, while an asynchronous layer to access data may seem to be the best solution, there is no way to guarantee that an update occurs in a timely manner. It is not difficult to envision a scenario where an update to a customer database is sitting in a queue, waiting for the database to free up while a data entry clerk is creating a sales transaction using the older data. RPCs may be slow, but they would never allow this kind of situation to occur. When using RPCs, updates are always applied in the correct order. In other words, if data integrity is more important than performance, RPCs may still be the best bet.

MOM vendors contend that synchronous middleware cannot support today's event-driven applications. Programs just cannot wait for other programs to complete their work before proceeding. Yet RPCs could provide better performance than traditional store-and-forward messaging layers in some instances. Then again, messaging could provide better performance, because the queue manager offers sophisticated performance-enhancing features such as load balancing.

Middleware is something that's difficult to explain and use. Users typically never see middleware's plumbing, as they do with application development and database products. In the future, however, we are going to see more user interfaces and business layers included with middleware products, where once only application program interfaces existed. Such is the case with newer middleware technologies such as application servers and message brokers. The presence of easy-to-use interfaces will take the power of middleware—at one time the exclusive domain of the developer—and place it in the hands of the business user. Clearly this is where middleware is heading, and it is ultimately how we are going to solve the EAI problem.

CHAPTER EIGHT

Transactional Middleware and EAI

"Real programmers can write assembly code in any language."

—Larry Wall

Transactional middleware, which includes TP monitors and application servers, provides benefits to distributed computing and EAI that cannot be found in traditional development tools. Scalability, fault tolerance, and an architecture that centralizes application processing are hallmarks of transactional middleware. In addition, transactional middleware has the ability to provide virtual systems and single log-on capabilities and, in many cases, has the ability to reduce overall system cost.

Transactional middleware is a good fit with EAI because the architecture provides for a centralized server that's able to process information from many different resources, such as databases and applications. Moreover, it ensures delivery of information from one application to the next and supports a distributed architecture (see Figure 8.1). However, despite its many advantages, the cost of implementing transactional middleware may preclude its use with EAI. Implementing transactional middleware is an invasive process because applications must be altered to use it.

Despite the fact that many transactional middleware vendors are promoting their products as the "ultimate EAI

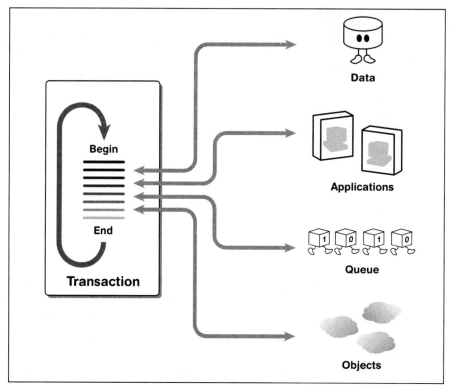

Figure 8.1　**Transactional middleware solves the EAI problem by coordinating the connection of many different resources.**

engine," there are limitations to what transactional middleware can accomplish within most EAI problem domains. None of the TP monitors or application servers that exist today support either "out-of-the-box" content transformation or message transformation services, at least not without a lot of programming. What's more, they generally don't support event-driven information processing.

What transactional middleware excels at is method-level EAI or, at least, the sharing of common business logic to promote EAI. However, if that is the only benefit, then much better options are available to the EAI architect or developer. Message brokers or traditional, message-oriented middleware are much better tools for the simple sharing of information at the data level or the application interface level. This is not to suggest that transactional middleware is not a good fit for some EAI projects, only that it is of greater advantage at the method level. As in all aspects of EAI, architects and developers need to understand the relative advantages and disadvantages of the options, if the correct choices are to be made.

In this chapter, we will examine transactional middleware from both a functional perspective and a developer's point of view. We will seek to establish those situations for which transactional middleware makes a good fit, and how to develop EAI around transactional middleware. The first half of the chapter will be devoted to basic transactional middleware features. Then we'll examine the integration of those features with "traditional" transactional middleware—TP monitors. Finally, we'll explore the new breed of transactional middleware—application servers.

Notion of a Transaction

Transactional middleware is nothing new. It originated *once upon a time* in the days of the mainframe, when most mainframe databases came with transactional middleware. These were, in fact, TP monitors that managed processes and coordinated access to the database.

Transactional middleware requires that complex applications be divided into bite-sized units called **transactions**. Transactional middleware controls transactions from their beginning to their end, from the client to the resource server, and then back again.

In these scenarios, transactions are either all or nothing. They either work or they do not. A transaction is never left incomplete. As a result, transactional

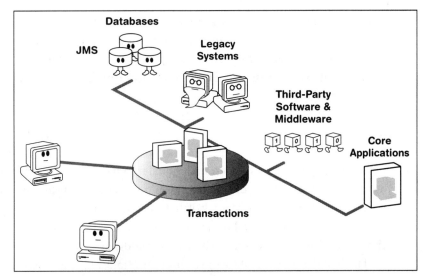

Figure 8.2   Using transactions to tie together back-end resources

---

Using Transactional Middleware for Heterogeneous Database Access

A common use for transactional middleware is to update several different databases during the same transaction. The transaction service is just a structured program that runs within either the TP monitor or application server environment, connecting to each database, and then updating it with the newer information before returning the success or failure of each transaction. Simply invoking the service from the client will result in all connected databases being automatically updated (see Figure 8.3).

A benefit to this process is that the transaction does not commit the updates to all the databases until *all* updates are complete. As a result of this feature, a problem, such as a database not working at the time, would cause the transactional middleware to roll back the transaction as if it had never been initiated. This "all or nothing" feature assures that updates occur on every connected database, or on none of them.

Transactional middleware provides load-balancing services, which allow it to support more than a thousand clients. As a result, the database servers themselves are never loaded down.

---

middleware always leaves the system in a stable state. This provides the developer with a consistent and reliable programming model. It makes transactional middleware a natural choice for distributed applications, which must deal with many different databases, queues, and batch interfaces running on heterogeneous platforms (see Figure 8.2).

The ACID Test

Before digging too deeply into transactional middleware, it might be a good idea to have an understanding of the concept of transactions. A transaction has ACID properties—Atomic, Consistent, Isolated, and Durable.

Atomic refers to the "all or nothing" quality of transactions. The transaction either completes or it does not. There is no middle ground. **Consistency** refers to the fact that the system is always in a consistent state, regardless of whether or not it completes the transaction. **Isolation** refers to the transaction's ability to work

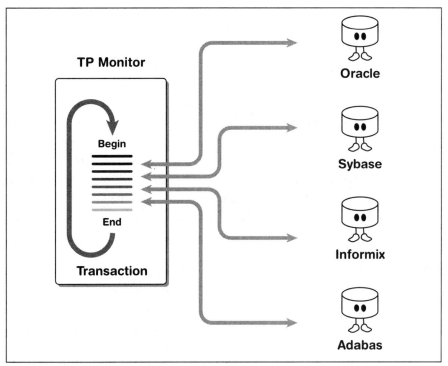

**Figure 8.3   Using transactional middleware to deal with heterogeneous
database management**

independently of other transactions that may be running in the same TP monitor
environment. **Durability** means that the transaction, once committed and complete, can survive system failures.

Although the ACID test might oversimplify the concept of a transaction, it
represents an easy way to remember the features and functions of transactional
middleware. Developers can count on a high degree of application integrity with
transactional middleware—even in heterogeneous environments comprised of
very different operating systems and databases. More importantly, a transaction
is secure. Even when other things go wrong, transactional middleware won't
allow those problems to affect any other transaction, application, or data.

Scalable Development

Transactional middleware processes transactions on behalf of the client or node
and can route transactions through many diversified systems, depending on the

requirements of the EAI problem domain. It's not unusual for a TP monitor, for instance, to tie together a mainframe, an NT server, a multiprocessing UNIX server, and a file server. Transactional middleware also provides load balancing, thread pooling, object recycling, and the ability to automatically recover from typical system problems.

Although transactional middleware is correctly—though only technically—referred to as middleware, it is much more than a simple middleware connection layer. It provides a location for the application code to run and, as a result, a location for business-processing and application objects to run, as well as a location where methods can be shared among applications. Transactional middleware can be used to enforce business rules and maintain data integrity or to create entire applications by building many transaction services and invoking them from the client.

Database Multiplexing

The real benefit to transactional middleware is the ability to multiplex and manage transactions that result in the reduction of the number of connections and processing loads that larger systems place on a database. With transactional middleware in the architecture, it is possible to increase the number of clients without increasing the size of a database server. For example, by using a TP monitor requiring only about 50 connections, more than a thousand clients can access the database server.

By "funneling" the clients' requests, transactional middleware removes the "process-per-client" requirement (see Figure 8.4). In this scenario (also known as "database connection pooling"), a client simply invokes the transaction services that reside on the TP monitor, and those services can share the same database server connections (threads and processes). If a connection overloads, the TP monitor simply starts a new connection to the database server. This ability is the foundation of three-tier architecture, and the reason three-tier architecture can scale to high user loads.

Load Balancing

When the number of incoming client requests surpasses the number of shared processes that the system is able to handle, other processes start automatically. This is the concept of **load balancing**. Some transactional middleware can distribute the process load over several servers at the same time dynamically or distribute the processing over several processors in multiprocessing environments.

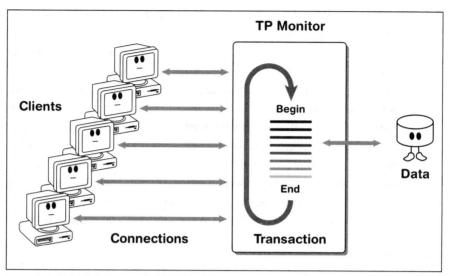

Figure 8.4   Database multiplexing

The load-balancing features of transactional middleware also enable transactional middleware to prioritize. As a result, developers are able to assure that VIP clients get top-notch service. Transactional middleware is able to handle priorities by defining "classes." High-priority classes kick up the process priorities. As a rule, developers use high-priority server classes to encapsulate short-running, high-priority functions. Low-priority processes (such as batch processes) run inside low-priority server classes. Moreover, developers can assign priorities by application type, the resource managers required by a transaction, high and low response times, and the fault-tolerance of a transaction. Developers can also control the number of processes or threads available for each transaction by defining any number of parameters.

Fault-Tolerance

Transactional middleware was built from the ground up to provide a robust application deployment environment with the ability to recover from any number of system-related problems. Transactional middleware provides high availability by employing redundant systems. For example, transactional middleware uses dynamic switching to reroute transactions around server and network problems. The transactions work through a two-phase-commit process to assure that the transactions complete and to guard against transactions becoming lost electrons when hardware, operating systems, or networks fail. Two-phase-commit also makes sure that reliable transactions can be performed on two or more heterogeneous resources.

In the event of a power failure, for example, transactional middleware alerts all participants of that particular transaction (server, queues, clients, and so on) of the problem. Any and all work accomplished up to that point in the transaction is rolled back, and the system returns to its "pretransaction" state, cleaning up any mess it may have left. Developers sometimes build transactions that automatically resubmit after a failure. This ability to create an automatic resubmit feature is highly desirable within the context of an EAI problem domain, because transactional middleware ensures delivery of the information being shared by the source and target applications. However, message brokers also understand the benefit of this feature. Many are moving to provide transactional integrity within their products.

Communications

Transactional middleware provides a good example of middleware that uses middleware, which includes message brokers. Transactional middleware communicates in a variety of ways, including RPCs (specialized for transactional middleware and called "transactional RPCs" or TRPCs), distributed dynamic program links (DPLs), interprocess communications, and MOM. Because transactional middleware is simply an API within an application, developers have the flexibility to mix and match all sorts of middleware layers and resource servers to meet the requirements of an application or EAI problem domain.

XA and X/Open

The standards that define how transactional middleware functions are the International Standards Organization (ISO) and X/Open's Distributed Transaction Process (DTP) specifications. Because **X/Open** defines the transactional middleware use of APIs, it is the standard that demands our attention in the context of the EAI solution.

In 1991, the X/Open created the "Transaction Processing Reference Model." In 1994 they published the "Distributed Transaction Reference Model." This model defined the features of transaction-based systems and how they communicate with outside resources. One outcome of this process was the **XA interface**, defining how a transaction manager and a resource manager (such as a database) can communicate.

The XA interface is a set of function calls, split between the transaction manager and the resource manager. Among the features XA provides are those functions provided by the transaction manager, which allow the resource manager to tell the transaction manager whether it is ready to work with a transaction or whether it is in a "resting state" and unable to respond.

Building Transactions

Building transaction services simply requires that you programmatically define the functions that the service will perform when accessed by the required TP monitor APIs. In Tuxedo, for example, the tpconnect() function call sets up the conversation with the participating service. tpsend() returns a response, and tpalloc() allocates buffer space.

A problem that many developers run into is that they are decoupled from the database, and as a result, can't work with the schema. This is a greater issue for the developer of specialized development tools (e.g., Visual Basic, Delphi, and PowerBuilder) because he or she usually works with the schema to construct an application. Likewise, it is a lesser issue for C++ developers who usually work with DLLs and APIs rather than directly with the schema from the development environment.

The client application generally communicates directly with the TP monitor through a TRPC. Sometimes another mechanism is invoked, such as RMI or IIOP. After receiving the communication, the TP monitor "talks" to the resource manager (native database API, ODBC, or a proprietary database-dependent network protocol such as Oracle's SQL*Net), using a native protocol or XA. With transaction services handled through a 3GL interface, the power to integrate many API services into a single transaction is there; however, this is a highly complex and laborious process.

Application Servers

To this point, we've discussed transactional middleware in general terms, highlighting the features and functions of TP monitors as prime examples of transactional middleware. While the importance of TP monitors should never be underestimated, the remainder of the chapter will focus on the new breed of transactional middleware—application servers. (Albeit, the press uses the terms

TP monitor and application servers to mean much the same thing, and clearly they are morphing into the same feature function set.)

Application servers not only provide a location for application logic, they also coordinate many resource connections (see Figure 8.5). Typically Web-enabled, they bring transaction processing to the Web through any number of mechanisms (see "Considering Object State Management and Application Servers," later in this chapter). The new application servers tend to support Java as both the native language and the development model (albeit, in different ways) as they move toward the new world of Enterprise JavaBeans (EJB, which is described in the section "Enterprise JavaBeans," later in this chapter).

Although application servers were created for Web-based transactions and application development, their usefulness to EAI is obvious, given their back-end integration capabilities (their ability to bind together several source and target applications through a series of connectors provided by the application server vendors—for example, SAP, PeopleSoft, Baan, relational databases, and middleware).

Application servers provide an up-to-date approach to sharing methods, as well as a mechanism for integration. However, each application server has its

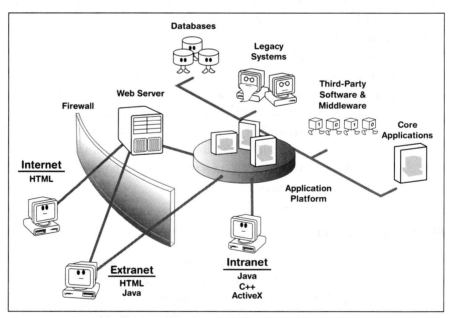

Figure 8.5   **Application servers provide both a location for application logic, as well as a mechanism to coordinate connections to remote resources.**

Considering Object State Management and Application Servers

Most application servers provide component processing environments using a stateless model, enhancing scalability through the recycling of an object in the memory of the application server. Rather than destroying and recreating objects for every connected node, the application server keeps a pool of objects ready to hand out to any external process requesting service.*

While the stateless component model has the advantage of improved scalability, it is burdened by two major disadvantages. The first is that it does not support multiple references to an object's properties. As a result, it does very little to support object reuse through the object-oriented programming model. The second disadvantage is that it has to create a new object for each database request, resulting in a performance hit when object data is loaded from a back-end database.

---

*Most TP monitors are able to maintain states, providing scalability through other mechanisms, such as load balancing and thread pooling.

---

own approach to how this happens. Therefore, making wise decisions regarding the selection of an application server—or application servers—for an EAI project requires an understanding of the category of features, as well as the problem at hand.

Evolving Transactions

Application servers are certainly nothing new. They've been used extensively over the years, along with enabling mechanisms such as distributed objects. However, new demands have resulted in a reexamination of this paradigm, adding more up-to-date products, such as those built around the notion of processing components with transactionality. Therein lies the evolution of the technology. However, application servers have yet to catch up with TP monitors in performance and reliability, although they do provide more advanced features such as an integrated development environment (IDE).

The benefit of application servers is clear. By placing some, or most, of the application logic on a middle tier, the developer can exert increased control over the application logic through centralization. Such a placement increases the ability to scale the application through a set of tricks, such as database multiplexing and load balancing, described previously.

The end result is a traditional three-tier client/server computing model, consisting of a presentation layer (the part that presents the information to the user), the application layer (the middle-tier application logic), and the data layer (where the data resides), as shown in Figure 8.6.

If this represents traditional, three-tier client/server computing, what has changed? To a large extent, the "change" is nothing more than the rediscovery of the value of this type of application architecture. Also, the change is being driven by a set of aggressive products, such as Netscape Application Server, WebLogic, Microsoft Transaction Server, and NetDynamics, which are new products that are much easier to use than traditional transaction-oriented products (e.g., TP monitors). The notion of leveraging reusable components within these environments and thus moving away from traditional procedural code also contributed to this change, as did the need to bind advanced application-development tools with transactions.

The two standards that dominate here are Java, with its Enterprise JavaBeans (EJB) initiative (also closely tied to CORBA), and ActiveX, integrating with products such as Microsoft Transaction Server (MTS), becoming MS AppCenter with Windows 2000. These technologies are more than a way to integrate components with transactions. They are providing the foundation for the next generation of applications, as well as an opportunity to integrate the enterprise.

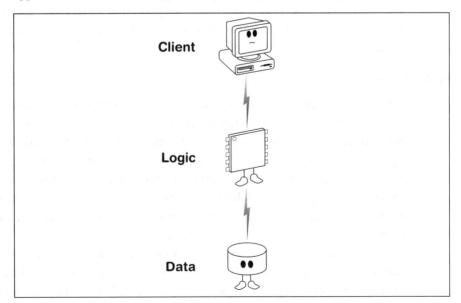

Figure 8.6   Application architecture, using an application server

Application Servers and Web-Based Application Development and Integration

In many EAI scenarios, enterprises will want to integrate their applications through a Web browser, thus providing a common interface for many different applications and data sources. This is also known as creating "portals," or views, into a broad array of information sources. Application servers provide one of the better solutions available to accomplish this.

There are three issues to consider in building Web applications: the enabling technology (Java, ActiveX, CGI, NSAPI, ISAPI, and so on), the architecture that works with the existing enabling technology, and the Web tools and technology needed to build the application around the architecture.

A Web site, like any distributed application, needs to be considered in terms of tiers. A traditional Web site has two-tiers—the Web browser and the Web server. More complex sites have three-tiers—the browser, the Web server, and a database server. The database server is connected to the Web server to provide data for the site. Traditional search engines are good examples of three-tier Web sites. The most complex architecture, four-tier, requires the presence of a Web browser, Web server, and database server, with an application server between the database server and Web server (see Figure 8.7).

The four-tier Web site architecture is not in wide use today, but its popularity is increasing as mechanisms to deploy mission-critical e-commerce applications to sites for use inside and outside the organization are explored. Four-tier architecture provides developers with the flexibility to create Web applications that can scale, recover, and support all the advantages of distributed processing. Although this area is still in flux, there are currently three basic types of technologies: TP monitors, distributed objects, and application servers.

TP monitors add another layer of technology for business application processing between the Web server and the database. In addition, they provide some advanced application-processing capabilities. This architecture works by allowing the Web client to access the TP monitor services from a CGI, NSAPI, or ISAPI application using server-side

continued

Application Servers and Web-Based Application Development and Integration (*continued*)

scripting or a traditional programming language (e.g., C++). The TP monitors then process the transaction service and communicate with the database server on behalf of the Web server process (if required). The information is then returned to the process, which returns the results to the Web client as HTML. By extending the same concept, the server-side process can communicate with other middle-tier technologies, such as standard distributed objects, remote program interfaces (e.g., SAP APIs), and other types of middleware (e.g., messaging middleware). CORBA and DCOM (Distributed Component Object Model) are the two most popular distributed object standards in use today.

A movement has been in the works to combine both Java and CORBA as a single distributed object offering, resulting in the ability of Java-enabled standards, such as server-side Java and EJB, to function as traditional distributed objects.

As with our TP monitor example, the Web-server application can access methods contained in a distributed object or a group of distributed objects. Once a method—or a series of methods—is invoked, the distributed objects perform application processing on behalf of the server-side process linked to a Web client. The distributed object can even access a database. Once again, at the conclusion of the processing, the information returns to the server-side process that, in turn, returns the results to the Web client. Because the server-side process can communicate with any number of distributed objects that exist on any number of application servers, this Internet architecture supports n-tier (four or more tiers) and provides a mechanism to offer a divide-and-conquer approach to distributed application development. Visigenic and Iona are examples of vendors selling CORBA-based distributed objects, while Microsoft is giving DCOM away as part of the Windows environments.

The advent of Web-enabled distributed objects means developers can place distributed objects at the client and the Web server. For example, Netscape supports CORBA within the browser while Microsoft supports DCOM. Rather than communicate with the Web server using traditional HTTP, the Web client runs a distributed object and communicates with the

Web server using a native object protocol such as CORBA's IIOP or Microsoft's DCOM RPC. Unlike HTTP (Hypertext Transfer Protocol), these protocols are dynamic and can use states. As a result, they make dynamic application development easier for developers.

Developers can also mix and match distributed objects at the client, the Web server, the database server, and all points in-between to meet the requirements of the application.

While it is possible to use standard distributed objects, such as those from Inprise and Iona, or standard TP monitors, such as Tuxedo, many site builders opt for easier, more distinct solutions—in other words, application servers built exclusively for use with the Web. Examples of these application servers include iPlanet's Application Server and the Inprise Application Server. (Albeit the line between traditional TP monitors and application server has blurred, as we've seen in this chapter. Each provides some Web-enablement capability these days.)

There are a number of advantages to using Web-enabled application servers over the more traditional technology. First, they are geared for Web development only. As a result, they provide the developer with many different mechanisms to build Web applications using an application server. Many are enabled for popular Web-development and authoring tools. Distributed object and TP monitors are more general-purpose application servers (although all TP monitor and distributed object vendors have done a good job with Web-enabling their products). Second, it's less costly to build applications with this technology. The application servers are less expensive, tools are plentiful, and less time is needed.

Enterprise JavaBeans

Application servers are different from traditional transactional middleware (such as TP monitors) in that they are able to function around the notion of transactional components. Almost all application servers using this transactional component type architecture are looking to employ EJB as the enabling standard. However, many are doing so in their own special way. What's more, the standard

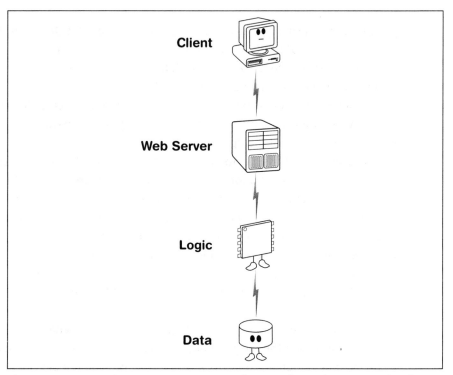

**Figure 8.7   Four-tier Web development/integration using an application
server**

is still in a state of flux, and Sun is in the process of correcting that, as well as
building a certification process.

While EJB are really a Java-enabled middleware (and therefore, a topic to be
covered in Chapter 12), it is appropriate to discuss them here, in the context of
application servers. This is due to the fact that EJB add the most value to transactional middleware.

The EJB specifications (see www.javasoft.com) define a server-side component model for JavaBeans. EJB, simply put, represent specialized JavaBeans that
run on a remote server (known as the "EJB container," see Figure 8.8). EJB look
very similar to distributed objects such as COM and CORBA, at least from the
point of view of architecture.

Using the same architecture as traditional JavaBeans, EJB can be clustered
together to create a distributed application with a mechanism to coordinate the

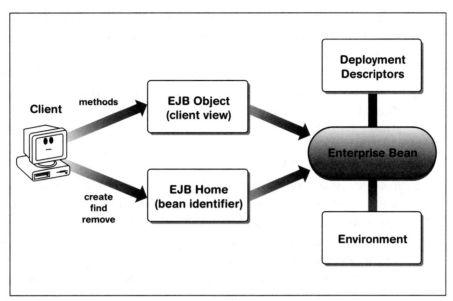

Figure 8.8   EJB define a server-side component model.

processing that occurs within the JavaBeans. Thus, they reside on application servers, which are able to process the beans as transactional components.

The EJB model supports the notion of implicit transactions. EJB needn't specify the transactional demarcation point in order to participate in distributed transactions. This feature represents an essential benefit to the model. The EJB execution environment automatically manages the transaction on behalf of the EJB with transaction policies that can be defined with standard procedures during the deployment process. Moreover, transactions may be controlled by the client-side applications.

The EJB model defines the relationship between an EJB component and EJB container system. EJB do not require the use of a specific container system. Furthermore, any application execution system, such as an application server, can be adapted to support EJB by adding support for services defined in the EJB specification. The services in the specification define relationships between EJB and a container. They also provide a portability layer. Thus, EJB can run in any execution system (EJB container) supporting the EJB standard.

The EJB execution system is called the "EJB Server." It provides a standard set of services to support EJB components. EJB and the EJB Server are analogous to traditional transactional systems. Thus, an EJB Server must provide access to a standard distributed transaction-management mechanism.

An EJB container implements the management and control services for a class of EJB objects. In addition, this system provides life cycle management, transaction control, persistence management, and security services. The overarching idea is to allow a single vendor to provide both the EJB Server and the associated EJB container.

Transactional ActiveX

In a strategy similar to the one employed with EJB, Microsoft is seeking to support transactionality through ActiveX and MTS. MTS, which is morphing into AppCenter with Windows 2000, provides an environment to process transactional ActiveX components, providing traditional TP monitor features such as support for ACID, database access, and recoverability.

MTS is based on Microsoft's COM and uses that model extensively as both a programming standard and a method of communications. In other words, MTS is COM, and COM is MTS.

MTS has been shipping since 1996, making it one of the first commercial software systems to combine transactions with components. Unlike EJB, which is a specification, MTS is a *product*. COM is the relative standard here, but it's really an ORB standard, not a standard of transactionality. While this might be somewhat confusing, the essential message is that transactional ActiveX with MTS is a product strategy, not a standards strategy.

MTS is best described as a container for transactional components like EJB. MTS applications are a collection of ActiveX server components (known as a "package") that are able to work either with other ActiveX components on the client or with other technologies such as Java, CORBA, or a more traditional application.

MTS applications must invoke themselves as in-process COM servers (ActiveX components). For all practical purposes, ActiveX components are analogous to DLLs (Dynamic Link Libraries) that load into the MTS environment. They are managed through several subsystems that react to requests made by the loaded ActiveX component. These subsystems provide MTS and the transactional ActiveX component with features such as automatic transactions, configurable security, database connection pooling, thread support, and component state management.

MTS also has some of the best tool support available, with direct integration with Visual Basic (which provides the tightest integration with MTS), Visual C++, Visual J++, and others.

The Big Two Application Servers

There are two major players in the application server world: Netscape Application Server from Netscape (www.netscape.com) and NetDynamics Application Server from Sun (www.netdynmics.com). Recently, Sun has taken over the Netscape Application Server as part of America Online's acquisition of Netscape, and the integration is called iPlanet.

The Netscape Application Server, acquired together with Kiva Software, supports a high volume of concurrent users through optimizedd end-to-end performance features. Netscape Application Server is able to provide these features by supporting caching and pooling, results caching, data streaming, and fully multithreaded, multiprocess architecture. Scalability features include dynamic load balancing and application partitioning. These allow Netscape Application Server to support thousands of concurrent users on a single server. Failure-recover features include auto-detection and auto-restart of failed servers and processes. This product also supports distributed state and session management.

The application is built within Netscape Application Server using Netscape Application Builder (sold separately). Application Builder supports both C++ and Java, although other third-party tools, such as Visual Café Pro from Symantec, can also be used.

The NetDynamics Application Server, based on CORBA and Java, integrates with a variety of systems and applications, enabling delivery of applications that draw from multiple sources of data. Delivered in an intranet, extranet, or Internet configuration, the user interface can be presented in an HTML, a Java, an HTML/Java, a Windows, or a mainframe terminal client. Like Netscape Application Server, the NetDynamics product supports thread pooling and load balancing and provides recovery services. The NetDynamics Application Server can be programmed using Java or C++, or through an ActiveX interface.

Because MTS uses COM objects, MTS applications support most languages and tools that support COM, including the ones mentioned previously. It is possible to create components using these COM-enabled tools and then place them inside the MTS environment (see Figure 8.9).

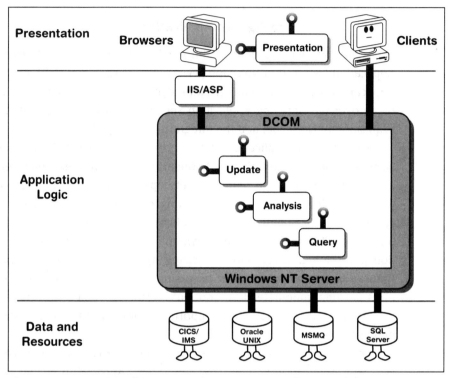

Figure 8.9   MTS provides a container for transactional ActiveX components.

Future of Transactional Middleware

What is the future of transactional middleware, and how should it be applied to EAI?

Despite the lack of hype, TP monitors will remain the dominant transactional middleware because they provide the best mix of standards, scaling features, and reputations. They are also proven workhorses. IBM's CICS has been around for decades, and Tuxedo continues to process billions of transactions a day.

However, there is no intrinsic reason to cling to "traditional" technology. The new line of application servers holds out great promise, with easy-to-use development features and the ability to leverage hype-driven standards such as EJB and ActiveX.

The transactional middleware technology that becomes dominant will be the technology that most often finds itself solving the EAI problem.

TP monitor vendors are certainly not sitting out the application server revolution. Both IBM and BEA have enhanced their TP monitors with transactional servers (TXSeries and M3, respectively) that can function in a distributed computing environment. However, the current state of TP monitors only brings up some more questions. Are application servers going to look more like TP monitors in the future, or are TP monitors going to look more like application servers? (Thus far, application servers have yet to match the robust transactional model and integrity controls provided by TP monitors.)

EJB are a step in the right direction; however, the specification does not give detailed definitions of the exact nature of the technology, such as thread pooling, concurrency control, and resource management. While the ambiguity provides vendors with an excuse to differentiate their products, it also allows them to stray in different directions, using different proprietary mechanisms. Fortunately, Sun understands this and is establishing a certification program to insure that all of those promoting their products as being EJB compliant, actually are. What's more, they are accelerating the progress of EJB, providing vendors with the ability to adopt this standard sooner rather than later. We shortly should be able to create a set of EJBs within any compliant tool and run those within any compliant container.

Traditional TP monitor environments, as well the new line of Java-enabled application servers, will prove to be the best place for EJB. For example, count on seeing EJB together with TP monitors such as IBM's CICS or BEA's Tuxedo. New component transaction servers such as MTS are also logical environments for EJB as well. There will also be other CORBA-compliant distributed objects working with EJB, and Sun is working closely with the OMG to make this a reality.

MTS (now AppCenter) and ActiveX, on the other hand, have a head start on EJB, just not as much hype and play in the media. Just as COM has crept onto desktops over the last several years, MTS and transactional Java are stealthily moving there as well. Enterprise software may be created using ActiveX and MTS for no greater reason than the wonderful convenience of it all.

The most compelling concept of MTS—that it's a product, not a standard—could be its downfall as well. Many organizations burned by proprietary products are cautious about wrapping enterprise applications around a product rather than a standard.

On the other hand, EJB is a standard that will cross many different product lines. However, it's difficult to tell how much protection will come with that.

Everyone implements standards in different ways. In fact, many consider standards to be more about marketing hype than about real technological value.

Problems that MTS needs to solve may include scalability and integration with other environments. We've yet to see how scalable EJB really is due to the immaturity of the standard and the lack of real life applications. Perhaps neither of these technologies will live up to its promise. At least, not initially. To do transactions today may mean to continue to rely on more traditional technology, such as TP monitors.

The coupling of transactional middleware with EAI is clear. EAI problem domains that need to support transactions between applications, share logic as well as data, and are willing to incur the cost of changing all connected applications, are perfect for transactional middleware–type solutions. EAI architects and developers, however, have to carefully consider the integration requirements (both technical and business) before committing to transactional middleware. In fact most EAI problem domains will need a suite of middleware, transactional and nontransactional, to meet their ultimate business requirements. Unfortunately, the problems are too complex to apply one generic solution, as we'll see in the following chapters.

CHAPTER NINE

RPCs, Messaging, and EAI

"The computer programmer is a creator of universes for which he alone is responsible. Universes of virtually unlimited complexity can be created in the form of computer programs."

— Joseph Weizenbaum

Our discussion in this chapter will be brief for two reasons. One, message-oriented middleware (MOM) and RPC-based middleware tend to be traditional, point-to-point middleware. As such, they are not effective solutions for most EAI projects. Two, there is not a great deal we can add to the material that has already been published. Our discussion will therefore center on the application of this technology to the new EAI space and to the evolution of this technology in support of EAI.

The question presents itself, "Given the preceding observations, is a discussion of this technology really necessary?" The answer is yes. It is important to understand point-to-point middleware in order to integrate it within the enterprise. Middleware itself is a common point of integration for source and target systems. Despite the limitations of this technology for EAI solutions, the appropriate tradeoffs in both technology and product decisions may make the inclusion of this middleware important to a particular EAI problem domain.

RPCs

Building on our discussion in Chapter 7, we note that RPCs are nothing more than a method of communicating with a remote computer, in which the developer invokes a procedure on the server by making a simple function call on the client (see Figure 9.1). RPCs hide the intricacies of the network and operating system using this mechanism. It should also be recalled that the client process that calls the remote function must suspend itself until the procedure is completed.

While RPCs are easy to use and understand, they can be problematic when being incorporated into an EAI problem domain. Stopping an application from processing during a remote call could diminish the performance of the application. In addition, because there is a high level of network communication between the client and the server when using RPCs, RPC architecture requires a high-speed network.

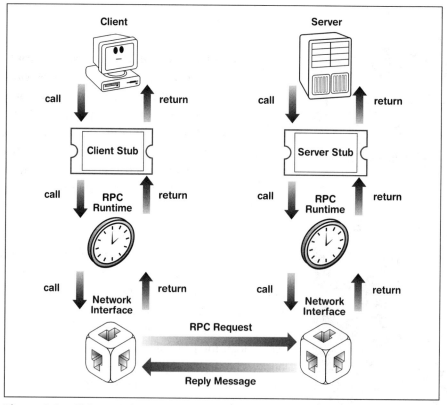

Figure 9.1   Using RPCs

RPCs were the base middleware layers of the early client/server systems. In addition to many database-oriented middleware layers, they are capable of running network operating systems, such as Sun's Network File System (NFS) and Open Software Foundation's DCE. Distributed object technology, such as COM and CORBA, leverage RPCs effectively in order to provide object-to-object communications.

DCE

DCE is a complex, but effective, middleware solution. Developed by Open Software Foundation (OSF), DCE makes many diverse computers function as a single virtual system—the ultimate in distributed computing (see Figure 9.2). As such, it is certainly relevant to EAI. However, the heart of DCE is a classic RPC mechanism. Because of this, every limitation inherent in RPCs—including blocking and the need for a high-speed network—exists in DCE as well.

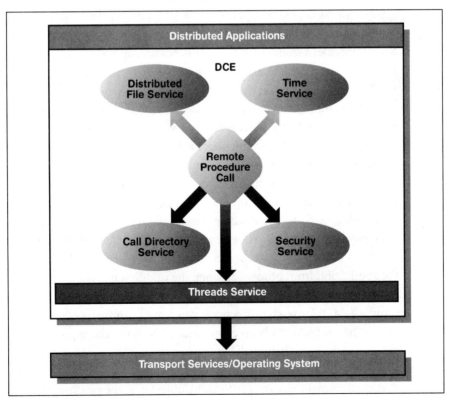

Figure 9.2   The DCE architecture

Despite its limitations, DCE is a key infrastructure component in many larger organizations. Developers can use DCE as a middleware layer to span every system in the company, tying together many systems, applications, and users. While DCE provides a comprehensive multivendor network operating system solution, many enterprises are moving away from it, opting for messaging technology, such as message brokers and other MOM.

The heart of the DCE is its RPC. It lets developers reach across platforms to access many types of application services, including database, distributed objects, and TP monitors. DCE also provides a sophisticated naming service, a synchronization service, a distributed file system, and built-in network security. DCE is available on most platforms.

Message-Oriented Middleware (MOM)

In the absence of a bandwidth to support RPCs, or in a situation where a server cannot be depended upon to always be up and running, message-oriented middleware (MOM) may be more advisable for an EAI project. Like RPCs, MOM provides a standard API across hardware, operating system platforms, and networks (see Figure 9.3). MOM is also able to guarantee that messages will reach their destination, even when the destination is not available.

MOM utilizes one of two "macro-messaging" models: process-to-process or message queuing. In the process-to-process model, both the sending and receiving processes must be active for messages to be exchanged. The queuing model allows messages to be stored in a queue, so only one process needs to be active. The queuing model is most beneficial when communication is taking place between computers that are not always up and running, over networks that are not always dependable, or when there is a limitation on bandwidth. We seem to be moving from process-to-process to queuing, considering current MOM usage.

Unlike RPCs, MOM is asynchronous. Consequently, MOM does not block the application from processing when the middleware API is invoked. (As noted in Chapter 7, RPCs, on the other hand, block processing until the procedure call returns.) MOM message functions can return immediately, even though the request has not actually been completed. This allows the application to continue processing, assured that it will know when the request is completed.

The queuing model is most useful for transaction-oriented EAI applications that must transverse many platforms. Unlike DCE, the platform does not have to be up and running for an application to request services. If the server is down,

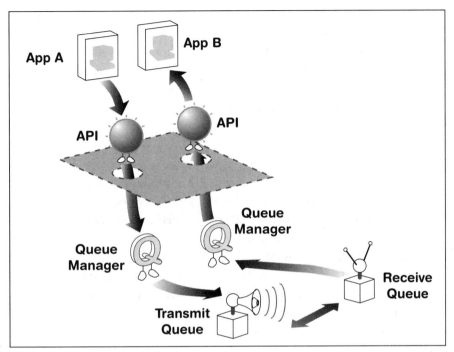

Figure 9.3 **MOM (in the case of queuing middleware) provides an API to allow programmers to access its services.**

the request remains in a queue. When the server comes back online, the request will be processed. In addition to these queuing features, MOM provides concurrent execution features, allowing the processing of more than one request at the same time.

So, when should MOM be applied? MOM is a good fit for store-and-forward communications or when dealing with applications that are not expected to be reachable at the same time. MOM is a natural choice for many EAI problem domains, at least at the transport level. MOM also makes sense for "defensive communication," when the network between applications frequently fails. MOM is also a good choice for journaled communications, when communications between processes need to be logged.

MOM and messaging tend to be better EAI fits than RPC-based middleware. Unfortunately, MOM alone does not provide the complete infrastructure necessary for EAI. Message brokers add value to traditional MOM products by providing data and schema transformation functions, as well as **intelligent routing** and event-driven processing to move information throughout an enterprise. Such a scenario relies on MOM products as little more than functional transport layers (see Figure 9.4).

Each MOM product implements the notion of messaging in its own way. For this reason, it is useful to examine two of the most popular MOM products— MSMQ from Microsoft and MQSeries from IBM. (Note: Java Message Service [JMS] is discussed in Chapter 12.)

MSMQ

MSMQ (Microsoft Message Queue) server is a Windows NT–based and COM-enabled MOM product. It is also a key product in Microsoft's foray into the enterprise-computing arena. MSMQ joins Microsoft Transaction Server (MTS), Internet Information Server (IIS), SQL Server, and Microsoft's Active Platform strategy in complementing an impressive array of products, technology, and tools that finally allow Microsoft to scale.

MSMQ provides a set of ActiveX components that implements an API to all MSMQ features. ActiveX allows these other Microsoft products to access MSMQ. In addition, MSMQ can be accessed from such traditional Windows applications as Excel and Word, or through any ActiveX-enabled development tool.

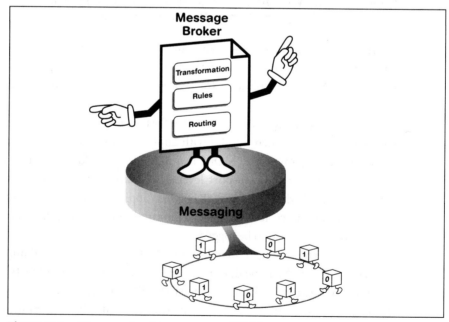

Figure 9.4   Message brokers may use MOM to transport messages.

MSMQ can guarantee the delivery of messages by utilizing disk-based intermediary storage and log-based recovery techniques. (This feature is, however, optional.) Although clearly beneficial, it is wise to bear in mind that logging diminishes performance.

MSMQ leverages most popular network protocols, including IPX/SPX and **TCP/IP**. Using MSMQ as a common translation mechanism, protocols can even be mixed and matched.

Like MQSeries (discussed in the section that follows), MSMQ supports transactions. In the MSMQ environment, transactions either work, or if they fail, they recover completely. The participating system is never left in an unstable state. For example, in a database update operation, any abort condition will cause the database updates to roll back by stopping the send operation. As with transactional middleware, operations are never completed until the transaction is committed.

MSMQ is tightly integrated with MTS. When MTS is present, its services automatically participate in the MSMQ transaction.

MSMQ administrators work through the MSMQ Explorer. Explorer is able to manage all machines in the MSMQ environment from a single administration workstation by using shared and replicated directory services to manage the configuration information. MSMQ is able to layer into the Windows NT security subsystem, leveraging the NT Access Control List facility.

The following are MSMQ features:

- One-time, in-order delivery, which assures developers that messages are delivered to their destinations only once and in the order they were sent. (A common complaint about primitive MOM products is that messages are out of order when they hit another application or resource server.)
- Message-routing services, which give the EAI applications the ability to send messages to their destination using least-cost routing. (An administrator defines the cost of each route, and MSMQ will automatically calculate the most economical path for the message.)
- Notification services, which inform the sender that the message was received and processed. They also handle messages that time out, giving developers the opportunity to take corrective action.
- Message priorities, which allow developers to assign priorities to messages. High-priority messages are placed before low-priority messages in the queue. (Allowing, for example, larger orders or orders from preferred customers to be processed before other orders.)

- Journaling. The journaling subsystem maintains copies of messages moving through the system. Developers can select messages and queues for the journal. This allows developers to recover from failures by bringing the messages into synch with the journals.

Using MSMQ

Building an EAI application using MSMQ is not particularly complicated. When an application needs to place a message in the queue, it uses the MSMQ Open API, which has an ActiveX control wrapped around it. By passing in the name and destination queue, a queue handle is created, allowing MSMQ to identify the destination queues to the MSMQ server sending the message.

Once a queue handle has been created, the next step is to create a message by allocating local memory and adding information to the message. It is at this step that parameters can be added (such as time-out values, names of response queues, and priorities). The message is then sent through the MSMQ Send API (MQSendMessage). Finally, the application closes the queue handle using the MSMQ Close API (MQCloseQueue). The queue handle can be left open if additional messages are slated to go out later. Opening and closing queues too often degrades application performance.

The receiver application requires the Open API, along with queue identification information, to create the queue handle. When calling the MSMQ Receiver API, MSMQ will pass back a pointer with control information to the message (such as the name of the response queue). After receiving the information, the application will close the connection to the queue. Figure 9.5 shows the architecture of MSMQ and the foundation for this process. (MSMQ supports both blocking and nonblocking receives.)

MSMQ is capable of Internet/intranet application integration. An MSMQ queue can be accessed directly from IIS, using Active Server Page (ASP) scripts. In addition, CGI and more traditional APIs for C and C++ can also be used.

IBM MQSeries

In the world of MOM, IBM's MQSeries is the proverbial 600-pound gorilla. Dominating queuing middleware with a market share of over 65 percent, it can do just about anything it pleases. Although it isn't the most feature rich of messaging middleware products, MQSeries sits atop the EAI world as the preferred messaging layer for moving information throughout an enterprise.

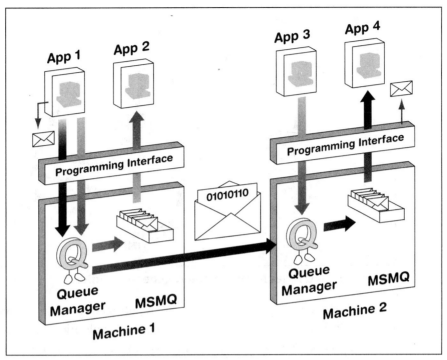

Figure 9.5   The architecture of MSMQ

Perhaps most notable about MQSeries is the number of platforms it supports. MQSeries works with IBM OS/390, Pyramid, Open VMS, IBM AIX, NCR UNIX, UP-UX, Solaris, OS/2, Windows NT, SCO UNIX, and MacOS, as well as others.

MQSeries supports all the features of MSMQ, including support for transactions, journaling, **message routing**, and priorities. MQSeries also provides a common API for use across a variety of development environments and on a variety of platforms. However, those interfaces are sold by third-party vendors.

MQSeries products provide a single, multiplatform API. As a result, messages can be sent from a Windows 2000 workstation and routed through UNIX, VMS, or even a mainframe, before reaching their final destination. The platforms running MQSeries can work in concert, assuring that messages are delivered to their destination (see Figure 9.6), and they can even route around network and system failures. MQSeries can be used as a transactional recovery method and a mail transport mechanism, assuring the delivery of messages.

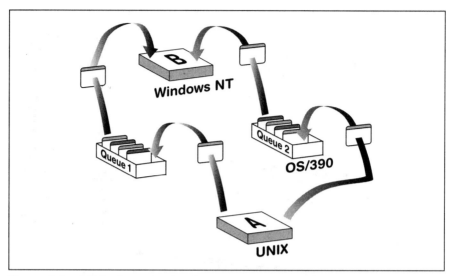

Figure 9.6   MQSeries MOM is a heterogeneous solution.

MQSeries supports what IBM refers to as "advanced message framework," a framework that consists of three layers: customer application options, trusted messaging backbone, and comprehensive communication choices (see Figure 9.7). The customer application options provide services such as basic messaging, transactional messaging, workflow computing, mail messaging, option messaging, cooperative processing, data replication, and mobile messaging. Transactional messaging allows developers to coordinate message flow with updates to other resource managers. For example, several databases on different platforms can be updated at the same time. The mail-messaging feature allows any Vendor Independent Messaging (VIM) or Mail API (MAPI) application to leverage the power of MQSeries' messaging infrastructure to transmit e-mail securely and reliably. MQSeries supports messaging between distributed objects and facilitates cooperative processing between two or more processes.

MQSeries' trusted messaging backbone guarantees that messages are delivered to their destinations and that the information encapsulated in those messages is secure. MQSeries' comprehensive communication choices allow it to leverage any number of protocols and networks for message traffic.

MQSeries Upgrade

The newest version of MQSeries may offer a glimpse of "things to come" in messaging middleware. While traditional MOM focused on simple A-to-B

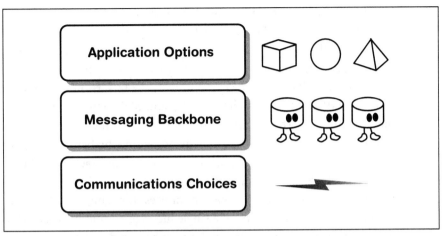

Figure 9.7   The three layers of MQSeries

asynchronous message passing, MOM now provides many value-added services in an attempt to compete with other MOM vendors, as well as other middleware products.

The original concept of MOM certainly never included the encapsulation of transactions. Today, most MOM packages can take advantage of the notion of a transaction (a "unit of work"), with the ability to maintain states. MOM can maintain message persistence and logging. Therefore, it can provide enhanced manageability and fail-over capabilities.

The best queuing products (like MQSeries) are trying to reinvent themselves with the addition of a publish-and-subscribe engine. This is a very positive development, and one intended to gain entry into the exploding world of information dissemination middleware products such as existing publish and subscribe middleware from vendors such as TIBCO.

MQSeries Features

The new MQSeries has taken the leap from version 2 to version 5, stepping up to the IBM installation procedures that put it on a par with other IBM products. MQSeries has always been notoriously difficult to install. Perhaps with this upgrade, the frustration has been adequately addressed. In addition to easier installation, IBM is claiming that the new version of MQSeries works better with its DB2, Transaction Server, and other Software Server components. Other new features include Database-Message Resource Coordination (DMRC) and smart message distribution.

Long available on a large number of server platforms, MQSeries now supports Windows NT and OS/2 as well.

Before this latest version, MQSeries required a transaction manager or a sophisticated application program in order to combine database updates and messaging activity into a single unit of work. With version 5.1 and the introduction of DMRC, MQSeries includes MQ and **SQL** activity support through the new MZBEGIN verb to register a unit of work. This means that subsequent work can be committed, or backed out, depending on whether the procedure(s) succeeded. MQSeries clearly supports the notion of a transaction, without having to employ a TP monitor or application server.

Smart message distribution minimizes the amount of network traffic required to distribute a copy of a single message to multiple users whose queues reside on a single node. MQSeries 5.1 is able to send a single copy of the message to each target MQ system, using a list of recipients at the target systems, each of which receives a copy. At that point, the receiving MQ system will produce and queue the copies locally.

In addition, the package includes performance enhancements, including fast messages (which means changes to MQSeries' message channel agents reduce the time and resources required to move nonpersistent messages) and enhancements to internal channel architecture and trusted bindings.

Another significant improvement in this upgrade is the ability to support large messages. The previous limit of 4MB per message has been extended to 100MB per message. Additionally, messages may now be built or retrieved in segments. MQSeries can also pass messages by reference.

MQSeries Publish/Subscribe

The publish and subscribe feature in the newest version of MQSeries automates the distribution of relevant information to people and applications that want it. Using the new pub/sub engine, MQSeries developers can make sure that what the client receives is exactly what the client wants, because the client has to subscribe to a topic to receive the information. Of course, behind the scenes MQSeries is using the MQ messaging infrastructure to move the messages throughout the enterprise.

Publish and subscribe removes the requirements for an MQ-enabled application to understand anything about the target application. It only needs to send the information to be shared to a destination contained within the pub/sub engine, or broker. The broker can redistribute the information to any interested application. The real advantage to MQSeries offering pub/sub is the degree of reliability MQSeries delivers.

The most significant downside is to those pub/sub vendors who now find themselves competing against Big Blue (IBM). TIBCO has dominated pub/sub but now could find that the new features included in MQSeries will finally threaten its "king of the hill" status in the world of finance. In addition, the pub/sub features of MQSeries are the same as many features offered by traditional message brokers, albeit without schema and content transformation facilities.

IBM has adopted NEON's message-brokering features, and placed them on top of MQSeries—the MQ Integrator.

It is clear that IBM's ultimate goal is to become the information bus for the enterprise. With this latest release of MQSeries, it is taking a giant step closer to achieving that lofty goal.

Getting the Message

MSMQ provides the best tool support "out of the gate." This is, simply, because it has been developed by Microsoft. Its ability to layer easily into most Windows-based development tools means that users of native Windows client/server applications will encounter minimal resistance with MSMQ. MQSeries, while able to work with most development environments, is not as easily integrated with popular client/server development products. This is, to a large degree, the result of MQSeries' "need" to be all things to all platforms.

MSMQ also has the advantage in tools and price. MQSeries has the advantage in scalability, maturity, and platform support. MQSeries' ability to work with a broad spectrum of hosts, servers, and workstations means that developers can support the standard hodgepodge of platforms that exist in most organizations and bring them all together to form client/server applications. While there are some third-party attempts to port MSMQ to non-Windows platforms, for the time being, MSMQ is homogeneous to Windows.

Scalability comes with platform support. Because MQSeries is able to support larger, more powerful platforms, it follows that it provides a better opportunity to scale to higher processing and user loads. MQSeries also has the advantage when it comes to fault tolerance, message delivery, time-of-day dispatching, access to databases, and broadcasting. Finally, MQSeries deserves credit simply for being a mature and well-tested product on most platforms.

Considering the tradeoffs, and the past behavior of EAI architects and developers, MSMQ appears to have the best chance for success for the low-end EAI development marketplace, which is where most application development occurs. Microsoft's strategy of giving products away, combined with the popularity of Windows NT, means that most IT managers looking for MOM will turn to MSMQ—if only because it's already there. This has been the case with IIS and Internet Explorer. However, it appears that MQSeries will continue to dominate the high-end, heterogeneous market. All that said, these products still have to evolve before they can support general-purpose EAI.

All MOM products have some EAI strategy. MSMQ, for example, is seeking to leverage Microsoft's SQL Server as message broker. It would be able to transform and route messaging using MSMQ as the underlying transport layer. MQSeries uses its MQ Integrator product (created by NEON) to add message broker services to MQSeries. SAGA Software's Sagavista is also able to leverage MQSeries for transport (in addition to JMS [Java Message Service] and their own EntireX MOM layer).

MQSeries is looking to build many of the features found in traditional message brokers into the base messaging layer. It's conceivable that MQSeries will be queuing software as well as message brokers in the years to come. In the meantime, other MOM, including MSMQ, will likely evolve along much the same path.

CHAPTER TEN

Distributed Objects and EAI

"The danger from computers is not that they will eventually get as smart as men, but we will meanwhile agree to meet them halfway."
—Bernard Avishai

Depending on the goal, distributed objects could have nothing to do with EAI—or everything. On the scene for nearly a decade, distributed objects technology creates an infrastructure to share methods by providing an additional location for application processing and for interoperability among processes. It provides a standard mechanism to access shared objects, objects that run on any number of servers. Distributed objects technology also provides access to any number of shared methods. As such, it is applicable to method-level EAI.

In the context of EAI, distributed objects give EAI architects the ability to create applications that share common methods or composite applications that support method-level EAI. "EAI nirvana," the integration of applications by sharing a common business logic, lies along this path. However, as we have already warned, the path is risky and studded with expensive obstacles. Such is the promise, and those are the pitfalls of distributed objects and EAI.

What Works

Distributed objects work best for EAI problem domains that need to share a large number of common methods and need to do so using a distributed computing model. For example, a human resources department may have four major applications:

- Employee tracking system
- Employee benefits system
- Resume database application
- Salary planning system

While each of these applications functions independently, they have a number of methods in common. These may include:

- Add_Employee()
- Edit_Employee()
- Delete_Employee()
- Promote_Employee()

For these methods to be shared, an additional shared application layer must be created (physical or virtual), one with an enabling technology that allows applications to share methods. Application servers, TP monitors, or distributed

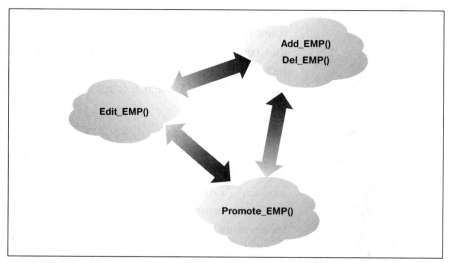

Figure 10.1   Using distributed objects

objects are the best options for such a layer. Each has distinct advantages and disadvantages, which should be apparent by now.

If method-level EAI is the chosen approach, then the EAI architect and developer may seek to create a set of distributed objects that houses these common methods. Using a common structure, interface, and communications mechanism (e.g., IIOP, or RPCs, which are discussed in the section "What's So Easy?" later in this chapter), distributed objects provide the enabling technology for sharing these methods (see Figure 10.1).

What's So Difficult?

Distributed object vendors are quick to suggest that using distributed objects is easy—a simple matter of making changes to several applications and exposing application methods using distributed object technology for access by other applications or, more commonly, among the distributed objects themselves. Simple. However, for this method to be successful in an application like the preceding example, the common methods would have to be stripped from all the human resource applications and then be redeployed within some sort of distributed object technology. Code would have to be changed everywhere. Each application would need to be tested and then redeployed. This is a monumental task, but one that could very well be worth the effort if it ultimately achieves the business objectives. This makes distributed object–based EAI an invasive integration approach, meaning that a lot has to change in order to accommodate this technology.

This translates into a straightforward truism: A solid business case is required to justify leveraging method-level EAI and enabling technology such as distributed objects. The calculus is simple—assess what is to be gained from the EAI project against the resources necessary to complete the project. If the resources required far exceed the gain, then other EAI levels will likely prove to be better approaches. However, if it appears as if the return on investment is there, then method-level EAI is the most elegant of EAI solutions. The failing in too many organizations is an absence of strict candor and realism in making this assessment. Organizations that talk themselves into EAI projects using distributed objects based on exaggerated claims by both the media and vendors are very often in for a rude awakening. Failed distributed object projects outnumber the successes. *That's* the reality without the hype.

What's So Easy?

Once the disadvantages of distributed objects are understood, the advantages can be focused on. The single, greatest advantage of distributed objects is the adherence to an application development and interoperability standard. CORBA and COM (now COM+) are mere specifications, not technologies. The vendors adhere to the established standard and therefore provide a set of technologies that can interoperate. Because the standard is open, vendors discover that interacting with distributed objects is not at all difficult because all the interfaces are well defined.

As the distributed object technology matures, vendors are adding new features that address many previous shortcomings, namely: scalability, interoperability, and communication mechanisms. Distributed objects are now able to provide better scalability through the ability to support transactions and therefore offer the same scaling tricks as application servers and TP monitors. The OMG is now endorsing CORBA's OTS (Object Transaction Services), while Microsoft is looking for MTS to bring transactionality to COM. Interoperability continues to improve as common protocols are defined, protocols that include CORBA's IIOP and Microsoft's COM RPC (loosely based on the DCE RPC).

One Standard—Many Different Instances

In truth, interoperability with standards such as CORBA is a very recent occurrence. In the early days of CORBA, distributed object vendors (all adhering to the CORBA standard) were unable to communicate with one another. The fault for this "failure to communicate" lay not with the vendors but with the standard itself, which was much too loose. It failed to describe enough detail to enable the objects to share information.

Over the years, the standards have matured, becoming more detailed. As a result, the communication mechanisms have become much more compatible. However, even with this progress, there remains a great distance to travel before distributed objects can truly "talk." With the next generation's specifications, both the vendors and the standards organization are promising seamless compatibility. All fine and good, but it may be wise to create a pilot project to test that promise before building an EAI project on what could turn out to be more hype.

Objects created by different vendors can share information by using a common object-to-object protocol as the least common denominator. Finally, where traditional distributed objects leverage simple, **synchronous communication** mechanisms based on the RPC (the case with both CORBA and Microsoft), they are now providing asynchronous messaging mechanisms as well. (CORBA is providing its own message service as part of the standard, while Microsoft is learning to leverage MSMQ as a way to bring messaging to COM.)

The result of all this? While distributed objects were once difficult to deploy and provided few advantages over more traditional alternatives, they are now easier to use and provide many more features that benefit an enterprise development technology. In short, distributed objects have become a key enabling technology for method-level EAI.

What's a Distributed Object?

Although distributed objects entered the systems scene in the early 1990s, their potential for EAI development is a recent occurrence. Several variables have contributed to this change in status:

- We now move toward multitiered application development. Developers are realizing that the enabling technology of distributed objects "gets them there." Distributed objects give EAI architects and developers the ability to create portable objects that can run on a variety of servers and can communicate using a predefined and standard messaging interface. EAI is exploiting this aspect of distributed objects.
- For the last several years, CORBA was the one, real standard available (see the section "CORBA," later in this chapter). Microsoft entered the distributed object marketplace with the Distributed Component Object Model (DCOM). DCOM promises to provide a distributed object infrastructure with Windows-based operating systems, along with the ability to tie applications created with traditional tools. The object request broker (ORB) is part of the operating system and therefore a giveaway.
- We learned to take ORBs to the desktop through the use of components. Application components, such as ActiveX, let developers create applications by mixing and matching components, piecing together an application like a jigsaw puzzle. This is the nirvana of application development, the ability to assemble applications the way the Ford Motor Company assembles Mustangs—from prebuilt component parts.

• The rise of the Web renewed interest in distributed objects. Technologies and standards, such as CORBA's IIOP, promise to provide both an enabling technology for dynamic application development and a better application-to-application, object-to-object transport layer. Now that powerhouse Web companies, such as Netscape, have put their weight behind ORBs, Web developers will continue their rush to ORBs.

The General Idea

With so much resting on ORBs, the question that seems to beg for an answer is: "What's an ORB anyway?" ORBs provide developers with standard objects to communicate with other standard objects, using a standard interface and line protocol. Like traditional objects (such as those found with C++, Java, or Smalltalk), ORBs can access methods of other ORBs locally or over a network (see Figure 10.2). The ability to access methods gives ORBs their distributed capabilities. ORBs can also exchange data and are platform independent—that is, able to run on many connected servers.

For example, a CORBA ORB can pass requests from object to object. The clients invoke ORB services through the ORB core and the Interface Definition Language (IDL) stub. Another invocation method is through a Dynamic Invocation Interface (DII) (IDL and DII are described in the next section

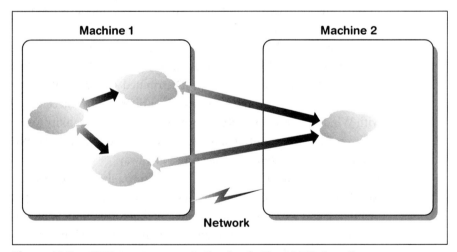

Figure 10.2   ORBs can access methods of other ORBs locally or over a network.

"CORBA"). The stub provides mapping between the language binding (e.g., C++ and Java) and the ORB services. This process describes how instructions are given to the ORBs. At the next step, the ORB core then moves the request to the object implementation, which receives the message through an up-call, using the IDL skeleton, or dynamic skeleton.

CORBA

In 1989, OMG, a consortium of technology vendors, began work on the first, cross-compatible, distributed object standard. OMG included such object powerhouse vendors as IBM, Apple, Sun, and many others. In tackling this endeavor, OMG promised object reuse regardless of platform, tool, or programming language—in other words, a common binary object that would work anywhere for any application, an object that would allow developers to mix and match objects for distributed computing application development. The result, CORBA, was first released around 1991. However, even with this promising beginning, there still remained a long road ahead before EAI and distributed objects could work together.

The first CORBA specification freed developers from their C++ compilers. With a standard finally in place, they were able to purchase objects to create applications. However, as with so many things in the distributed application development world, there was a catch. The first CORBA specification came in two parts: the Interface Definition Language (IDL) and the Dynamic Invocation Interface (DII). Both of these components exist within every CORBA ORB, and each provides a communications service between ORBs—either locally (intra-computer) or over a network (intercomputer).

The IDL, at its core, defines an object's structure and provides the developer with an API to access the object services during runtime. The IDL is the tool CORBA ORB developers must grapple with in order to build application-dependent features into an ORB.

The DDI is an API as well, one that provides developers with dynamic construction of object invocations. In contrast to the IDL, DDI allows developers to do things while the objects run. The client can establish the objects and operations, including any parameters.

Shortfalls

CORBA's first release, CORBA 1.1, had many limitations. For example, as we mentioned previously, it did not provide enough detail to allow ORB vendors to create CORBA-compliant ORBs that were able to work together. While CORBA 1.1 did define an object standard, it had no real value due to lack of interoperability. In short, version 1.1 was the first step but only the first step. OMG's 1994 release of CORBA 2.0 made great strides to solve the interoperability problem. CORBA 2.0 contained specific syntax for a network protocol. As a result, ORBs were able to communicate with one another. Version 2.0 also defined a TCP/IP-based inter-ORB protocol backbone, along with an inter-ORB communication service that allowed components to generate IDs for any of the interfaces they supported.

The guts of CORBA ORBs remained the same in 2.0 as in 1.1. They included support for an IDL and a DDL. However, while CORBA 1.1 only included mapping to C, a nonobject language, version 2.0 included mapping to C++, Smalltalk, and, later, Java.

CORBA 3.0 promises to "go the remaining distance" in solving the shortcomings in CORBA 2.0. In many regards, OMG is finally getting CORBA "right," providing a robust specification to define transactionality, **asynchronous communications**, and a better development environment. Along with OMG, the vendors who dominate the CORBA-compliant ORB marketplace, such as Iona, IBM, and Inprise, are also making good on those promises.

CORBA Internals

Because a great deal of information is available, what we hope to do here is provide an overview of distributed objects and their application to EAI. If CORBA (or COM) is being considered as the enabling technology for an EAI project, this information should prove helpful.

There are four main parts to a CORBA ORB (see Figure 10.3):

- Object Request Broker (ORB)
- Object services
- Common facilities
- Application objects

These features exist in other ORBs, such as Microsoft's COM/DCOM, or even proprietary ORBs, such as those sold by NEXT Software, Forte, and Dynasty.

ORB

The ORB is an engine that shares information with other ORBs. Together, they create a distributed object. ORBs exist as background objects, functioning

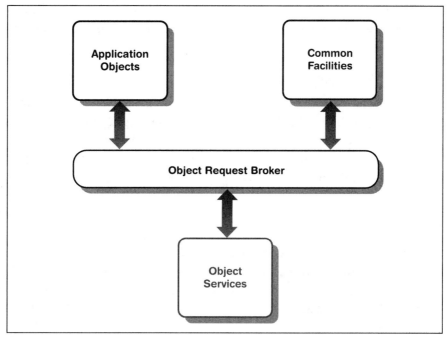

Figure 10.3   Four parts of the CORBA ORB

behind the application. Applications are also layered on top of ORBs, providing the distributed infrastructure. This is the reason why ORBs make such effective middleware layers—many communication services already exist in ORB services (such as CORBA-compliant ORBs). Layering also provides heterogeneous application portability and interoperability. It is this interoperability feature that makes ORBs most valuable to EAI.

Object Services

CORBA mandates object services, which are groups of services that leverage object interfaces for communications between services. These are the basic services developers expect in an ORB: security, transaction management, and data exchange services. Developers use object services as a base class upon which to build applications.

Common Facilities

Common Facilities, optional for CORBA, are a collection of services that link with the client. Common facilities allow developers to build component characteristics in CORBA-compliant ORBs. Developers consider common facilities whenever they need to implement CORBA-compliant component-based objects.

Application Objects

Application objects support the application development features of a CORBA ORB, as defined by the ORB/application developer. This is where "the rubber meets the road" in ORB development, where ORBs can be turned into something useful. These features are built into ORB with the IDL, which assures interoperability with other CORBA-compliant ORBs.

COM

The dynamic that both complicates and drives the distributed object world right now is the emergence of Microsoft's component object model (COM), along with the further development of Microsoft's ORB into COM+. Microsoft invented COM using its existing Object Linking and Embedding (OLE) model as its design basis.

Although the great ORB debate rages on with great emotion on either side, the bottom line is that COM is as much an ORB as CORBA. ORB provides an object standard (that isn't really object oriented [e.g., the ability to support inheritance], but then, neither is CORBA) and a common mechanism for inter-ORB communications. COM is based on automation (using the COM model), a standard on most Windows desktops and a feature of most Windows-based development tools. For example, Visual Basic, Visual C++, Visual J++, Delphi, and PowerBuilder all support the creation of COM-enabled automation servers—servers an application can share through DCOM.

Automation

Automation (also known as "OLE automation") lets EAI architects and developers take advantage of the services of other COM-enabled applications that, for example, allow access to the services of a PowerBuilder application from Visual Basic or that run a Visual Basic object from Word for Windows. Automation provides a standard interface to expose methods for access by other automation servers or containers.

There are two types of automation: the automation controller and the automation server. The automation controller is, in actuality, the COM client.

The controller invokes the services of an automation server through the common COM interface (see Figure 10.4). Automation servers are ORBs that expose method functions available for use by other automation servers.

There are two types of automation servers: in-process and out-of-process. In-process servers are typically DLLs, which run in the same process and memory space as their clients (see Figure 10.5). ActiveX components offer the best examples of in-process OLE automation servers with some component features built-in. By contrast, out-of-process servers run in separate memory and process space from their clients (see Figure 10.6). Out-of-process servers are typically EXEs that communicate with other COM applications through a "lightweight" RPC mechanism (intracomputer). As with any ORB, out-of-process OLE automation servers can invoke the services of other COM ORBs either locally or remotely through DCOM.

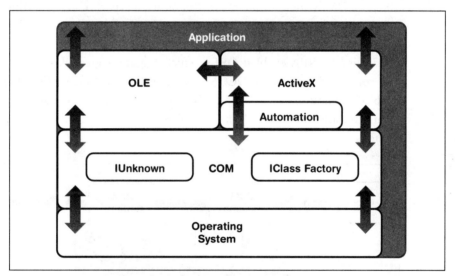

Figure 10.4   The OLE automation controller invokes the services of an OLE automation server through a COM interface.

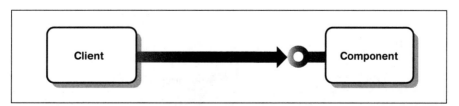

Figure 10.5   In-process automation server

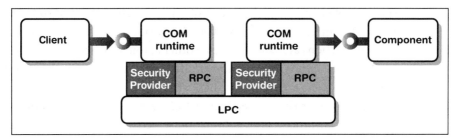

Figure 10.6   Out-of-process automation server

Moving to DCOM

The power of COM is lost without the ability to distribute COM-enabled ORBs. With DCOM, developers can create automation servers and make them available for other COM-enabled EAI applications on a network (see Figure 10.7). DCOM is not a commercial ORB; rather, it is part of the operating system. DCOM was first released with Windows NT 4.0 and is a part of Windows 98 and Windows 2000.

Unlike CORBA-enabled ORBs, which require a great deal of integration and coordination to work, DCOM simplifies things. With DCOM, the COM-enabled application checks the registry of the Windows operating system to locate and use remote COM-enabled ORBs, finding and invoking the service it requires.

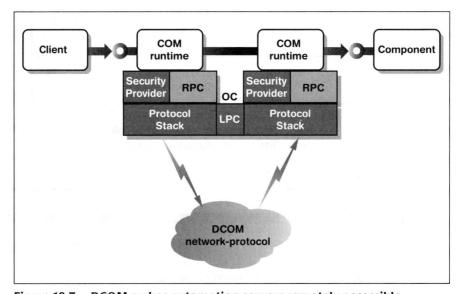

Figure 10.7   DCOM makes automation servers remotely accessible.

As suggested previously, DCOM differs from the CORBA architecture in that it is built into the infrastructure of the operating system, rather than as a product of an ORB vendor. DCOM is backward compatible with existing COM-enabled development tools, as well as with tools that were not created specifically for the development of distributed objects. Although not so by design, these tools are now in the distributed object business simply because DCOM can distribute the automation servers they create.

With the exception of Inprise, CORBA has had trouble attracting mainstream tool vendors. This lack of tools translates into a lack of CORBA interest in the development community. In sharp contrast, COM is already a part of most Windows-based development tools.

For all its advantages, there are drawbacks to DCOM. It will always be a Windows-bound ORB (in spite of the fact that there are DCOM implementations on UNIX, VMS, and even OS/390 from Software AG). Because of this, CORBA is the better choice for most EAI applications in a heterogeneous computing environment. In addition, DCOM is still immature and does not provide the performance of CORBA (not that CORBA is anything to write home about). However, when either develops to the point of incorporating mature transactionality, it may finally become the darling of the enterprise.

Quite simply, DCOM's strength is Microsoft. Microsoft's strategy has been to make complex, high-end software (such as ORBs) a widely available commodity. The availability of tools, coupled with the popularity of Microsoft operating systems, will assure a place for DCOM.

The Realities

There is both good news and bad news in considering the role of distributed objects in EAI. While distributed objects do provide EAI developers with an advanced distributed architecture to develop and deploy distributed applications, there remain issues that make them unsuitable for mission-critical EAI computing. For example, most commercial ORBs don't perform well at all, even with the transaction and messaging extensions. What's more, few recovery mechanisms are built into ORBs (CORBA and COM), and most ORBs don't perform garbage collection functions, load balancing, or concurrency control. This means they don't scale well, despite the fact that they support multitiered EAI architectures. Consequently, if method-level EAI and scalability are requirements, then application servers, or TP monitors are likely to be better solutions (albeit, these products may include ORBs within their internals).

Middleware needs to be considered as well. Most ORBs, COM and CORBA, use the synchronous communications model and still lack support for asynchronous messaging. Finally, the ORB code is still not completely portable from platform to platform. As with every other shortcoming, vendors and standards bodies plan to address these problems in new releases of specifications and products.

When all is said and done, do distributed objects and EAI work together? Absolutely. However, as with all things, careful consideration must be employed in making a decision. The marriage of technology and EAI is like any other—the partners have to mesh well to prosper over the long haul. In EAI (and, perhaps, in people), this is intrinsic to the architecture.

CHAPTER ELEVEN

Database-Oriented Middleware and EAI

"If a train station is where the train stops, what's a workstation . . . ?"
—Anonymous

Database access is a key element to EAI, especially data-level EAI. While there was a time when databases were proprietary and difficult to access, there are currently so many solutions for accessing data that a problem rarely arises when either retrieving information from any database or placing information in any database. Not only do these solutions make EAI a much easier proposition, they speak directly to the notion that the capability of modern middleware drives the interest in EAI.

As with most things, however, the situation with databases and database-oriented middleware grows complicated. Database-oriented middleware is no longer just a mechanism to "get at" data, it has also become a layer for placing data within the context of a particular common database model or format, known as a **virtual database**. For example, if data contained in a relational database is to be viewed as objects, the database-oriented middleware can map the information stored in the relational database so it appears as objects to a source or target application. The same thing can be done "the other way around"—mixing and matching models such as hierarchical, flat files, multidimensional, relational, and object-oriented (see Figure 11.1).

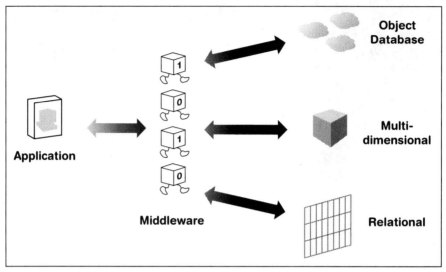

**Figure 11.1   Database-oriented middleware allows the viewing of data
using any model, no matter how the data is stored.**

Database-oriented middleware also provides access to any number of databases, regardless of the model employed or the platform upon which they exist. This is generally accomplished through a single, common interface such as Open Database Connectivity (ODBC) or Java Database Connectivity (JDBC), both discussed later in this chapter. As a result, information stored in your Adabas, DB2, Oracle, or Sybase databases can be accessed at the same time through a single interface (see Figure 11.2). By taking advantage of these mechanisms, it is possible to map the difference in the source and target databases to a common model, making them much easier to integrate. This process also supports the notion of a common enterprise metadata model presented earlier in this book.

It should be clear from these examples that database-oriented middleware plays a very significant role in the world of EAI, allowing a large number of enabling technologies to process information coming and going from the source or target systems. If a message broker or an application server requires information contained in a database, then database-oriented middleware becomes the logical solution for accessing that information. Many EAI products, such as message brokers and application servers, already contain the necessary database-oriented middleware to access the most popular databases. In fact, most message brokers and application servers come prepackaged with the appropriate adapters to access most relational databases, such as Oracle, Sybase, and Informix. Clearly, database access is now a problem solved, with plenty of inexpensive and proven solutions available.

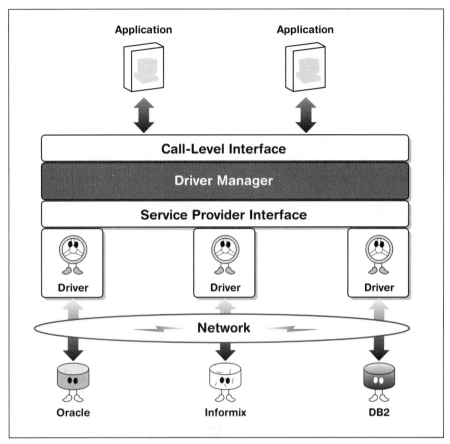

Figure 11.2 Database-oriented middleware provides access to a number of databases at the same time.

However, it's important to understand the role of database-oriented middleware in the context of EAI in order to get to the larger picture. Let's face it, databases are going to serve as the primary point-of-integration for most EAI solutions over the next few years, and the mechanism you select to move the information in and out of the databases can make or break your EAI project. What's more, the integration with more modern middleware solutions is essential and carries with it its own complexities and opportunities.

What's Database-Oriented Middleware?

Database-oriented middleware provides a number of important benefits (see Figure 11.3), including:

- An interface to an application
- The ability to convert the application language into something understandable by the target database (e.g., SQL)
- The ability to send a query to a database over a network
- The ability to process a query on the target database
- The ability to move a response set (the results of the query) back over the network to the requesting application
- The ability to convert a response set into a format understandable by the requesting application

In addition to these processes, database-oriented middleware must also provide the ability to process many simultaneous requests, as well as provide scaling features, such as thread pooling and load balancing. All this must be presented along with management capabilities and security features. As in other contexts,

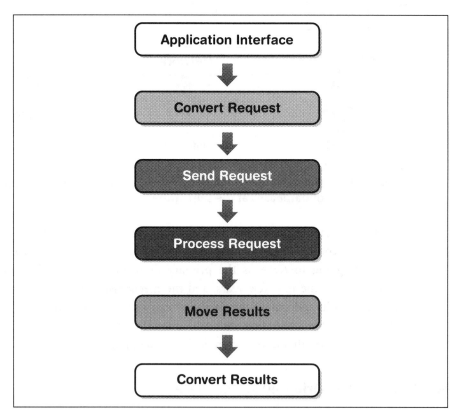

Figure 11.3   Functions of database-oriented middleware

the approaches to providing these benefits vary greatly from vendor to vendor and technology to technology.

Types of Database-Oriented Middleware

As has been the case at other times in this book, we will not present a lot of information that is readily available from other sources. Rather, we hope to present information that provides an overview to the types of database-oriented middleware available to apply to your EAI problem domain. That said, we will cover JDBC in detail in this chapter. Also note that this book includes a chapter on Java middleware (Chapter 12), and certainly JDBC is Java middleware. We'll touch on JDBC in the next chapter as well, just to put it in perspective.

In short, database-oriented middleware is "all the software that connects some application to some database." Like primitive middleware layers, database-oriented middleware allows developers to access the resources of another computer, in this case, a database server, using a single, well-defined API. While database-oriented middleware appears straightforward in its architecture, many products and standards make up this market, and each accomplishes the task in very different ways.

Although several types of database middleware exist, they are all basically native middleware—call-level interfaces (CLIs) and database **gateways**. That is, native middleware is middleware created for a specific database. For example, middleware provided by Sybase to access the Sybase databases from C++ is native database–oriented middleware. Native database–oriented middleware provides the best performance and access to native database features (such as stored procedures and triggers) because the middleware has been created for a particular database. However, once the links to a database have been created using native middleware, major renovations will be required in order to change databases.

CLIs, such as ODBC and JDBC (both discussed later in this chapter), provide a single interface to several databases. CLIs are able to translate common interface calls into any number of database dialects, as well as translate the response sets into a common response set representation (see Figure 11.4) understandable by the application making the request to the database.

Database gateways are able to provide access to data once locked inside larger systems, such as mainframes. They can integrate several databases for access from a single application interface. They can remap archaic database models (flat files,

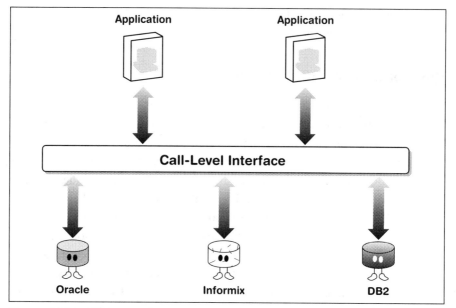

Figure 11.4   CLIs use a single, common interface to access several different databases.

ISAM, VSAM, and so on), so they appear more traditional, and translate queries and information as they move in and out of the database gateway software (more on this in the section "Database Gateways," later in this chapter).

ODBC

ODBC is really not a product but a standard that Microsoft created several years ago just after the Windows revolution. ODBC is a CLI that simplifies database access from Windows (as well as a few other operating systems) by allowing a developer to make a single API call that works with most relational databases, along with a few that don't follow the relational model.

Simply put, ODBC is a translation layer (as is JDBC). Like all middleware layers, ODBC provides a well-defined and database-independent API. When using the API, ODBC utilizes a driver manager to determine which database the application would like to communicate with and load (and unload) the appropriate ODBC driver (see Figure 11.5). As a result, an application using ODBC is database independent. However, if there are any database-specific calls (such as passing SQL directly through to the database or invoking a number of stored procedures and triggers), that application is no longer database independent

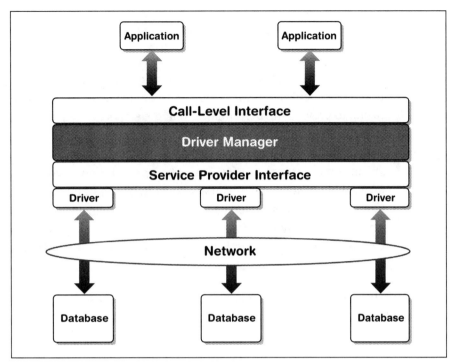

Figure 11.5   The ODBC driver manager

because it's bound to a particular database brand. In that case, it may make more sense not to use ODBC but rather move to a native database middleware layer.

ODBC is currently available in a 32-bit version, and most relational databases have ODBC drivers available. Although ODBC is free, the drivers are not. These drivers can be purchased from the database vendors or through third-party ODBC driver vendors. Most popular application development tool vendors provide database access features using ODBC. In fact it's the only way Microsoft's Visual Basic and other Microsoft tools can talk to a database.

Bottom line, ODBC is good enough for most EAI projects, especially those using Microsoft platforms. ODBC should be considered when operating in a multidatabase environment that requires access to several different databases from the same application or integration server (message broker or application server). ODBC is also a good fit if a database is likely to change during the life cycle of the application (such as scaling to a larger user load).

Using ODBC enables an EAI solution to move from database to database quickly. However, ODBC should be avoided if one is wedded to a particular

---

Does ODBC Hinder Performance?

There is a great deal of debate concerning ODBC's ability to provide performance, to access database features, and to provide a stable application deployment platform. While it is true that ODBC had a rough start, failing to provide the performance that developers were looking for, the ODBC of today (generally speaking, because performance is driver dependent) provides high-performance database access.

In some instances, ODBC has outperformed the native middleware layer. What's more, ODBC can access most of the native database features, such as accessing stored procedures and triggers, tracking transactions, and recovering from errors—albeit without the same degree of control as when using middleware that's native to a particular database.

---

database or if an EAI solution requires a large number of proprietary database functions.

JDBC

Now an accepted and stable approach, JDBC from JavaSoft was the first standard Java-enabled database API. Functionally equivalent to ODBC, JDBC provides Java developers with a uniform interface to most popular relational databases from most Java-enabled development or application-processing environments.

The JDBC API defines a set of Java classes that allow an applet, servlet, JavaBean, or Java application to connect to a database. In most cases, such an applet is one that links back through the network to remote relational database servers, such as Sybase, Oracle, or Informix. The native Java JDBC classes, sold or given away by the database vendors, exist with the custom application classes and provide a "pure Java" and portable mechanism for database access. These allow you to link to any database from any platform that supports Java. At least, that's the idea. JDBC also provides uniformed database access for many EAI-enabled middleware products, such as message brokers, application servers, and even traditional MOM (e.g., message queuing software).

JDBC Java classes allow the developer to use native Java to issue common SQL statements to request information from a remote database, as well as process the result set. Because JDBC is another translation layer, like ODBC, Java applications that employ JDBC are database independent and can access any number of databases through a single JDBC interface. For example, you may gather data from an Oracle database running remotely, update a local Sybase database, and delete a record from a DB2 database running on a mainframe, all from the same Java applications using one common interface, JDBC.

Two major layers make up JDBC: the JDBC API and the JDBC Driver API (see Figure 11.6). The JDBC API provides application-to-JDBC Manager communications. Developers use this API to access database services using standard Java mechanisms. It is incumbent upon the database vendor to provide the JDBC driver interface. Vendors may also use a traditional ODBC connection through a JDBC to ODBC bridge.

As alluded to previously, the drivers are really a group of Java classes (including java.sql.Connection, java.sql.Statement, java.sql.PreparedStatement, java.sql.CallableStatement, and java.sql.ResultSet). When developers want to access a database with JDBC, they can use these classes from the native Java applications, which can link to the database, send a request, and process the returning result set.

The java.sql.DriverManager interface handles the loading and unloading of the proper DBMS driver. The java.sql.Connection interface exposes the database to the developer, representing the connection as a set of objects. The java.sql.Statement interface provides the developer with a container for execut-

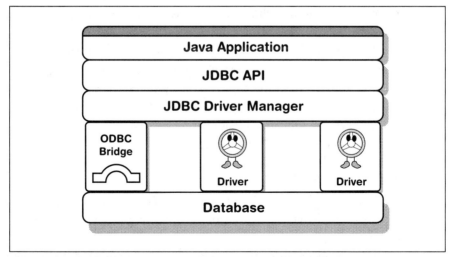

Figure 11.6 **JDBC features two layers: the JDBC API that provides application-to-JDBC Manager connections and the JDBC Driver API.**

ing SQL statements using a connection to the database. The java.sql.ResultSet interface exposes the requested data as native Java for processing by the Java applet or application.

The JDBC Manager, just as the ODBC Driver Manager, loads and unloads database drivers as required by the Java applet or application. JDBC supports a connection either to a single or multiple database servers. This means that an applet can connect to the inventory database in the warehouse as well as a public database on the Internet—at the same time.

The DBMS supports JDBC through the JDBC driver interface with each driver providing an implementation of the java.sql.Connection, java.sql.Statement, java.sql.PreparedStatement, java.sql.CallableStatement, and java.sql.ResultSet classes. What's more, the driver must implement the java.sql.Driver interface for use by the java.sql.DriverManager interface.

If a developer needs to access a database from Java, he or she obtains the java.sql.Connection object directly from the JDBC management layer and the java.sql.DriverManager. The Driver Managers leverage the URL string as an argument, allowing the JDBC management layer to locate and load the proper driver for the target database. The driver manager performs this "magic" by looking at each driver, finding the only one that can connect to the URL. Sometimes the URL may require a subprotocol that the driver supports (see the section "Types of JDBC Drivers," later in this chapter). Once all of this is complete, the driver connects to the DBMS and returns the proper java.sql connect object for accessing the database.

In order for the Driver Manager to locate the correct driver, each driver has to register with the Driver Manager using the DriverManager.registerDrive method, invoked from the applet. JDBC, using Java's rather limited security, is only able to use drivers coming from the local file system or from the same class loader. These are limitations that the tool vendors are overcoming through their own custom JDBC implementations.

Types of JDBC Drivers

JDBC drivers fit into one of four categories: JDBC-ODBC bridge driver, a native-API part-Java driver, a net-protocol all-Java driver, and a native-protocol all-Java driver.

JDBC works with ODBC by providing a JDBC-ODBC bridge to translate JDBC calls to functions understandable by the ODBC API. Although JDBC and ODBC are similar, they take slightly different approaches toward connecting to databases. Therefore, when using this architecture, developers must endure the overhead of a translation layer communicating with another translation layer.

The JDBC-ODBC bridge driver provides Java developers with JDBC access using most ODBC drivers. Not only is this the most flexible method, it is also the most homogeneous. Typically, the ODBC binaries must be loaded on each client machine using the driver. That being the case, it is likely that the Java application will be locked into the Windows platform where ODBC is more native. An easier option may be to access a shared set of ODBC binaries existing on an application server using JDBC. However, the architecture involved is much more complex and adds time to a development project.

The ODBC bridge is a requirement of JDBC if the standard is expected to support the vast majority of relational databases (and sometimes nonrelational databases) currently available. This is the result of failure on the part of some of the database vendors and gateways of larger systems to offer JDBC drivers. Eventually, middleware vendors will offer the JDBC drivers, thus eliminating the need to communicate through more than a single translation layer. However, the performance hit will not be as significant as might be anticipated.

A native-API part-Java driver is a "middle-of-the-road" approach. This driver converts JDBC calls into calls on the client API for any number of target databases (including Oracle, Sybase, Informix, and DB2). However, for this option to be successful, some binary code must be loaded on the clients. As a result, it has many of the same limitations as the JDBC-ODBC bridge driver but does not require access to ODBC.

The net-protocol all-Java driver translates JDBC calls into a DBMS-independent net protocol, which is again translated into a native DBMS protocol by a server. As a result, this driver can connect its pure Java clients to any number of databases with the database vendor specifying the native protocol employed. This is one of the most flexible of all JDBC solutions and is typically seen on intranets. For Internet access, this architecture must support additional security requirements. Database vendors are working to assure that they support net-protocol all-Java drivers.

Finally, a native-protocol all-Java driver directly converts JDBC calls into the network-native DBMS network protocol. This driver architecture provides direct calls from the client to the database server. This architecture is most popular for intranet access because it not only uses pure, portable Java but, by taking a direct route to the data, also provides the best performance.

Database vendors need to provide for this solution. Most have, or are working on, drivers for this architecture.

Other JDBC Features

The beauty of JDBC goes beyond its ability to link to and retrieve data from remote DBMSs to its robust array of database features. JDBC is able to access binary large objects (BLOBs)—handy for moving large amounts of binary information to and from the database. There is a data conversion mechanism as well, allowing JDBC to map the data back into Java by converting some SQL types into Java types. In addition, JDBC is able to support threading for pooling database connections, thus providing the source or target application (or integration server) with the ability to operate against the database asynchronously.

The ability to support transactions is a useful feature. Utilizing this JDBC native feature, developers can define a starting point and end point in a set of homogeneous or heterogeneous database operations. There are a few options here. Developers can set the JDBC transaction manager to "auto-commit," meaning that each database command is carried out as the applet invokes it. Developers may decide to turn "auto-commit" off, allowing them to define several database commands as individual transactions, something that will complete all operations successfully or put everything back the way it found it. This option allows complete recovery if any of the commands in the transaction fails. For example, an operation that records a sale in three separate databases (e.g., inventory, sales, and customer list) is a good candidate for a JDBC transaction because the failure of any of the updates would result in none of them completing. This maintains database integrity. Most popular DBMSs (such as Oracle) provide native transaction features. JDBC simply extends those features to the Java applets or application.

JDBC supports database cursors as well, using the ResultSet.getCursorName() method of JDBC. A database cursor allows the developer to return a cursor name that points to the result set that actually still resides, as a cursor, on the database server. This saves the network the overhead of having to send the entire result set down to the requesting application. Using this feature, the Java applets or applications can move through the data, bringing only the data required across the network. This feature also allows positioned updates and deletes to be invoked. However, the target DBMS must support this feature in order for JDBC cursors to work. Fortunately most do.

There are even more benefits, such as the use of SQL escape syntax. This allows developers to map escape syntax to DBMS-specific syntax. Stored procedures from JDBC can be invoked as well, simply by invoking them from JDBC and passing in the proper arguments. Finally, scalar functions are available, such as ABS(), DEGREES(), WEEK(), and DAYNAME().

Java, JDBC, and EAI

The use of Java as a development language and architecture for EAI is widespread. At this time, JDBC seems to be filling the enterprise space more than the Web space. That trend will most likely continue as the future brings a Web-enabled, existing corporate database. So, while JDBC will exist on the Web, its real value will be on the inside of the firewall.

In many respects, JDBC is bringing the traditional, complex multitiered world of Web-enablement back to the EAI problem domain. With the advent of server-side Java (e.g., EJB and application servers), JBDC does not have to be client-only anymore. Many tool vendors are employing both RMI (Remote Method Invocation) and JDBC to provide a flexible and complex architecture to solve a number of application problems, problems that include EAI. The trade-off, however, is complexity and proprietary approaches. When a standard is used in such a way as to make its architecture proprietary, then the value of that standard is diluted. The danger is that JDBC is heading toward that unhappy ending.

OLE DB

OLE DB, referred to by many as the big brother of ODBC, is a specification that defines a set of data access servers capable of facilitating links to any number of data sources. As a result, developers have the ability to manage different data sources as a single virtual database. OLE DB allows access to data using a standard COM interface.

OLE DB gives developers the means to access data that resides in relational databases, documents, spreadsheets, files, and electronic mail. Developers, through COM, can easily integrate object-oriented and multidimensional (real cube) databases with OLE DB. When using OLE DB, the database simply becomes a component known as a **data provider**. Any component that uses a native data format and exposes methods through an OLE DB interface is considered a data provider, including relational databases (using ODBC), an ISAM file, a text file, e-mail, a Microsoft Word file, or a data stream (see Figure 11.7).

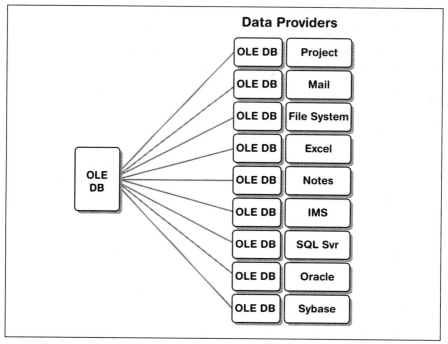

Figure 11.7   OLE DB

The idea here is to create an individual OLE DB component object to deploy additional features that are layered on top of the data providers. These individual OLE DB components are called **service providers**. Service providers are like query processors in that they allow applications to take advantage of providers that interconnect different combinations of data (homogeneous or heterogeneous). The data, regardless of model (object-oriented, relational, multidimensional, and so on), exists as single view. This solves the relational-bond limitations when using ODBC.

The other side of data providers are OLE DB data consumers, applications written to a single data provider or generic consumers that work with any number of data providers. For example, Microsoft's Excel, Word, and Project can become data consumers.

ODBC remains a piece in the puzzle but in a diminished role. It is simply a mechanism to communicate with relational databases from OLE DB. Microsoft has an updated ODBC Driver Manager with an OLE DB provider, making OLE DB compatible with any ODBC-accessible database.

So how is OLE DB programmed? OLE DB provides 55 new interfaces grouped into 7 object types: DataSource, DBSession, Command, Rowset, Index, ErrorObject, and Transaction. An object type is simply a set of methods (interfaces) that an object must expose. For example, developers will define the Transaction Objects using a group of methods that any data consumer can request from a transaction service.

It is likely that few EAI developers will have to deal with the OLE DB interface directly. Microsoft is perfecting a new set of products and development environments that allow developers to build applications with OLE DB hidden behind many easy-to-use layers. This OLE DB interface is analogous to the relationship with ODBC and development tools.

Going Native

In addition to ODBC, JDBC, OLE DB, and other database translation interfaces, there are many other native database-oriented middleware products. These are APIs provided by a database vendor or a third party with access to a particular database. In the past, these were often older C and C++ libraries. Now, most EAI development tools ship native database-oriented middleware with their products.

The advantage of using native database-oriented middleware rather than ODBC, JDBC, or OLE DB is the ability to provide high-performance database access, along with the ability to access features native to a specific database. However, using native database-oriented middleware binds the user to that middleware vendor, because the EAI application uses calls specific to that particular database. That's the tradeoff.

Database Gateways

Database gateways (also known as **SQL gateways**) are APIs that use a single interface to provide access to most databases residing on many different types of platforms (see Figure 11.8). They are like virtual database middleware products, providing developers with access to any number of databases, residing in environments typically not easily accessible, such as a mainframe. For example, using an ODBC interface and a database gateway, it is possible to access data residing in a DB2 on a mainframe, Oracle running on a minicomputer, and Sybase running on a UNIX server. The developer simply makes an API call, and the database gateway does all the work.

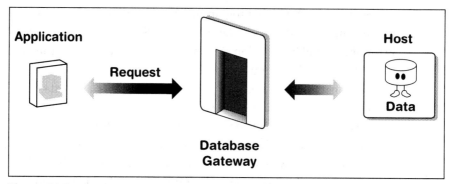

Figure 11.8   Database gateways

Database gateways translate the SQL calls into a standard format known as the **Format and Protocol (FAP)**, the common connection between the client and the server. It is also the common link between very different databases and platforms. The gateway can translate the API call directly into FAP, moving the request to the target database and translating the request so that the target database and platform can react.

A number of gateways are currently on the market such as Information Builders' Enterprise Data Access/SQL (EDA/SQL), in addition to standards such as IBM's Distributed Relational Data Access (DRDA), and ISO/SAG's Remote Data Access (RDA).

EDA/SQL

EDA/SQL is a wonderful, general-purpose database gateway for several reasons. It works with most database servers and platforms, bridging many enterprises where dozens of servers might be running on dozens of different platforms needing to be accessed from a single application—perfect for EAI. It uses ODBC as the interface rather than a proprietary API.

EDA/SQL can access more than 50 relational and nonrelational database servers and can access all these databases using ODBC. There are several EDA/SQL components including the API/SQL, EDA/Extenders, EDA/Link, EDA/Server, and EDA/Data Drivers. API/SQL provides the call-level interface (ODBC), allowing the developer to access the EDA/SQL resources. EDA/Extenders are really redirectors of SQL calls, which route the request across the network. EDA/Link provides the network connections by supporting more than 12 communication protocols, and EDA/Server resides on the target database, processing the requests on behalf of the requesting application or integration server. Finally, the EDA/Data Drivers, like ODBC drivers, provide access to more than 50 different target databases.

RDA

RDA is not a product. It is a standard for developers to access data. RDA uses OSI and supports dynamic SQL. RDA also allows the client to be connected to more than one database server at the same time. However, it does not support typical transaction-related services, and due to lack of vendor support and its inability to snap into popular EAI development environments, it's no longer relevant for EAI.

DRDA

DRDA is an IBM database connectivity standard that has the support of many database heavyweights such as Sybase, Oracle, IBI, and Informix. Like other database gateways, DRDA attempts to provide easy database connectivity between any number of databases operating in multiplatform environments.

DRDA defines database transactions as remote requests, remote units of work, distributed units of work, and distributed requests. A **remote request** means that one SQL request is sent to one database. A **remote unit of work** means that many SQL commands are sent to one database. A **distributed unit of work** means that many SQL commands are sent to many databases. However, each command is sent to one database. Finally, a **distributed request** means that many SQL commands are sent to many databases, and each command can execute on several databases.

While DRDA is a well-defined standard, the fact that DRDA requires that databases comply with standard SQL syntax diminishes the benefit of DRDA to organizations where many different systems run many different databases at different stages of maturity.

Ready for Prime Time

The strongest point in support of database-oriented middleware is that the technology is very mature, well tested, and ready for most EAI applications. In other words, database access should not be a major concern for most EAI projects.

Problems that remain to be solved for database-oriented middleware include the ability to make it more scalable. As things stand now, a TP monitor or application server will have to be employed to multiplex the database connections on behalf of the application or EAI solution. **Multiplexing** (or **connection pooling**), the ability to remove the one-connection-per-request restriction from database-oriented middleware, is becoming part of many database-oriented middleware layers, including JDBC and ODBC.

Moreover, as interest is renewed in nonrelational database models, such as multidimensional, hierarchical, and object-oriented, middleware is learning how to emulate and translate data from model to model. Today it is possible to view a relational database using the object-oriented model, and a hierarchical database as a relational database. These emulation and translation services make EAI a much easier proposition because they make it possible to map very heterogeneous environments to a common database model, and thus provide an easier starting point for integration (See discussion of federated database middleware in Chapter 20.) Certainly this adds the most value to data-level EAI.

This world won't change much, even as EAI grows in popularity, due to the simple fact that solutions to most of these problems exist. Isn't it nice to come upon an area of technology where few problems are left to solve?

CHAPTER TWELVE

Java Middleware and EAI

"f u cn rd ths, u cn gt a gd jb n cmptr prgmmng."
  —Anonymous

Java, a seemingly revolutionary method for building Web-born applications, is now maturing enough to be of benefit to the enterprise and to EAI. Today's Java is pumping up an already growing middleware marketplace. While Java was once "joined at the hip" to the browser, it has become the mechanism of choice for application servers, component-based development, and now EAI.

Recognizing that applets, servlets, and beans were of little use standing alone, JavaSoft has been promoting middleware standards for Java since before the release of the 1.0 JDK (Java Development Kit). JavaSoft can now claim many successful standards (including JDBC, JMS, RMI, and the Java IDL for CORBA—all described in this chapter, with the exception of JDBC, which is described in Chapter 11). These standards are all applicable to EAI in that they provide a Java-enabled infrastructure.

We should note that JavaSoft does not create products. It becomes partners with vendors who wrap *their* products in JavaSoft standards. Vendors in partnership with JavaSoft write their products to JavaSoft specifications, thus assuring that their products will grow as Java grows. Consequently, our discussion in this chapter is centered on specifications and the products that use those specifications.

We spoke earlier of the "re-revolution" in application servers—another form of middleware. Most servers now exploit the hype, the language, and the platform that Java offers. Just as Java has ignited the world of middleware, it will ignite EAI—with many EAI solutions leveraging Java as the middleware platform. This is not mere "crystal ball predicting." The thousands of Java developers at work today guarantee this eventuality.

Categories of Java Middleware Standards

The idea of Java-based middleware should sound complex for one simple reason—it *is* complex. In order to create order of Java's hype-driven standards and products, it is useful to establish categories of Java middleware. We identify the following six major categories:

- Database-oriented
- Interprocess
- Message-oriented
- Application-hosting
- Transaction-processing
- Distributed object technology

Database-Oriented

Database-oriented, Java-enabled middleware is the oldest and best supported of these categories. It follows that, in order for Java to be successful, it would have to access most relational databases. The JDBC specifications have become the ODBC for the world of Java and are now found in most tools and application servers that support Java. You'll find detailed information about JDBC in Chapter 11.

Interprocess

In addition to connecting to databases, JavaSoft provides Remote Method Invocation (RMI). RMI is a simple synchronous mechanism that allows applets to communicate with other applets, invoking each other's methods, as needed. For instance, you can download an applet that's able to connect to an Enterprise JavaBean running on a remote Web server, and invoke a method that updates a database with customer information. This communication can take place in the same machine or over a network. A useful perspective on this process is as "a poor man's distributed object." RMI benefits EAI projects by sharing information with other applets and servlets scattered throughout an enterprise.

With RMI as an intramachine and intermachine IPC (Inter-Process Communication) mechanism for Java applets and applications, there are those who claim that RMI and CORBA provide the same value. This view is strengthened by JavaSoft's and OMG's exploration of the integration of RMI standards with CORBA standards. While the ultimate corporate strategy here might be to "gang up" on the Microsoft COM middleware revolution while adding value to each set of standards, the benefit to an EAI solution is less certain, depending on the specific requirements of the particular EAI project. In other words, don't buy into the message being spouted by that guy on the soapbox—at least, not yet.

There are many things to consider when comparing RMI to CORBA. First, RMI-enabled applets and applications can communicate only with other RMI-enabled objects. As a result, forget about invoking methods written in other languages, such as C++. In addition, RMI fails to provide a language-neutral messaging service. Unlike Java, RMI does not provide support for a wire protocol for security. Neither does it support the notion of transactions. RMI is unable to provide support for self-describing objects or dynamic invocations.

As always, before rushing forward based on exaggerated claims, the EAI architect and developer must "take a deep breath" and look at the specific project at hand. If the EAI project is "Java and nothing but Java" and there is no requirement to link external resources, or wire-level security—in short, if the EAI project skirts wide of the shortcomings of RMI—then RMI is fine. However, the architect and developer should remember that the decision to use RMI means conceding features that may be required as the application matures.

The bottom line here is that RMI technology is lightweight and bound to Java, while CORBA is robust and language neutral. RMI lacks the basic features of IIOP, and Java is not providing features that are found in most ORBs.

Message-Oriented

Some traditional, message-oriented middleware products like IBM's MQSeries support Java. However, the real story in this context is a new standard from JavaSoft called JMS (Java Message Service). JMS is attracting a critical mass of messaging vendors seeking to bind their products tightly with Java. Some of the larger vendors include BEA, IBM, SAGA Software, Active Software, and Oracle.

JMS adds a common API and provider framework that enables the Java developer to dispatch and receive messages with other Java-enabled applications or applets existing anywhere on the network (see Figure 12.1). JMS defines a common set of messaging concepts and programming strategies. JMS provides a good mix of the messaging features common to most messaging products— important but hardly revolutionary. The difficulty is to support these concepts and strategies from JMS-compliant vendor to JMS-compliant vendor. If successful, the resulting products will not only share common characteristics, but will have the ability to share messages as well—something that has yet to be perfected with more traditional, message-oriented middleware products.

JMS is comprised of three major entities: the JMS provider, JMS messages, and JMS domains. The **provider** implements JMS for a particular product (for example, a Java applet, servlet, bean, or application supporting JMS). The JMS **messages** are a set of messaging interfaces that define a common mechanism and format for moving information from providers. JMS messages consist of several parts, including the header, properties, and body (see Figure 12.2). The **header** supports the same set of header fields as are supported in traditional messaging products. Both the JMS client and provider use the header to identify and route messages. The JMS message **properties** allow developers to add additional information to the standard header, information such as application-specific properties, standard properties, and provider-specific properties. The **body** contains the data that is being transported.

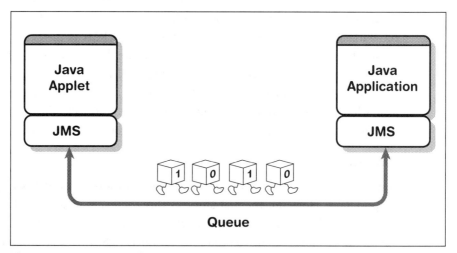

Figure 12.1   JMS provides message transport services for Java.

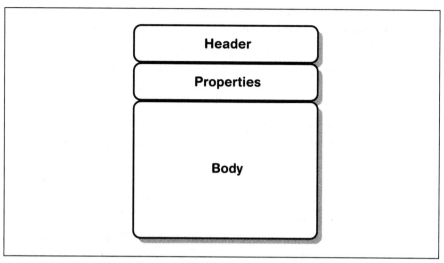

Figure 12.2   JMS message structure

Messaging Models

JMS **domains** provide for the classification of messaging paradigms, including point-to-point and publish-and-subscribe. **Point-to-point** messaging generally relies upon queues to transport messages. **Publish-and-subscribe**, as you may remember from an earlier chapter, addresses messages to some node in a content hierarchy. As we've noted earlier, pub/sub is particularly useful to EAI projects because there it does not require an understanding about the resource that is being subscribed to. JMS provides client interfaces created for each type of domain.

The question remains for the architect and developer: Which model to use, and when? The JMS point-to-point defines how a client works with queues. For example, it defines how a JMS-enabled application finds queues, sends a message to them, and/or receives messages from them. The JMS client is able to send a message to a specific queue. The receiving applet or application need not be engaged in order for the message to be placed in the queue. The receiver picks up the message from the queue when it has time. In other words, this is an asynchronous messaging model. It is one best applied when applications need to communicate with one another but, in doing so, do not need to delay the target or source application from processing tasks.

As with traditional queues, JMS queues may contain a mixture of messages. A shortcoming of JMS is that it does not define facilities to administer queues.

However, this is not as significant as it might first appear because JMS implementations leverage static, not dynamic, queues.

There are several Java concepts to keep in mind when working with JMS queues. Among them are: the Queue object, the TemporaryQueue, Queue-Connection Factory, QueueConnection, QueueReceiver, QueueSender, and a QueueSession. Together, these represent a set of classes that a developer can leverage within a JMS-enabled application.

The **Queue object**, the heart of this beast, encapsulates a provider-specific queue name. This object identifies a queue to a JMS method from the client. A **QueueConnection** is an active connection to a JMS point-to-point provider. The JMS client leverages the QueueConnection to create instances of **QueueSessions**, which produce and consume messages.

The **TemporaryQueue** is created for the duration of the QueueConnection. True to its name, it is a system-defined queue, only available to the Queue-Connection object that created it as a temporary storage location. The **Queue-ConnectionFactory** creates an instance of a QueueConnection object within a JMS provider. The client uses a **QueueReceiver** to receive messages that exist in a queue. A **QueueSender**, in contrast, places messages in a queue.

If the point-to-point model doesn't meet the needs of the project, the JMS pub/sub model might. The JMS pub/sub model describes how JMS clients publish messages and subscribe to them from a well-defined node by using a content-based hierarchy structure. This model, as we have noted in our earlier discussion of middleware models, is superior to simple, point-to-point models and is most practical when considering JMS for use with traditional EAI projects. (Although either model can be used with EAI implementations.)

JMS refers to these "nodes" as "topics." A **topic** is, in fact, a small message broker that gathers and distributes messages from other entities (see Figure 12.3). JMS uses topics as quasi-intermediaries. They create messages that are separated logically from subscribers. Topics are adaptive. They can adjust as subscribers and publishers appear and disappear.

By drilling down to the next "topic level," it becomes apparent that a topic is really nothing more than a Java object that encapsulates a provider-specific topic name. Most pub/sub vendors group topics into hierarchies, allowing subscribers to subscribe to any part of the hierarchy. JMS does not place such restrictions on its users. Instead, it organizes topics and the granularity of subscriptions in a completely open manner. There are no set policies for how developers should do this. This "openness" is a step in the right direction because strict pub/sub policies are, by definition, limiting.

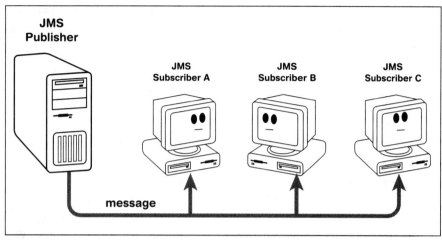

Figure 12.3   JMS is able to gather and distribute messages throughout an enterprise.

JMS and Application Development

Because JMS is just another Java-enabled API, application development comes down to being a simple matter of linking to and leveraging the proper JMS objects within an application. A JMS application can be created and deployed as a single unit, or JMS clients can be added to an existing JMS-enabled application or applet. Generally, JMS plays an important role in creating distributed Java applications or linking non-JMS messages into the world of Java. For example, IBM is in the process of insuring that its MQSeries is able to exchange messages with JMS. Other MOM vendors will soon follow.

A typical JMS client application must go through a standard procedure to get up and running. This procedure includes using the Java Naming and Directory Information (JNDI) to find a ConnectionFactory object and then finding one or more destination objects. To create a number of instances of a JMS session, the ConnectionFactory object is used to create an instance of a JMS connection and the Connections method. Finally, the JMS client must use the Session and the Destinations to create the MessageProducers and Message-Consumers required for the application. From this point, the connection to the queue or the pub/sub engine is set, and the application may use JMS as a mechanism to transport data in and out of an application.

There remain a number of key issues that JMS must address. These include load-balancing, fault-tolerance, and error notification. It is likely that JMS-compliant software vendors will build such features into their products. It would be nice if they all chose to use a consistent paradigm and mechanism but don't count on it. As we mentioned above, there is no notion of administration built into JMS's specifications. IBM discovered that a weak administration hurt MQSeries initially, and so they responded by fixing the problem. At this point, there is no such fix in sight for JMS. In addition, security seems to be an afterthought to JMS. Unfortunately, this seems typical in the world of middleware.

Beyond JMS, Java integration with the big MOM products, such as MQSeries, is having a significant impact. With over 65 percent of the point-to-point, message-oriented middleware marketplace, MQSeries is the dominating product. Providing Java links will only add value to that domination. IBM is "Java-tizing" just about everything these days. Clearly, Java is going to be the least common denominator between CICS, Component Broker, and MQSeries. This represents the largest enterprise growth area for Java, with JMS supporting smaller systems at first.

Application-Hosting

Calling application servers "middleware" is a bit misleading. However, because that is the way they are generally classified, we do the same here. As we discussed in Chapter 7, an application server is any product that provides a host for application logic and that processes all (or part) of an application. For example, an interface logic can be defined by using client-side development tools, with all business logic processes server-side using a remote application server. The benefit to this scenario is that both application logic and access to resources can be shared through a centralized entity.

The new generation of Java-enabled application server vendors (WebLogic, iPlanet, and Inprise) provide a hosting environment for server-side Java. These environments do a number of things, including accessing remote resources such as database servers, mainframes, ERP applications, and even other Java applications (see Figure 12.4).

Application servers control access to these environments by using "units-of-work," or transactions. By using a transactional paradigm, they are able to recover from system- and resource-level problems and to scale to high user and processing loads. To accomplish this, they use tracks, such as multiplexing database requests. However, every product implements such features in unique ways and so should be explored carefully before being implemented.

These environments include integrated development environments (IDEs). IDEs assist the developer in creating the logic for the application server, using an

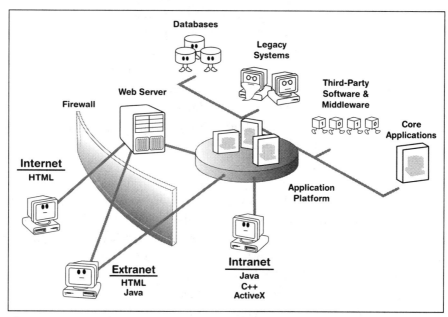

Figure 12.4   Typical Java-enabled application server architecture

easy-on-the-eyes graphical user interface. They may also provide client-side tools or client-side development features through a partner.

How then do these application servers differ from Java-enabled TP monitors? From an architectural or features point of view the answer is, "not much." However, TP monitors generally do Java only as an afterthought at the interface level. Java-enabled application servers are built from the ground up to support transactional, server-side Java.

TP monitors, such as BEA's Tuxedo and IBM's CICS, are best known for providing transaction-processing capabilities. With several traditional TP players entering the market using Java as a programming mechanism, as well as a way to draw more attention to themselves, these well-known TP monitors have had to adjust. They say you can't teach an old dog new tricks. Well, these old dogs are definitely learning new tricks. Both Tuxedo and CICS are providing Java links to their TP monitor environments. This creates a situation in which it is possible to build applications using a Java client and invoke transactions housed within a TP monitor environment. These transactions may be built in any of the number of languages that the TP monitor supports.

The benefits of this capability should be clear. The two largest TP monitor vendors are moving in this direction, adding Java language capabilities within their environments. The result of this development will be that "traditional" programming languages such as C or COBOL will no longer have to be used to create transactions. It will be possible to simply use Java.

What we are seeing is a blurring of the once-clear line between TP monitors and the new application servers. These new products are moving aggressively to make sure that they don't lose their market share to the less-mature, Java-enabled application server. While these products have yet to provide the scalability and the fail-safe environments traditional TP monitors provide, they are generally much easier to build applications around.

Distributed Objects

Although there has been a great deal of talk about linking Java, CORBA, and other distributed object technologies, the number of software development projects using this type of technology are few and far between. In other words, the talk has been, thus far, mostly talk. However, as many application servers look to merge with distributed objects, the talk is growing more serious.

CORBA extends the distributed features of Java using CORBA infrastructure. Even with the integration of RMI, Java applets were not designed to communicate across application address spaces. RMI provides an easy-to-use approach to distributed computing but does not support the advanced architectural features of CORBA-compliant ORBs.

CORBA allows Java applets to communicate with other objects written in different languages across different address spaces by using the common pipe of IIOP (Internet Inter-ORB Protocol, see Figure 12.5). This allows developers to create truly distributed applications using any number of languages. CORBA provides a rich set of distributed object services that are built on top of the Java language. For example, the developer may create the client-side ORBs using Java, and the business logic at the middle-tier using C++.

Java lends little to the world of distributed computing save for a very nice, object-oriented programming language, and a very nice binary application distribution mechanism. Still, Java is a good match for CORBA. Java's infrastructure seems to "pick up" where CORBA's "leaves off." All the while, it allows CORBA to do what CORBA does, which is provide a distributed object infrastructure that allows applications to extend their reach across networks, component boundaries, operating systems, and programming languages.

The integration of Java and CORBA lets developers do such things as move intelligent behavior from one ORB to another using the common infrastructure and interfaces of CORBA. As a result, both clients and servers are able to dynam-

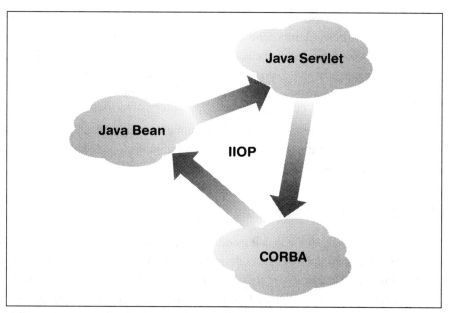

Figure 12.5   Using IIOP to allow Java applets, servlets, beans, and applications to communicate

ically gain behavior as required for the application development effort. CORBA also provides a language-independent partitioning technology, as well as the technology to allow applications to run on a client or server without having to recompile (albeit, adaptations must be made for each platform).

A Java ORB is an ORB that supports a Java language mapping of the IDL. In most cases, Java ORBs are implemented in Java itself. The language mapping, or language binding, allows CORBA-compliant ORBs to be implemented using Java. Unfortunately, not all Java ORBs available today support the complete CORBA functionality.

In the simplest form of the Java-enabled CORBA ORB architecture, the client and the server are both implemented in Java. Using this architecture, the Java virtual machines on each platform allow each applet or application to execute. The applet or application shares a common ORB, which provides interprocess communication services. The client communicates with the ORB in order to transmit a request for an operation invocation to the server. The server, in turn, sends the results of the ORBs back to the client.

Iona and Inprise are the two dominant players in the Java/CORBA space. Inprise sells Visibroker for Java, with native implementation of the IIOP.

Visibroker supports the OMG's IDL-to-C++ mapping and the OMG's IDL-to-Java mapping, maintaining full compliance with the latest from the OMG, the CORBA 3.0 standard. Inprise's strategy is to combine Visibroker with the suite of application development tools that they offer, including JBuilder. Iona offers OrbixWeb, a Java-enabled CORBA ORB that provides many of the same features as Visibroker, including the ability to create CORBA ORBs using Java. In spite of the fact that Inprise has more experience with Java and CORBA and seems to have a tighter integration with a solid set of tools, Iona seems to be cornering the CORBA ORB market.

The Future of Java and Middleware

The future of Java-enabled middleware is as difficult to read as tea leaves in the wind. Depending on who is doing the "reading," the future can look very different. If database vendors are doing the reading, then Java will become an integral part of most core database technology, providing a common mechanism to build and deploy applications, as well as program the database itself. If ORB guys are doing the reading, they'll say that Java is a good language and platform to further promote the ORB religion. They'll say that Java brings some much-needed hype to a dying market. The messaging guy will say that Java will become the preferred access method for most popular MOM products.

Basically, everyone is looking to "Java-tize" his or her middleware of choice, and the product vendors are only too happy to oblige.

The real advantage of Java is more than the sum of these parts. Java has finally brought about a general consensus on language and platform. Middleware is only adding power to that reality. With the help of such heavy hitters as IBM, Java is morphing into a full-blown, enterprise class, application development and processing environment. Middleware support is simply a natural progression from that reality.

So, the future? Count on message-brokers written entirely in Java—transactional component environments and even Java-enabled intelligent agent technology. This is the next generation of Java-enabled middleware, representing another set of explosive growth opportunities that will add significant value to the EAI space.

CHAPTER THIRTEEN

Implementing and Integrating Packaged Applications— The General Idea

"If you can't beat your computer at chess, try kick-boxing."
—Anonymous

Traditional packaged applications are too often virtual prisons, locking away the information and business processes. The difficulty in accessing this information from within these popular applications is the primary reason for the increased interest in EAI. Correctly applied, EAI frees this information, making it available to other systems or end users who may need it.

Although packaged application vendors have begun to see the value in opening up their architectures and technologies by allowing external applications and middleware to access their data and methods, they continue to do so using proprietary approaches. As a result, EAI architects and developers must understand the ins and outs of the packaged applications they are attempting to integrate. SAP, PeopleSoft, Baan, and Oracle represent only the tip of the iceberg. Hundreds of packaged applications are available, some easy to integrate, most difficult.

We'll look closely at packaged applications in the next several chapters. In this chapter, we will explore the basic integration, installation, and configuration issues of packaged applications. Although we will devote the next chapters to examining a number of packaged applications, it will be necessary for you to seek detailed information about a particular packaged application by contacting the application vendor or through another publication. Our concern here is with basic integration issues. (More general information about packaged application interfaces and application interface–level EAI can be found in Chapter 3.)

Why Packaged Applications?

For the past several years, there has been a "refocusing" from custom applications to packaged applications. For many developers this represents a significant change in paradigm as well as process. What it ultimately represents is a tradeoff in the types of problems both application architects and developers are solving. A tradeoff, unfortunately, of technology and opportunity.

The reasons for the rise in packaged applications are not difficult to discern. First, organizations share many of the same business processes and services. Such processes as accounts receivable and accounts payable don't vary much from company to company, nor do purchase order systems or inventory control. Second, it is finally possible to reuse common services through common applications. Historically, the software development industry has done a poor job of sharing objects, functions, and components. Finally, there is a reduction in the time-to-delivery and the number of quality problems when dealing with packages.

It is simply impossible to deliver a custom application in the time it takes to install and configure a package. Still, most packaged applications require some customization. It is here, in this need for customization, that most companies confront the real tradeoff.

Time-to-delivery remains the greatest advantage to packaged applications. Fortune 500 organizations no longer have to wait through lengthy development cycles to realize the benefits of an enterprise application such as an inventory control system, a sales order system, a customer care application, or a general ledger application. While many companies compete in the packaged application market, SAP, PeopleSoft, Oracle, and Baan lead the industry (see Figure 13.1).

In what now seems like ancient history, packaged applications meant older systems and green-screened terminals. Today most packaged applications are based on state-of-the-art client/server or Internet/intranet application architectures. Modern packaged applications run alongside standard office automation applications, becoming as familiar and at least as easy to use.

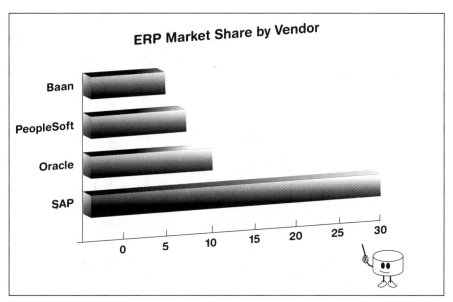

Figure 13.1   Revenue of packaged application vendors

This revolution in using prebuilt applications has given rise to multibillion dollar consulting opportunities, driven largely by the bigger accounting firms. The subsequent demand has also created a shortage of qualified applicants who are skilled in the ways of SAP, Baan, and PeopleSoft. This boom industry, still in its infancy, has led to a new way of looking at application architecture. Once upon a time, everything was built from scratch. Now organizations are discovering that the best value is to "purchase and integrate best-of-breed." Although this seems like a straightforward process, it is not. Failed package installation projects continue to outnumber the successes.

In short, while attractive, "purchase and integrate" is still not a perfect solution. Packages have limitations as well as opportunities. An organization must recognize that "what you see is what you get" when it comes to packages. Either the organization takes what the package has to offer, or it spends a great deal of money using proprietary languages and tools to customize it. More to the point, the architecture of the package must be accepted, regardless of whether or not it fits into the enterprise. As the ERP (Enterprise Resource Planning) package vendors (such as SAP, Baan, and PeopleSoft) move into most of the Fortune 1000 information infrastructures, the real obstacles are becoming clear, as are the opportunities.

The ability to overcome the obstacles and seize the many opportunities can be summed up in a single word: integration. While ERP and other applications seem to work well as an island of automation unto themselves, they lose value quickly when companies attempt to link services and data with external systems. Thus, it's difficult to share resources between ERP application brands (SAP, Baan, PeopleSoft), as well as ERP packages and custom applications. It is here, in the nexus that is integration that EAI adds a tremendous amount of value.

Installing Packaged Applications

A common problem when installing and integrating packaged applications is preparation. There is the incorrect notion out there that SAP and Baan will install as easily as Word. No way. The cruel fact is that integrating enterprise-class packaged software installations with existing infrastructure is, in many ways, more complex than building a customized application.

Preparing for a package installation and integration project demands a detailed understanding of the user requirements and business issues. It requires the answers to many questions. For example, how many end users will use the system on a daily basis? What are the hardware and software requirements for the package? What about sharing information and processes with other external systems? How long will it take for users to learn the new software? Each of these questions opens a minefield of other questions and problems. The difficulty and complexity of the task make it a good idea to document these requirements, feeding them back to the user to assure there is no miscommunication.

It is a simple fact of life that it will take a good deal of time to get a set of larger UNIX servers up and running and even more time to define the points of integration with other systems. A successful transition depends on a great deal of coordination. If this coordinated effort is not begun early in the installation and integration process, then the project is at risk before it has a chance to get off the ground.

Business Drivers

The lack of a clear vision regarding the business drivers is another potential project killer. Bottom line—the package must somehow solve some problem and thus make money for the company. If it doesn't, the company should nix the installation before it begins. For example, if the sales department is not able to keep up with customer demand, then there is a genuine business problem. In this case, the value of the business driver is having a faster system in place to keep up with customer demand. As a result, the company will make more money. Using this as the "value proposition," it becomes straightforward to put the metrics in place to assure that the system lives up to expectations after going live. If there is no clear set of business drivers, nor a value proposition, then the organization may want to consider other solutions or doing without a system altogether.

Architectures Drive Success

Neglecting the application architecture is a common problem during installation. Too often, the organization moves forward on the assumption that a packaged application installation effort does not require any formal application architecture. While it's true that installing and integrating a packaged application presents different architectural problems than a custom application, there are still technical problems to solve. A common difficulty arises because most organizations don't accept the package as bundled. Instead, they make modifications to the business service and interface layers of the packaged application. Such modifications are often tantamount to a reengineering and application development activity. Requirements must be gathered, interfaces designed, and business processes redefined. Also, a plan must be formulated to use the proprietary technology of these functions. Most vendors of packaged applications understand the requirements of application architects. As a result, they often bundle design and development tools. For example, SAP sells the ABAP Workbench, a repository-driven development platform for client/server applications not unlike (at least in concept) other client/server development packages on the market today.

Packaged application vendors are also providing CASE-like tools to assist their customers in reengineering and redesign efforts. R/3 Business Engineer, for example, provides such services. It provides business process configuration services for R/3 installations. R/3 Business Engineer provides a mechanism for business process improvement and is the core enabling tool for SAP's R/3 installation and configuration methods called AcceleratedSAP. The concept driving this application is to make all configuration decisions using the modeling tool with the model tied to the corresponding customizing tasks. The tool lets the R/3 application architecture see how changes in the business process will affect the system before the changes are actually implemented.

PeopleSoft provides a similar tool called the Business Process Designer. Using this tool, PeopleSoft application architects can define business processes by creating visual models that reveal activities, steps, and workflow routings. These models provide an overview of the process and allow application architects to navigate to the application components they need during a PeopleSoft installation and integration project.

Testing What Has Already Been Tested

Custom applications invariably underwent rigorous testing when they were installed. Unfortunately, many organizations fail to put packaged applications through the same process. This is a mistake. A rigorous testing process assures that the newly installed system is meeting performance, interface, and business expectations. This is especially important in an EAI problem domain where the fundamental issue is not so much that the system performs well by itself, but that it performs well when sharing information with any number of external systems.

There really are no shortcuts when it comes to testing, other than to create a test bed for the package and run it through its paces. There are three levels of package testing: performance, process, and interface. **Performance testing** is a direct examination of the throughput of the packaged application as well as the entire system it is connected to (see Figure 13.2). For example, how long will it take an order to appear on the warehouse PC after it has been entered in sales? How long does it take the package to locate a customer in the database? What about sharing information with external systems? It is critical to uncover performance problems as early as possible because the only real fixes are rearchitecturing the application and ordering new hardware and software. Any shortcomings with performance after installation could delay a project for months and cost the faith of clients and/or users.

Process testing is a quick look at the accuracy of the system, as well as its ability to function at the level required by the business. For example, does 2+2=5? Or

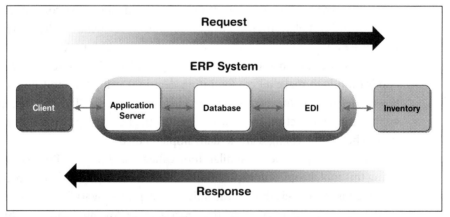

Figure 13.2   Performance testing is a direct examination of the throughput of a packaged application, as well as the entire system it is connected to.

Testing Tools for SAP

Most packaged application vendors understand the need for testing. They provide either their own testing tools or interfaces to external tools. For example, SAP provides the basis: Automated Testing Tool interface (BC-ATT), a combination of SAP graphical user interface presentation server software and the Desktop Developer Kit interface. BC-ATT provides third-party testing tool vendors with the ability to execute under Windows 95 or Windows NT on SAP's Presentation Server PC, which communicates with the R/3 application server.

---

does the inventory report reflect the data feed into the system? Within an EAI problem domain, it is also necessary to validate that the information remains correct as it moves from system to system. This is most important when testing systems that have undergone significant customization and therefore have new processes that have not been tested by the package vendor.

Typically, test scenarios come from a test plan. Simply put, the test plan includes the tests to be run on the new system, the input, and the expected results. It is impossible to overstate the importance of this sort of testing considering that bugs in processes (e.g., processing all sales at a discount) could cost as much as a million dollars in lost revenue.

Interface testing provides a quick look at how well the interface works with the human beings that have to use it. Too often, such testing is minimized or overlooked completely. Ultimately, if the end user has trouble with the interface, there will be problems with the system. Therefore, it is wise to work directly with the end users during the entire installation process, gathering requirements and assuring the user that the requirements are met in the final product. This is especially important for those users, such as telephone sales operators, where a bad interface can translate into slow sales order response on the phone and thus lost sales.

Implementing Specific Packages

Truth be told, each application suite has its own architecture, customization features, installation procedures, and level of complexity. As a result, it is impossible to approach the installation of all packages in the same manner. This reality has led to specialization in the consulting world. SAP R/3 is the most popular package among ERP applications and thus receives the most coverage in this book.

SAP uses a thin-client, three-tier architecture that is essentially proprietary. The real processing occurs at the middle tier, or the application server (see Figure 13.3). R/3 leverages a transaction model, using a proprietary transaction processor. The R/3 clients are basically data collectors for the middle-tier transaction processor. The client defines its behavior by invoking transaction services on the middle tier. SAP R/3 uses off-the-shelf databases such as Oracle and Sybase for the database layer.

SAP's ABAP Development Workbench includes a repository, editor, and dictionary, as well as tools for tuning, testing, and debugging R/3 applications. This is where ABAP developers will customize the SAP software to meet the exact requirements of the enterprise. SAP layered this tool deep into the R/3 middleware layer. As a result, it is able to communicate with the application server as well as with the R/3 clients.

In addition to providing tools and technology for a SAP installation, as mentioned previously, SAP offers an implementation methodology called AcceleratedSAP. AcceleratedSAP is divided into several phases, including Project Preparation, Business Blueprint, Simulation, Validation, Final Preparation, and Go Live & Support. (Although AcceleratedSAP is being examined in some detail here, other packaged applications have their own installation and integration methodologies/approaches that must be considered.)

If a particular developer bristles at a packaged methodology approach to integrating a SAP system, there is no need to worry. Each consulting organization has its own approach or methodology that are basically checklists to assure the client organization that all bases are covered with the installation phases. They

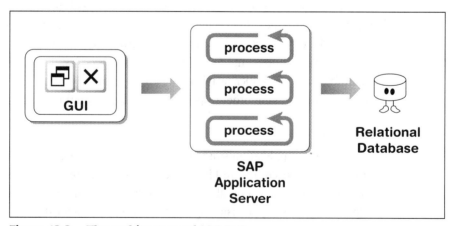

Figure 13.3   The architecture of SAP R/3

also assure the consulting organizations a rather hefty fee when the integration and installation project is complete. Many times they are worth the cost. These canned methodologies reduce most of the project risk.

PeopleSoft provides PeopleTools. Like SAP's ABAP, PeopleTools provides a set of methodologies and tools for installing and customizing its ERP application. PeopleTools is a rapid application development environment, which provides both application architects and developers with the ability to tailor PeopleSoft applications to the business requirements of the enterprise. Features of PeopleTools include a workflow designer, development subsystem, administration tools, reporting tools, and integration tools that link other products to PeopleSoft.

Scopus is another example of a packaged application. Scopus is a suite of customer care applications. Its installations are customized using ScopusWorks, a complete set of integrated configuration, customization, and administration tools usable across all Scopus customer care applications. ScopusWorks provides a graphical interface to Scopus' metaobject architecture to design, layout, and configure the windows and forms of the Scopus application. In addition to supporting templates for frequently used fields and objects, these tools support the ability to integrate ActiveX controls into traditional Windows applications. Finally ScopusWorks streamlines business rule development and redevelopment and customizes workflow between forms and objects found in Scopus applications.

Where SAP has ABAP, PeopleSoft has PeopleTools, and Scopus has Scopus-Works, Baan has Dynamic Enterprise Modeling (DEM). DEM is a framework to adapt an organization's software to dynamic organizational structures, business practices, and operational procedures. The DEM framework is a layer on traditional ERP, allowing a developer or application architect to match specific business processes with the new layer.

Packaged Application Tools

While many "soft issues" are encountered when installing, deploying, integrating, and managing an application, a tremendous amount of technology is available for leveraging as well. Tools can be divided into service management, system administration, and production control.

Service management tools support the highest levels of application management building on the strength of the production control and system administration tools. Such tools add tremendous value to a packaged application installation, providing high availability and integrity. These tools are helpful once

---

Available Server Management Tools

When considering production control tools, there is a choice among many tools from vendors such as BMC, CA, Legato, and Tivoli. BMC's R/3 solution includes Patrol Knowledge Modules (KMs) for SAP R/3. The KMs provide a common interface for monitoring and analysis of critical application resources. The KMs collect information on events, performance, and printers.

The events KM gathers information from the SAP R/3 MIB and CMS log and includes a specialized ABAP program to extract data from R/3. The collection of Patrol KMs provides R/3 administrators with an in-depth view of performance statistics for all SAP subsystems, storing the information in a central database.

---

the EAI solution is up and running, assisting in monitoring performance, insuring availability, and taking corrective actions. More to the point, many of these tools are able to monitor custom applications and databases, allowing the EAI architect or developer to take into account all of the integrated systems and to assess how well they are sharing information or processing.

It is possible to divide service management tools for packaged applications into a few subcategories: reporting, availability, and performance (although each has a tendency to provide features outside of its core competencies). Reporting tools, such as those from Candle Envive and Luminate, provide developers and administrators with the ability to determine the status of an application during runtime. They also make it possible to track historical data, trend the data, and react to problems. Availability tools help the packaged application to remain up and running. These tools typically spot problems before a system interruption occurs, and may correct the problems automatically. Performance tools monitor application performance at the system and component levels. By doing this, administrators can spot performance problems and take corrective action, as well as tune a system for optional performance.

Database Issues

Each package has to leverage a database to store and retrieve the data for the application. Database support varies from package to package, but most support the most popular databases such as Oracle, Sybase, Informix, DB2, and

SQLServer. Typically, each package will come with its own set of DDL for each target database supported. Then, it is just a matter of running the DDL (database definition language) against the database, creating the proper physical schema as well as all relevant stored procedures and triggers. Unless only a few users are being supported, the database should reside on its own server.

Scalability is another issue when considering the database. Most ERP vendors (for example, SAP and PeopleSoft) leverage a transaction or application server (three-tier client/server) that's able to multiplex the database connections and thus buy increased scalability. Others leverage two-tier client/server. In this scenario the clients are going directly to the database and require one connection per client. As with traditional client/servers, two-tier packages aren't as scalable. This reality needs to be considered when the architecture is being created.

Web Enablement

All packaged applications have some sort of Web-enablement strategy to deploy an application either to the Internet or, more likely, an intranet (see Figure 13.4). While they all differ somewhat, the basic idea is to replace the client with a Web browser that is able to link to, and invoke, transaction services on the application server. Sometimes the application server needs to support these new features. Sometimes that Web client appears as a traditional client and thus does not require an upgrade to the infrastructure. Most advanced ERP applications are leveraging Java at the client to provide dynamic behavior to the end user, but some still only provide primitive solutions, such as generating static HTML. If Web enablement is a requirement, the wise course is to begin to ask *a lot* of questions.

PeopleSoft, version 7, offers two new applications: the Web Client and Universal Applications. The Universal Applications is the Java-enabled, server-side portion of the architecture that serves up the applets to any number of Web clients. The Web Client is downloadable from the Web server and is able to run on multiple browsers on multiple operating systems. All of the data transmitted between the Web Client and the application server is encrypted. In short, PeopleSoft is simply creating a new Java-based Web-enabled client to communicate with their standard application server (see Figure 13.5).

SAP Web-enablement architecture is a bit more complex. R/3 provides a Java component that is able to communicate with components residing on a remote application server. The mechanism is straightforward—the application server invokes application services through Business Application Programming Interface (BAPI, discussed in the next chapter), and then it is purely traditional

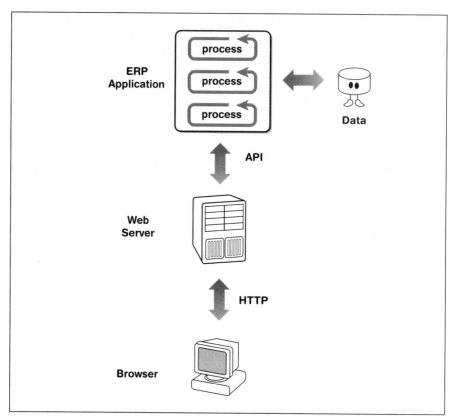

Figure 13.4   Most packaged applications provide some sort of Web-enablement facility.

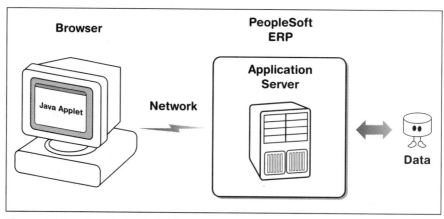

Figure 13.5   PeopleSoft's Web-enablement solution

SAP after that. SAP creates a whole new architecture at the application server layer to support Web enablement (see Figure 13.6).

Scopus provides a product on the customer-care side of the packaged application world they call WebTeam. By using WebTeam, it is possible to generate Web applications directly from new or existing Scopus applications. It's just a matter of regenerating HTML from an existing application. However, the Scopus Web strategy is focused on providing relevant data to customers via the Web, and not on a method to redeploy all of their application modules.

The Opportunity

Why care about linking together disparate ERP systems? Three reasons come to mind: supply chain integration, enterprise integration, and Web-enabled business-to-business or business-to-consumer selling. We have concentrated on discussing enterprise integration thus far in this book. It is appropriate here to look at Web-enabled business-to-business or business-to-consumer selling and the supply chain, as well as how these approaches relate to the packaged application movement. (Supply chain integration or, as we call it, Inter-Enterprise Application Integration, is so important that we've dedicated Chapter 16 to it.)

Web-Enabled Selling and EAI

Web-enabled selling is certainly big news these days. Virtual companies are competing for space to sell their wares all along cyberspace Main Street. Sending information to a customer using a browser via a Web server is not a difficult proposition these days. However, the back-end integration still requires a lot of

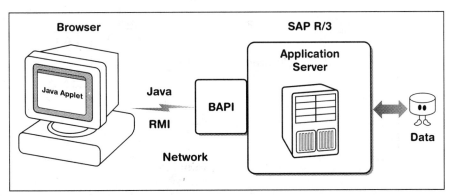

Figure 13.6   SAP's Web-enablement solution

heavy lifting. This reality applies to business-to-business as well as to business-to-consumer selling (see Figure 13.7).

Simply put, it is important to gather information from many packaged and custom systems in order to support Web-enabled selling. For example, a bond trade made by an end user over the Web may touch as many as a hundred systems before it clears the trade. The middleware and the Web application must coordinate every aspect of this transaction, with EAI as the conduit. Without EAI, the end user (consumer or business) would have to navigate manually through these many systems in order to complete a single business event.

Integrating the Supply Chain (e-Business)

The supply chain (or value chain, as it's sometimes called) is the flow of goods and services from their points of origin to the ultimate consumer. This differs from business-to-business Web-enabled selling in that it is integrating systems at the back-end, inter-enterprise, instead of exposing the systems for access to end consumers over the Web. For example, a steel company produces raw sheet metal, which is sent to an automobile manufacturer who processes the metal into panels and assembles the car. The car is then shipped to the dealer, where it is sold to the ultimate customer. The sheet metal plant, the automaker, the dealer, and the customer are all members of the supply chain (known as trading partners).

Although supply chains have existed since the beginning of production, our economy has built systems to automate each supply chain member. That's the

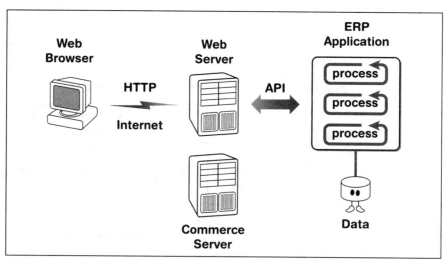

Figure 13.7   Web-enabled selling requires packaged application integration.

good news. The bad news is that we've done a mediocre job of sharing information and processing among the members. What should now be obvious to everyone is that there is a great value in integrating all of the supply chain member systems. For example, using our previous example, a number of customers purchase a certain model of automobile. This increases the demand for that model. The dealer system is able to spot this trend immediately and automatically order more of the popular cars from the automaker. The automaker system receives the larger order and automatically steps up production of that model by ordering all of the component parts required to manufacture more cars, schedule additional workers for overtime, and of course, order more sheet metal.

Once upon a time, not terribly long ago, this process took weeks, even months—not so, today. A fully integrated supply chain can react to consumer demand in a matter of minutes, automatically making the majority of the operational decisions (see Figure 13.8). The end result is the ability to react systematically—and immediately—to higher consumer demand by building and selling more cars. The bottom line is greater profits for every member in the chain. The integration of supply chain systems is a high-value opportunity for most businesses.

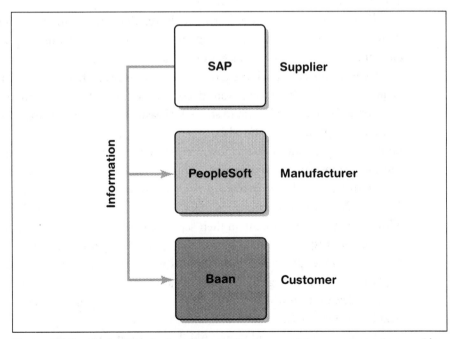

Figure 13.8   An integrated supply chain can react to consumer demand in a matter of minutes.

The potential and value is clear. Unfortunately, most members in a supply chain operate as discrete units, failing to share information by design or failing to share information because of the limitations of the systems (e.g., proprietary systems). Typically, these systems are traditional ERP systems that do a good job intraenterprise but don't provide the plumbing required to share processes and data with other ERP installations or custom enterprise applications. Again, this is the ultimate value of EAI and EAI-enabling technology (e.g., message brokers and application servers along with EDI [Electronic Data Interchange] and XML [Extensible Markup Language]).

Applying EAI to Packaged Applications

There are three ways to integrate supply chains and packaged applications: conformity, traditional middleware, and EAI-enabled technologies. Of the three, conformity is the easiest to understand. Unfortunately, it is also the most difficult to implement. Conformity requires going to every supply chain member and convincing it to use the same application, even the same physical system and database. The idea behind conformity is simple enough—if everyone uses the same system application services, database schema and data, then integration is not an issue. There is nothing to integrate.

Conformity's downside is cost and culture. Most organizations aren't willing to toss out their existing systems and absorb the cost (and hardship) of implementing new ones. With costs estimated at $10,000 per user for most system changeover projects (considering the amount of software, hardware, and services required), conformity starts to sound less wonderful. Perhaps more to the point, most organizations don't want to share data easily with other organizations. That sensibility represents a cultural barrier that is difficult to work around. While conformity is a good idea for post-merger systems integration, it's simply too radical for most supply chains today.

Traditional middleware (e.g., queuing or connection-oriented middleware), as we've discussed in previous chapters, is the most difficult to implement but allows the members to maintain their separate fiefdoms. Traditional middleware ties together disparate ERP systems through a common middleware layer that spans all member platforms. Typically, this means using the APIs that most ERP applications provide (e.g., SAP's BAPI) as a point of integration and then applying middleware to translate and carry the information from one system to the next (see Figure 13.9).

The downside of a traditional middleware solution is complexity, cost, and scalability. Because traditional middleware itself does not know how to make

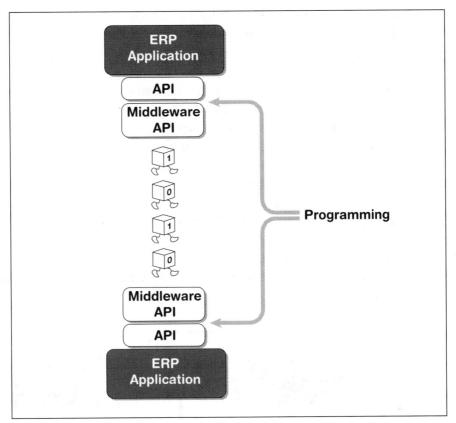

Figure 13.9   Using traditional middleware

connections between two or more ERP systems, custom programs will have to be created that use a middleware layer as the lowest common denominator. This means a large development project to create plumbing applications that are able to make API calls on one system must gather and send information to another system—using yet another API. If that sounds like a nightmare, it is. It is necessary to keep track of what service is bound to what data, and how application services and data maps from one system to the next.

While the database may be an easier point of integration (e.g., data-level EAI) for some systems, caution is required with ERP applications because the data is often bound to application services. Thus it's dangerous to read or update the database without a complete understanding of how the data is handled by the services.

Depending on the degree of integration required, the traditional middleware solution leads to a significant cost to integrate the member systems. This solution is further complicated by the fact that the convoluted architecture created by loosely coupling the systems may have so many bottlenecks that it does not have the capacity required to support all member organization users.

EAI-enabled middleware, such as message brokers with adapters and some application servers, provide middleware that's designed from the ground up to allow different ERP and other distributed systems to share processes and data as if they were a single system (see Figure 13.10). The real value of this new EAI-enabled middleware is that the mapping between the application services and the data is incorporated—there is no need to create the links and mappings.

EAI-enabled middleware is able to communicate with most packaged and custom applications present in an enterprise through adapters (see Chapter 18) and can define how processes and data are shared among them. EAI middleware accomplishes this by creating an infrastructure that allows applications to access most services and data encapsulated in different ERP systems so that they interact as if they shared a single API. This not only allows ERP systems to communicate, but allows other distributed and legacy systems to share information and services as well.

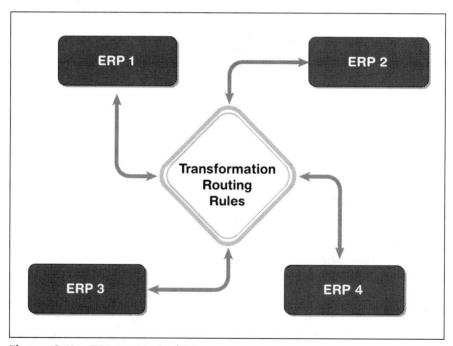

Figure 13.10   EAI-enabled middleware

Our Packaged Future

Organizations are finding that purchasing packaged applications, and modifying them to fit, is more valuable than in building them from scratch. Code is finally being reused through the use of packages. As these packages become ever more feature rich and customizable, the trend to buy rather than build will continue.

Even as this trend grows, problems must be solved. It is vital that the lessons learned from prior installations be leveraged and transferred to current projects. To quote George Santayana, "Those who cannot remember the past are condemned to repeat it." Too often, as an industry, we seem to be making the same mistakes over and over again. It is time to learn from past failings. We need to understand the vision for the application and not simply the current technology. The packaged application needs to grow with the organization and integrate with existing systems, adding value as time goes on, and not become a point of contention as so many of the previous enterprise-wide packaged applications have.

The future is clear. We are going to concentrate more on integrating existing packaged applications, as well as streamlining the customization process through new tools and techniques. As our base of understanding grows, so does our ability to carry out installation and integration projects effectively. Packaged applications are here to stay. We need to learn to leverage their power and potential through EAI.

CHAPTER FOURTEEN

Integrating SAP R/3

"Who's General Failure and why's he reading my disk?"

    —Anonymous

It is no surprise that SAP R/3, the most popular packaged ERP application for the enterprise, is the packaged ERP application that most EAI architects and developers will encounter. Architects and developers tend to be pragmatic people. Knowing that most EAI products are driven by the need to move information in and out of packaged applications like SAP R/3, they figure that, unable to break free from having to link into these beasts, they might as well learn to use them to their best advantage.

As with most things, connecting to SAP has an upside and a downside. The upside is that, unlike many packaged applications out there, well-defined and well-tested interfaces are built into SAP that adequately provide for the sharing of data and processes with the outside world. Of course, the downside is that these same interfaces are complex, their architecture is confusing, information is lacking as to how best to leverage them, and various other technical issues still require resolution. SAP is working toward resolving these issues but don't expect answers anytime soon.

In addition to these problems, there is the problem of what to do with the information once it's been wrenched out of SAP. In most cases EAI architects and developers will pass the information directly to a middleware layer (e.g., the application server or message broker), converting the information into something that's understood by the target system. This transformation and transportation difficulty needs to be solved as well. At this point, finding the proper solution is more an art than a science.

Finally, there is the question of SAP's future. With the popularity of more open interfaces such as Java, CORBA, and COM, SAP is looking to provide uses for these interfaces that access their underlying system. While this is an opportunity for SAP to open access to their system, it is important to consider just how the movement to these interfaces will impact a particular EAI solution. In many instances, the more traditional interfaces can be used now, but an upgrade to the newer interfaces will be necessary when they're available. It doesn't require a genius to see that that's having to do the integration work twice.

The Basic Problem

SAP, like most other packaged applications, was built as a monolithic solution never intended to communicate with the outside world. The later addition of interfaces changed that. They first allowed SAP systems to communicate with each other and then allowed SAP to interact with many different types of systems.

The original SAP R/3 architecture did not contain these interfaces. They were, in fact, added over several years. As a result, they often seem ill conceived and poorly structured. For example, there are many ways to extract the same information from SAP. Coming to a decision as to the exact method and manner is something of a crapshoot, with the correct choice not always obvious. A thorough knowledge of SAP, including data, process information, and business objects, is the only insurance that allows for the successful use and manipulation of SAP.

The nirvana of SAP access rests in the hands of the EAI vendors who are looking to place an abstraction layer on top of interfaces to SAP (see Figure 14.1). The purpose of this abstraction layer is to hide the interface complexities from those who need to integrate SAP with other systems. As a result, SAP will appear like a set of business objects, sharable among applications. The result is a shift in burden from the EAI architect and developer to the EAI solution itself—where it belongs.

While the use of abstraction layers remains the ultimate goal, users today must deal with intermediary realities—APIs and middleware layers. Although they may be ugly, they're all that's going to be available for a while.

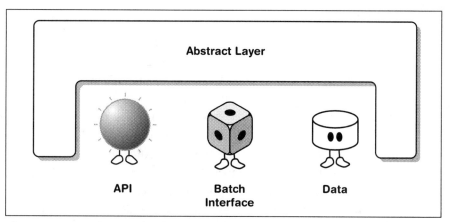

Figure 14.1   Using an abstraction layer to hide complex interfaces

SAP Adapters and Connectors

Most advanced middleware layers such as application servers and message brokers provide adapters or connectors to SAP R/3. However, most of these, while promising easy connections to SAP, typically solve only portions of the problem.

Middleware vendors provide adapters or connectors to better position and sell their middleware. This is a wise marketing strategy. After all, most enterprises leverage packaged applications such as SAP. Many middleware products are purchased less for their inherent merits than for the availability of adapters or connectors. Unfortunately, such purchases are mistakes. Each middleware vendor has its own definition of an "adapter." These can range from the most primitive API layers and simple exits, to very easy-to-use connectors that hide the complexity of the SAP interface from the EAI architect and developer. It is clear that the latter is the best solution—as long as the underlying middleware transport layer meets the particular needs of the solution set as well.

The moral here is the same moral of all purchases—*caveat emptor!* Buyer beware! Ask many questions when selecting an EAI-enabled middleware product or vendor-providing SAP connectors or adapters. For example: which SAP interface(s) do they leverage? How do they move the information? Do they handle transformation? How much custom programming is involved? A pilot test wouldn't be a bad idea either.

SAP Architecture

SAP uses a three-tier architecture comprised of a presentation layer, an application server layer, and a database layer (see Figure 14.2). SAP runs on smaller platforms and operating systems, including most popular flavors of UNIX and Windows NT. It is possible to mix and match operating systems at the client, the application server, and the database levels, making the SAP architecture both flexible and scalable. SAP uses the **Advanced Business Application Programming (ABAP/4)** language, along with the ABAP/4 development workbench and toolset to configure and customize R/3.

The other basic services supporting R/3 include printing, security, and communications. In addition to these services, R/3 allows the interplay of applications, user interfaces, and data. The movement of this information is provided through the use of standard interfaces, application interfaces, and open data

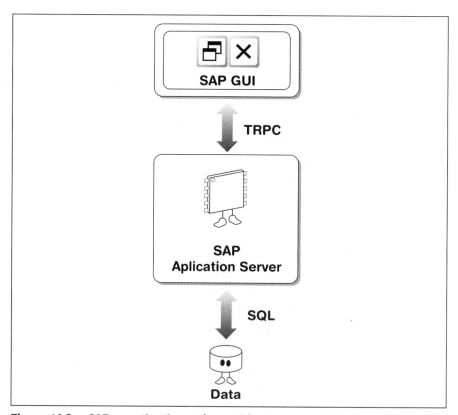

Figure 14.2   SAP uses the three-tier architecture.

formats. These services constitute the basis of SAP's ability to integrate applications. We will explore these services further later in this chapter.

SAP supports most major standards including TCP/IP, SQL, OLE, X.400/500, and EDI. It also supports its own **Remote Function Call (RFC)**, which enables remote calling to SAP functions from other systems. RFC was originally built by SAP for use by other linked SAP systems. However, as time has gone on, RFC has become the primary interface for most EAI efforts. We will discuss this in more detail later in this chapter.

The SAP Repository

SAP provides an advanced repository that contains a description of all metadata, modules, and processes. This information includes screen forms, business rules, and the location of application servers. In the SAP scheme, all applications are extracted from the repository and sent to the connected application servers, providing automatic updates for system upgrades.

The SAP Presentation Layer

The SAP clients are very thin, very terminal-like. The client communicates with the application server and presentation server and simply provides the interface to the end user. One such SAP client is a GUI that supports Windows 98/2000, Windows NT, OS/2, OSF/Motif, and Apple Macintosh.

The SAP Application Server Layer

The application server is able to perform all of the application and interface processing, in addition to providing such rudimentary transaction-processing features as load balancing and fail-over. The R/3 architecture allows the application tier to uncouple from the presentation and data tiers.

The SAP Database Layer

The database simply provides a location for data storage. It handles data access through the use of SAP SQL, which is, at its heart, a standard SQL called from within the ABAP/4 toolset. Because relational database systems offer different subsets of standard SQL functions, the ABAP/4 toolset supports SQL at two levels: SAP SQL and native SQL. The database interface translates SAP SQL into the native SQL dialect. It is possible to use either of these two levels (see Figure 14.3). It should be noted that most relational databases such as Oracle, Informix, and SQL Server work with SAP R/3.

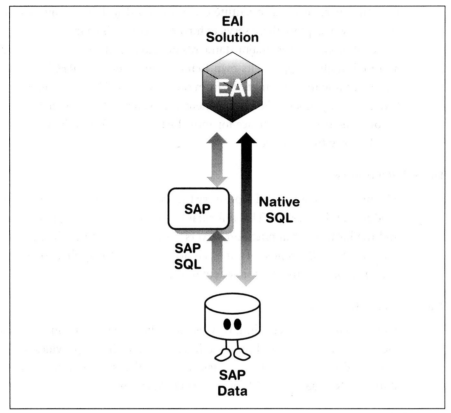

Figure 14.3   SAP provides two levels of database access, either of which can be leveraged for integration.

SAP Middleware

SAP uses traditional and proprietary middleware layers. Program-to-program communications are implemented with older **Common Programming Interface for Communications (CPI-C)**. RFCs are the most prevalent mechanism to mine SAP processes and data. The other layers, such as Java and COM access, are really nothing more than wraparound RFCs.

CPI-C

CPI-C, an older middleware layer left over from the days when traditional IBM mainframes roamed the earth, is part of IBM's System Application Architecture (SAA) of the late 1980s. The CPI-C is included in ABAP/4, allowing an ABAP/4 program to link to a CPI-C session. The program-to-program communication is always performed via an internal gateway that handles the conversion of CPI-C communications to external protocols, including TCP/IP and LU6.2.

If asynchronous communications are required, it is useful to know that SAP supports the notion of queues, allowing a system to create a queue for transmission to another SAP system at a later time. This process is handled by the Queue Application Programming Interface (Q-API). SAP is able to use this interface to accept information into the system through standard batch processing. Although some people judge this practice as inelegant and outdated, the simple fact remains that it's still in wide use today.

RFC

While CPI-C and Q-API provide mechanisms that allow SAP to communicate with the outside world, many people find these "traditional" middleware mechanisms limiting and unable to support SAP's more advanced features, including RFC, which is included in the ABAP/4. RFCs remain the mechanism for accessing the SAP program interface. They provide a standard procedural approach for moving all sorts of information in and out of SAP.

RFCs are callable from a multitude of platforms, development environments, and applications. The R/3 Automation Software Development Kit provides RFC libraries and RFC DLLs (Dynamic Link Libraries), user dialogs, in addition to an error-processing facility. Documentation and sample programs for RFCs are included in this software, allowing access to SAP processes and data from standard software such as MS Excel, PowerBuilder, Visual Basic, C++, and Java. Even more beneficial is the ability to access RFCs using other, more "standard" Microsoft interfaces such as COM, COM+, and OLEDB.

RFC brings the reality of program-to-program communications to SAP, allowing EAI architects and developers to incorporate business objects across several platforms, programs, and databases (see Figure 14.4). RFCs hide the layer of CPI-C calls (the actual communications mechanism used by SAP) from those using RFCs.

Transactions and RFCs

The question remains: "Why use RFCs when it is possible to go directly to the database"? While there are many reasons to do so, the most compelling is transactional integrity. It is simply too dangerous to read and write directly to the SAP database without using the application server, which controls access to the data and thus enforces database integrity. For example, simply updating customer

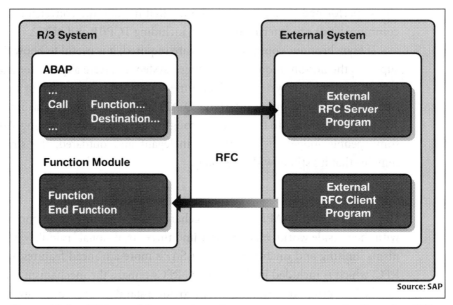

Figure 14.4   RFC provides program-to-program communications for SAP.

information within SAP could mean invoking a single transaction that is linked to several hundred tables. Without using the transaction contained on the application server, it would be necessary to update each table in the same order, making sure that the data is in the proper format. While it is certainly possible to do all this, why not take the easier and safer route of updating and accessing information using the application server layer, using RFC? Without question, doing so is the safest bet.

RFCs ensure transactional integrity by making sure calls are executed in the same order and within the same program context. In addition, RFCs guarantee that a single RFC is not invoked more than one time and that the status of an RFC call may be accessed at any given time.

RFCs are synchronous calls by nature (recall, they are really RPCs). It is, however, possible to use queues to place requests for RFCs for later processing or to process when the SAP server returns to life. It is also possible to leverage other middleware to make RFCs asynchronous. Message-brokering technology is particularly valuable in this regard. We'll discuss this aspect of message-brokering technology in Chapter 18.

At base, RFC technology is really a middleware technology meant to interface with other middleware. As a result, while it is possible to use an RFC to access a SAP system directly, it is more common to bind RFCs to a more traditional middleware layer, such as MOM, distributed objects, or application servers (see Figure 14.5). It is important to bear in mind that the links to RFCs don't magically occur. In most cases those links will have to be created from scratch—or leveraged from a SAP adapter that may come with the middleware.

ALE

With a knowledge of what's going on behind the scenes, we can turn our attention to the heart of EAI access to SAP. The beating heart of EAI access to SAP lies within the Application Link Enabling (ALE) technology, a technology that's able to combine business process with middleware. ALE provides a robust distributed architecture for SAP, providing transparent distributed access to both SAP data and processes. The ALE architecture is also essential for moving information to non-SAP systems and, ultimately, supporting the entire EAI effort.

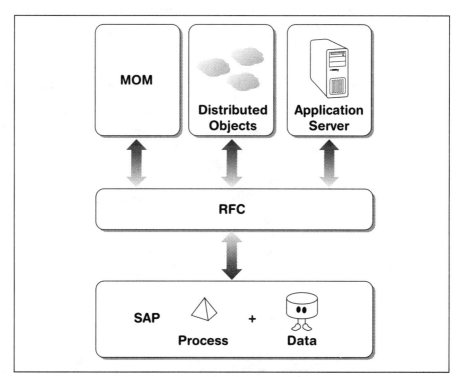

Figure 14.5   An RFC binds to most traditional middleware layers.

ALE allows EAI architects and developers to set up application modules and databases at various sites and then bind the sites at both the business process and the data levels (see Figure 14.6). In other words, they make several SAP sites appear to be a single monolithic system.

In addition to simple data exchange between SAP systems, ALE also allows external systems to access SAP. This benefit results from "tricking" ALE into thinking that it's communicating with other SAP systems. In this way, ALE is able to understand and route data required to support a business process.

ALE provides a competent mechanism that enables EAI architects, developers, and clients to achieve integration as well as the distribution of applications and data. SAP provides ALE technology with a set of tools, programs, data definitions, and methodologies that EAI developers or vendors may apply to unlock the information from traditional SAP systems.

ALE is comprised of three layers: the application layer, the distribution layer, and the communications layer.

The application layer provides ALE with an interface to the R/3 application. This is needed in order to send or receive messages to and from the SAP system you're attempting to integrate. The distribution layer, applying a predetermined set of rules, filters and converts the messages containing the information that is being moved in and out of the SAP system. This is required due to the different releases of SAP (R/2 and R/3). (This is not a substitute for transformation

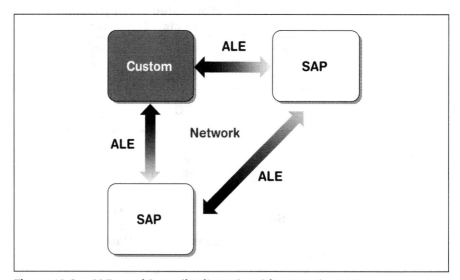

Figure 14.6   ALE provides a distributed architecture for SAP.

engines, such as message brokers, that make short work of EAI.) The communications layer carries out the communications between systems, both asynchronously (for the transmission of data) and synchronously (for the transmission of control information). The tRFC (transactional RFC) mechanism allows for the real-time exchange of information.

IDOC

An IDOC (Intermediate Document) is a structured information set providing a standard format for moving information in and out of a SAP system. In this regard, it represents a similar concept to EDI, but IDOC is not a standard. It is possible to invoke an RFC at the SAP level and get an IDOC as a result. That IDOC becomes a basis to structure a message that's transported through a standard middleware layer. For example, most message brokers are able to convert an IDOC into another format so it may be understood and processed by a target system.

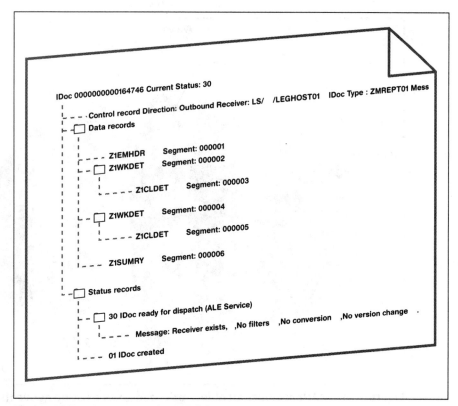

Figure 14.7   Structure of an IDOC

IDOCs contain a control record, a data record, and a status record (see Figure 14.7). Each IDOC is a single SAP business object. The control record contains several fields with information about the IDOC such as its type, sender, and receiver. The data record contains the application data, and the status record contains information on the state of the document.

As a single business object, an IDOC may contain only one shipment document. This represents both an advantage and limitation of IDOC; while easy to use (due to the simplicity of having only one business object per IDOC), a large number of IDOCs will have to be sent and received in order to handle real-time integration.

BAPI

BAPIs provide an object-oriented mechanism to get at the underlying proprietary SAP middleware technology, such as RFCs (see Figure 14.8). In addition to

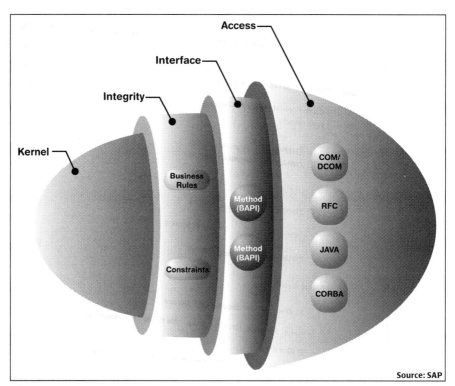

Figure 14.8   BAPI provides an object-oriented layer existing above the SAP middleware (e.g., RFCs).

providing access to the data and processes, a benefit once only possible by means of specific methods, a BAPI allows access to the SAP business objects held in the Business Object Repository (BOR), encapsulated in their data and processes. In other words, a BAPI provides a layer of abstraction above the primitive interfaces that SAP provides.

To use a BAPI method, an application program simply needs to know how to call the method, such as its structure and parameters. The BAPIs in the R/3 system are implemented as function modules, all of which are held in the Function Builder. Each function module underlying a BAPI supports the RFC protocol and has been assigned as a method to a SAP business object in the BOR.

The importance of BAPIs resides in the power they give developers to provide SAP access from many different tools and technologies. For example, using the BAPI interface makes it easy to build applications that are able to gather information from SAPs without having to drop down to primitive function calls. However, a BAPI does not provide everything needed to access SAP as a true set of objects. For example, a BAPI provides access to only a limited number of functions. That said, it is important to note that BAPIs are expanding their reach with every day.

Using the Repository

The SAP repository, as mentioned previously, contains most of its business engineering information, including business models, programs, and objects. The R/3 repository is also the container for all R/3's application information, including development and design information. The repository comprises the business- and application-related metadata and provides a means to explore the features and functions of a SAP system in order to provide better integration.

The advantage of using the SAP repository is the ability to discover as much as possible about the SAP system that is to be integrated. This knowledge enables the EAI architect and developer to automatically link SAP with other systems at the business object (method level) or data level, without having to create a common set of functions.

Although using the SAP repository requires a more sophisticated level of EAI, the ability to react automatically to changes to the source or target SAP system makes a compelling argument for going to that next level. Many who are integrating SAPs have leveraged the repository as a mechanism to intelligently integrate the system. The real value of this approach will come from vendors who are looking to create EAI solutions that link deeply into SAP. Currently, the SAP adapters are more at the RFC level and do not take into account the content of the repository.

SAP and EAI

It's important to note that SAP is a dynamic ERP and is constantly morphing into new, more marketable products. This will only drive the need for additional integration and will certainly add to the already formable challenge of integrating SAP. For example, SAP is going to sell Web-delivered application services for mid-market companies. Thus, there is no need to host your own copy of SAP. While this does provide a low-cost alternative to hosting your own SAP R/3 system (which runs in the millions of dollars), the integration complexities of this approach have yet to be considered.

It's a given that SAP will be a part of most EAI efforts where an ERP is involved. Fortunately, many people have already been down this road and cleared a trail of approaches, interfaces, and technology that make it possible to move information in and out of SAP. The question is, "How much is SAP going to change to accommodate the new interest in EAI"? As SAP matures, it has to provide better interfaces than it currently has, if it is to successfully open up. At this time, most SAPs accomplish this in such a way that they reach a wider set of technologies. In the end, ERPs may all have standard connections, allowing ERP systems to appear as databases, Java objects, or distributed objects. If that occurs, ERP systems such as SAP will be able to be bound seamlessly with existing enterprise applications—which is exactly where they'll have the most value.

CHAPTER FIFTEEN

Integrating PeopleSoft

"Programming today is a race between software engineers striving to build bigger and better idiot-proof programs, and the Universe trying to produce bigger and better idiots. So far, the Universe is winning."

—Rich Cook

Of all the popular ERP packages, PeopleSoft is the most open. Which is not to suggest that it is simple or easy to use. This beast is actually very difficult. It provides the least amount of information on how it can be integrated with the rest of the enterprise. In fact, obtaining information for this chapter was a bit of a challenge. Fortunately, there are enough projects, and vendors muddling through with them, to allow us to elucidate some basic approaches.

PeopleSoft is significantly less proprietary than SAP. As such, it provides greater opportunity for integration without forcing the EAI architect and developer to rely on the vendor interface. These interfaces are, however, hardly cut and dry. In order to create an optimal EAI solution, it is necessary to understand the native and enabling technologies of PeopleSoft.

This world, however, could be changing for PeopleSoft. PeopleSoft has already announced and loosely defined their Open Integration Framework (OIF). While OIF does not define their EAI technology in detail, it does more clearly outline the options that are available to those looking to integrate with PeopleSoft, including up-to-date mechanisms such as XML and their latest Business Component API appearing with PeopleTools 8 (discussed later in this chapter).

PeopleSoft Architecture

Like SAP, PeopleSoft uses standard relational databases for information storage, allowing for the possibility of mixing and matching databases between modules (see Figure 15.1). The databases provide the best point of integration—as long as there is no need to access the business processes that are encapsulated within the application itself. There are ways to accomplish this as well but not as readily.

Unlike SAP, the PeopleSoft application server is based on open technology—BEA's Tuxedo. Because there are tools and techniques to access transactions on the Tuxedo platform, there is another point of integration. In spite of this

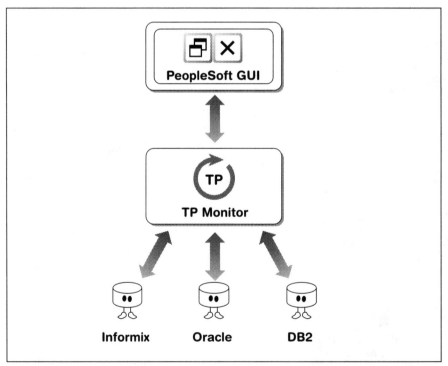

Figure 15.1   PeopleSoft is able to communicate with a number of relational databases.

additional benefit, PeopleSoft does not promote going directly to the application server (TP monitor).

PeopleSoft relies on a three-tier client/server architecture, with a client, an application server, and a database (see Figure 15.2). The client communicates with the application server, which in turn communicates with the database. This architecture provides PeopleSoft with good scaling capabilities as well as an extensible architecture.

The supplemental products offered with the PeopleSoft application solution include:

- PeopleSoft Financials
- PeopleSoft Distribution
- PeopleSoft Manufacturing
- PeopleSoft HRMS
- PeopleTools

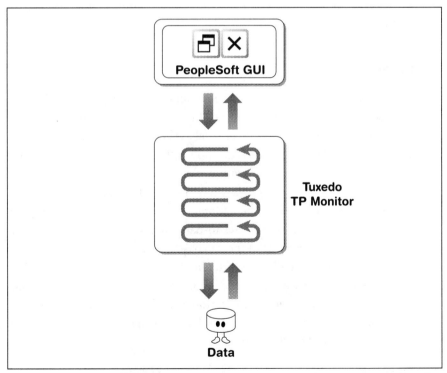

Figure 15.2   PeopleSoft, like SAP, uses a three-tier client/server architecture.

PeopleSoft Financials provides a general ledger system, payables, receivables, asset management, projects, budgets, treasury, and expenses. PeopleSoft Distribution provides purchasing, inventory, order management, billing, enterprise planning, demand planning, and product configuration. PeopleSoft Manufacturing provides bills and routings, production management, production planning, cost management, engineering, and quality management. PeopleSoft HRMS (Human Resources Management System) provides payroll, time and labor, pension administration, FSA administration, benefits administration, and stock administration. PeopleTools is an application development environment that enables the PeopleSoft developer to customize, maintain, and implement PeopleSoft applications without changing the PeopleSoft source code. PeopleTools provides facilities for modifying panels, records, and menus, as well as importing information from other systems. PeopleTools also provides a facility for reporting.

Although the methods for moving information in and out of PeopleSoft are not well defined, it is possible to define several approaches to PeopleSoft integration at the data and interface levels.

Data Level

Fundamentally, data-level PeopleSoft application integration is data-level EAI as described in Chapter 2. This means that information can be moved in and out of PeopleSoft-supported relational databases (including Oracle, Informix, and SQL Server) in order to integrate PeopleSoft with other external applications at the data level. This is accomplished with any number of database-oriented middleware products, message brokers, data migration software packages, or even with the replication and data link features contained in most popular relational databases.

In this, as in any other data-to-data integration effort, it is necessary to first understand the structure of the database or databases from which information is being extracted, as well as the structure and integrity features of the database that is receiving the data. PeopleSoft provides EAI architects and developers well-defined database schema information and a built-in database movement facility (although not real time). This includes the Data Mover and SQRs and leveraging the PeopleSoft Workflow interfaces.

Data Mover

The PeopleSoft Data Mover is a platform-independent PeopleTool that provides the user with the ability to transfer data between PeopleSoft databases. Data

Mover also provides the user with the ability to unload and reload data from other external, non-PeopleSoft databases. Data Mover may also be used for archiving data. Although this is a useful tool, more traditional database-to-database integration solutions may be the better choice.

SQRs and Moving Data

PeopleSoft provides a tool known as SQR, a reporting tool that's a part of all PeopleSoft applications. This tool allows for the exchange of data between two databases with different data structures. In order to use this tool for data movement, two SQR procedures must be written first. The first procedure runs against the source database, selecting the appropriate data. This information is then placed into a sequential file. A second SQR procedure is then created to read the sequential file and update the target databases (see Figure 15.3). PeopleSoft Process Scheduler allows the user to schedule regular transfers of this information. (This is not a real-time solution but more of a batch-oriented one.)

Workflow and Moving Data

Within the PeopleSoft environment, workflow activities and worklists can be triggered to established database agents. These database agents are able to monitor one or more tables in the databases, searching for conditions that should trigger an event. Using features found in most relational databases, such as database links, workflow activities can also be triggered by events occurring within remote databases.

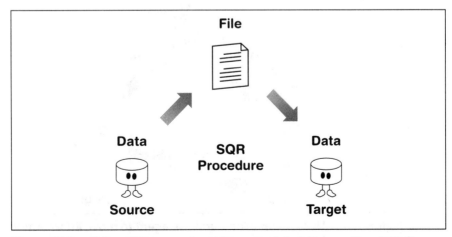

Figure 15.3   Using SQR procedures to move data between PeopleSoft databases.

Workflow activities for multiple databases are set up by first creating the appropriate external tables as database links from the source database (if supported), then creating an agent to monitor the tables awaiting an event (such as a change in state, deletion of a row, or insertion of a row). This mechanism may be leveraged for EAI by using the agent to watch for changes in the source database, such as a table update. When such an event occurs, a stored procedure or replication process could be fired off to move the appropriate data from a source database to a target (see Figure 15.4). In this way, a "mini message broker using intelligent agent technology" is being created. It should, however, be noted that this PeopleSoft mechanism was not designed for database movement exclusively.

Application Interfaces

There is nothing remarkable about PeopleSoft's database-level integration approach. It is independent of the application, leaving the user to deal with the package at the database and database middleware level. Leveraging some of the other interfaces that PeopleSoft provides for accessing not only the data stored in the application, but the business information as well (e.g., invoices, work orders, accounts receivable reports, and so on) requires a bit more sophistication. Grading this aspect of PeopleSoft earns it a C– (SAP isn't much better, earning

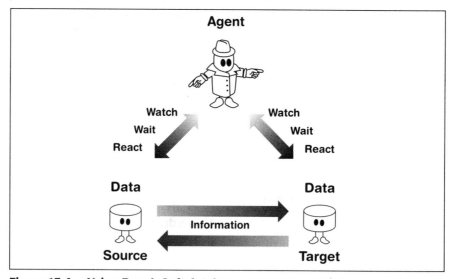

Figure 15.4   Using PeopleSoft database agent to move information between two databases

only a C) for the quality of interfaces that it provides for this purpose. Fortunately, most EAI middleware vendors (e.g., message broker vendors) provide interfaces to PeopleSoft. As a result, it may be possible to obtain appropriate technology and avoid having to understand the details of the interface.

Proper integration of PeopleSoft with the rest of the enterprise requires an understanding of other existing interfaces. As the PeopleSoft product matures, it's a good bet that PeopleSoft will enhance its business-oriented interfaces, opening up the PeopleSoft processes for other systems both inside and outside the enterprise.

Screen Scraping

Scraping screens to access application information has always been a viable option. In this regard, PeopleSoft is consistent with existing products. Using 3270, ASCII terminals, or even Windows user interface access mechanisms (e.g., COM automation), it is possible to extract information from PeopleSoft. In fact, most of the interfaces that PeopleSoft provides at the application level already scrape screens.

EDI

While there are many ways to move information in and out of PeopleSoft, most consider the Electronic Data Interchange (EDI), which exists to exchange business information with systems existing outside the enterprise, to be the best overall solution. Although the PeopleSoft EDI interface was not created for EAI, it certainly works effectively in the EAI domain.

The PeopleSoft EDI is like any other EDI interface in that it is necessary to map the information contained within it in order to transmit it outside PeopleSoft. Once outside the PeopleSoft environment, the information may move to any system that understands EDI or be reformatted by a middle-tier middleware layer, such as a message broker or an application server (see Figure 15.5). Such reformatting assures that the target system will understand the message.

In the context of EAI, EDI is a simple method to get at relevant business data. It represents a method of "tricking" the PeopleSoft system into believing that information is being moved to and from a system existing at a trading partner. In actuality the interface is being used to exchange information between systems within the company. The enabling technologies that will make short work of this include: EDI-mapping software, message brokers that can read and write

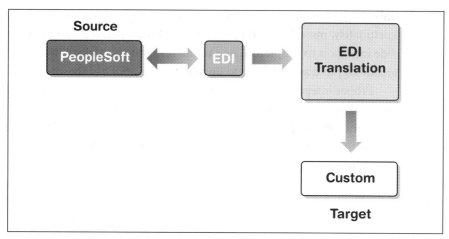

Figure 15.5   It is possible to use EDI to move information in and out of PeopleSoft.

EDI (EDI adapters), application servers with EDI connectors, and traditional queuing middleware such as MQSeries.

If this technology is not beyond the budget of the corporation, it could very well be the best bet for situations requiring the exchange of application information and not just simple data.

Workflow

The PeopleSoft Workflow subsystem enables the user to integrate rules, roles, and routing associated with the localized processing of the enterprise (workflow will be discussed in more detail in Chapter 19). Clever EAI architects and developers may incorporate this workflow mechanism as a method to integrate PeopleSoft with other applications. While the database agent has been discussed previously, it is possible to use similar techniques to send and receive electronic forms and messages.

Application Designer

The PeopleSoft Application Designer can be used as the graphical tool for creating visual business process maps to define workflow scenarios. Once again, while this feature was not created for EAI, moving information between PeopleSoft modules is particularly suited to the needs of EAI in that it creates the opportunity to move information out of PeopleSoft.

Message Agent API

The PeopleSoft Workflow subsystem provides a Message Agent API that allows third-party applications to integrate with PeopleSoft Workflow. This interface processes electronic messages sent to and from PeopleSoft. These messages may be sent through COM automation, a C program, or Windows DDE (Dynamic Data Exchange) as well.

Business Component API

PeopleSoft's Business Component API, new with PeopleTools 8, allows internal and external applications to invoke business rules encapsulated within PeopleSoft. The Business Component API is also able to perform simple data access operations. This interface provides a high-level abstraction layer hiding the complexities of the PeopleSoft system from developers that invoke the Business Component API.

The Business Component API employs online business component logic running through a set of processing events. When creating the logic, business component–specific events provide the infrastructure for sharing components between external applications and transition logic. This API is accessible through C++ or COM and is analogous to SAP's BAPI.

Workstation

In addition to moving information between databases, or using the workflow or EDI interfaces, it is possible to integrate PeopleSoft with other applications that traditionally exist on the desktop. By using utilities that are provided within PeopleTools, it is possible to invoke another workstation application. For example, the WinExec function can be run synchronously or asynchronously. This mechanism is used to launch such Windows applications as Microsoft Excel.

PeopleSoft also supports COM automation, allowing PeopleSoft to control a Windows application through this standard interface. PeopleTools includes a set of COM functions that allow PeopleSoft applications to appear as a COM automation client on a COM automation server existing on a Windows-based PC (see Figure 15.6). These functions include creating an instance of a COM automation object, obtaining COM properties, setting properties, and invoking methods existing on the automation server. DCOM may also be used to extend COM automation over a network as a true distributed object.

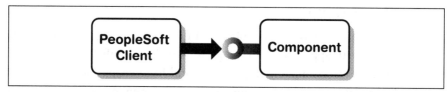

Figure 15.6   PeopleSoft is able to be a COM automation client to another application existing on a PC.

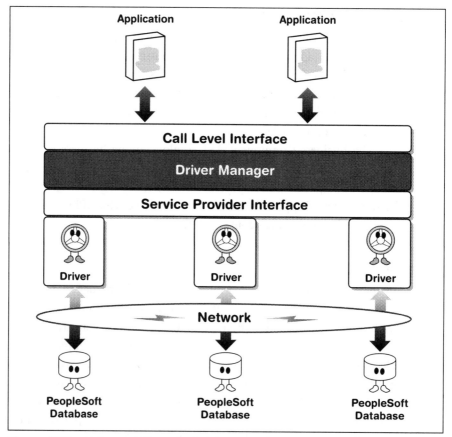

Figure 15.7   Using ODBC to access PeopleSoft data

In addition to supporting COM automation, PeopleSoft also supports external DLL using the PeopleCode scripting language. This feature allows PeopleSoft applications to call an external C function defined in a Windows DLL library, giving the developer a low-level interface to hook PeopleSoft into desktop tools and applications.

Of course, it is also possible to access PeopleSoft data by using ODBC and going directly to the databases. This method allows you to view PeopleSoft data within any Windows application that supports ODBC, such as Visual Basic and Excel (see Figure 15.7).

What's Best?

Before integrating PeopleSoft with other enterprise applications, it is necessary to understand the architecture, the modules, and the various interfaces available. In addition, it is advisable to be familiar with the details of the database schema along with the best mechanisms to get at the data. For most EAI projects, the best method to access PeopleSoft information is through the standard database interfaces. Standard technology—including database middleware, data replication and translation software, and message brokers—allows for access and movement of data, as well as the translation of the schema and content.

As with every other data-level approach, it is important to consider both data integrity issues and how the data is bound to the application logic. PeopleSoft provides most of the necessary information, but testing and then retesting is still a smart move to ensure that a particular EAI solution is the correct one.

The PeopleSoft application interfaces are adequate. The EDI interface is the best choice for moving business information in and out of PeopleSoft. It's designed to share information with external systems, making it a good mechanism to exchange business data with other applications both inside and outside the enterprise. Unfortunately, like most EDI-based EAI solutions, the enabling technology is expensive. What's more, it is difficult to move information out of PeopleSoft on a real-time basis, near time being the best to be hoped for.

While the workflow interface shows real promise, it's still not much more than a mechanism that uses agents to monitor and react to events as it moves data between databases. If PeopleSoft could build on this interface, and provide true message brokering features, it may be better able to open its business information to the outside world.

The workstation integration tools are little more than methods to integrate PeopleSoft with a Windows-based PC, providing only rudimentary mechanisms to share information and methods. Not only is this handy for client-to-PeopleSoft integration, it may also prove useful to EAI architects and developers looking to integrate PeopleSoft as a set of COM objects. PeopleSoft, however, needs to do some more work here to make complete integration through COM a reality.

PeopleSoft will continue to be a leading ERP in the packaged application marketplace, second only to SAP in the number of installations. As the People-Soft installations settle in for the long haul, integration will become the next big problem to solve. In an effort to solve this problem, look to PeopleSoft to shore up the interfaces into their software.

e-Business: Inter-Enterprise Application Integration

"I'd love to change the world, but they won't give me the source code!"

—Unknown

In today's business environment, organizations face fluctuating demand, abbreviated product life cycles, and significant customer attrition every year. Organizations able to align both their human and information resources to meet the demands of e-Business are positioned to own their market. These successful and innovative companies understand the need to bind the members of their e-Business. They also understand that technology is the glue that will hold that chain fast. EAI provides us with an opportunity to get our e-Business under control.

e-Business integration and EAI are "joined at the hip." EAI is the process of bringing together systems that reside within a single enterprise. e-Business integration is the process of joining systems that may exist in two or more enterprises. The technology, the approaches, and even the benefits are much the same. It is safe to say that the ability to create a tightly coupled e-Business is dependent on the success of EAI, along with such EAI technology as message brokers, application servers, and standards.

e-Business integration may represent the Promised Land, but the road leading to it is hardly smooth or straight.

A significant commitment to technological and organizational change must be made for e-Business integration to work. Companies with little corporate patience looking for short-term gains need not apply. The road to this Promised Land is filled with risk. Organizations willing to take the risk face new and changing technological approaches, significant fees to consulting fees, and the need to layer into other organizations not under their direct control. More frightening yet, those "other organizations" may even include a competitor.

There is no foolproof method for integrating e-Business. Organizations can take steps, however, to assure that they are, at least, minimizing the risks. The trick is to plan for the long term, implementing in the short term, and all the while keeping sight of the business reasons for e-Business integration. Perhaps most difficult of all is the need to keep the technology in perspective. It is there to be controlled, not to be worshipped. Ultimately, it is the tool, not the master. Finally, organizations must make decisions wisely. They need to avoid making decisions because they are "trendy" and base their decision-making on what adds the most value to the chain.

The risks should give every organization pause. However, the amazing opportunity of e-Business integration is beginning to outweigh the risks. Indeed, the greater risk might be in *failing* to integrate. Organizations can no longer afford to view their operations as if they existed in a vacuum. They need to collect comprehensive, accurate, and timely information throughout the e-Business. The first step is analyzing the information and its flow in order to better comprehend the causes and effects of the business environment on the core business. Armed with the relevant information, it is possible to make informed business decisions and to utilize information as a mechanism to gain market share.

Defining Your e-Business

Simply put, e-Business supports the flow of goods and services from their origin to their endpoint, the customer. The components of the e-Business may include the original suppliers, multiple production operations, the logistics operations, retail, the customer, and even the customer's customer. For example, an organization that builds birdhouses has an e-Business that includes the lumber company that processes the trees into lumber, the plant that turns the lumber into birdhouses, the company that supplies the paint for the birdhouses, the logistics department ensuring the availability of supplies, sales, shipping, the retailer, and the customer who ultimately purchases the birdhouse (see Figure 16.1). As we noted previously, not all of these organizational components may be under direct control of the organization that heads the value chain.

e-Business management depends on the planning and control of the flow of goods and services, information, and money back and forth throughout the e-Business. It determines the speed and time-to-market, as well as the inventory an organization must carry at any given time. Therefore, e-Business management determines the overall cost-of-goods-sold as well as customer service and satisfaction.

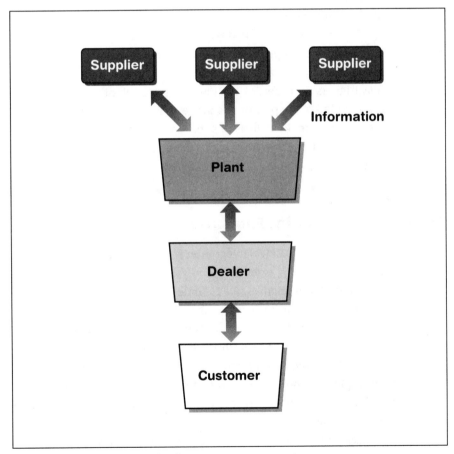

Figure 16.1   Example e-Business

> ### Saturn Leverages e-Business to Ensure Success
>
> Saturn's ability to deliver a quality low-cost vehicle depends on its e-Business management operations. Saturn keeps inventory costs low by practicing "just-in-time-inventory" through a sophisticated information system. The company doesn't maintain inventory beyond what is required to complete a certain number of cars. Saturn is successful because it not only manages the automobile manufacturing facility and the logistics operations, but also the operating systems that encompass their parts suppliers and dealers. This gives Saturn the ability to determine demand and then to react to that demand by ordering more parts and building more cars.
>
> Saturn has this high degree of e-Business integration because it insists that its suppliers tie into their information systems in one way, shape, or form. As a result, the purchase of a Saturn vehicle *automatically* triggers an order for the inventory and plant time to build another car. People are *not* part of this process. The technology exchanges information and makes decisions based on the criteria determined by management. This is the mark of a well-integrated and automated e-Business—essentially no human intervention.

Extending EAI outside the Enterprise

Consideration of e-Business integration is really a consideration of extending the enterprise. Just as an extended family might include aunts, uncles, second cousins, and distant relatives, the extended enterprise comprises all of the members of a company's e-Business, such as the various legal units within the company, suppliers, supplier vendors, and customer organizations.

In order to extend the enterprise, it is necessary to leverage technology, such as EAI-enabled middleware and Web-enabled application development tools. For example, common network infrastructures must be in place, such as those offered by value-added networks (VANs), proprietary wide area networks (WANs), or the Internet. The Internet has the ability to level the playing field for smaller organizations seeking to leverage the power of e-Business integration. Using the common links of the Internet and the common platform of the Web, it is very possible to become part of a set of informally connected systems. While some organizations may be fighting this evolution, the Internet has, on one level, already accomplished the task by creating its own natural e-Business.

For example, consider a typical direct-order apparel company. Consumers access the company's Web site where they are able to browse through the available merchandise. The consumer is able to get an immediate price for the order, including tax and shipping charges, as well as a ship date, estimated time of arrival, and a confirmation number to track the order as it progresses through the chain. The value for the consumer is the ability to shop without sales pressure and time constraints, as well as having an enormous amount of information about the costs, timing, and status of the order. While Web-enabled commerce has yet to take off as predicted, online storefronts are doubling sales every year and, in the process, adding value to the concept of e-Business.

Web-enabled commerce has many benefits for the company as well as the consumer. Because orders are collected directly from the consumer, point-of-sales data is immediately available to the e-Business systems. This data provides real-time feedback to various points within the organization's business processes. For example, suppliers are made aware of the demand for a particular garment, enabling them to adjust production. Sales knows the success or failure of a product line before its effect reaches the bottom line. If a company not only automates its own business processes, but is able to integrate its systems with the systems of the e-Business partners, then as a team they can build a mechanism for dealing automatically with the volatility of the most aggressive markets.

Binding the Home System to a Stranger's

As we've noted, integration of information and business functions is the first step in effective e-Business management. Those individuals responsible for automating e-Business must analyze the information to determine the required courses of action. The best systems should automatically trigger a corresponding transaction by looking at conditions and provide the decision-makers with enough data to make effective decisions.

Communication barriers must be removed so that the flow of information can be improved among all members of e-Business. The degree of difficulty in creating links to members—and opening up this flow of information—ranges from very easy to very difficult. Most members already have information systems in place, but the types of information retained, and the standards they rely on, vary greatly. For example, many information systems are proprietary in nature and fail to provide points-of-integration. In addition to being difficult to integrate with e-Business, such proprietary technology results in higher cost and diminished value.

The Internet provides the e-Business chain with an inexpensive network for sharing information between members. The Web also provides the additional benefit of linking unknown users (e.g., customers) into the e-Business. Those responsible for integrating e-Businesses should look at this Web-enabled customer base as a mechanism to extend e-Business integration, not merely as a simple link to it.

The Process

While a number of methodologies are promoted by the Big Four consulting firms, the process of creating an automated e-Business is really more like traditional system development—with a twist. The first step is to automate and optimize all of the major business processes within each member organization. It is impossible to integrate an e-Business unless the members have their core systems in place. The second step is to extend the enterprise to incorporate all members in the e-Business. This is the most difficult and time-consuming part of the process. It is here that EAI technology and techniques add the most value. At the heart of this process is a system architecture and design effort that extends the enterprise systems to the member organizations. Thus, not only is the enterprise being automated and the process flows, object models, database models, and so on being created, but the way in which all of this integrates with other systems in other organizations (which is, in a way, analogous to the integration process outlined in regard to the levels of EAI) is being defined. The end result is a common information infrastructure that integrates all member business systems with those of customers and suppliers.

It is here, once such an infrastructure is in place, that the new family of EAI technology—message brokers and application servers—creates the best new opportunity to get the e-Business problem under control. Using message brokers, e-Business integrators can bind systems, even custom proprietary systems belonging to a trading partner, with their own enterprise systems. The solution is not significantly different than the solution to similar integration problems *within* the enterprise. In this case, the problem domain is simply extended to include the relevant systems owned by the trading partners (see Figure 16.2).

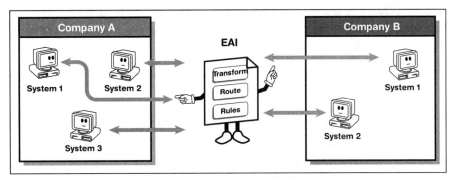

Figure 16.2   e-Business integration extends EAI techniques and technologies outside the enterprise.

It is important to look for opportunities to add value to the e-Business system, such as real-time decision support to increase responsiveness—for example, defining triggers to automatically perform business processes such as reordering inventory, increasing the marketing budget for a best-selling product, or informing management of other issues that need to be addressed. Other examples include an organization's leveraging systems to automatically select suppliers based on price and availability, freeing the staff from performing a complete analysis of the business drivers.

This type of sophisticated processing lends itself well to the process automation aspect of EAI, the ability to create a workflow/process automation layer on top of the existing enterprise or, in this case, inter-enterprise processes. A real-time solution brings with it the greatest degree of flexibility because changing a process or a flow is a simple matter of dragging icons around a screen.

Near-time decision support information is important as well. Almost all e-Business systems need to leverage the power of data warehousing technology to provide decision-makers with information they need to drop a product line, increase promotional activities, or normalize the number of participants in the e-Business.

In addition to the technical issues these solutions raise, it is important to focus on human issues as well. e-Business integration is not complete unless it is accompanied by a reinvestment in re-educating and reorienting employees, suppliers, and other interested parties. Too often "techies" forget about the soft aspects of e-Business integration.

Absent from this process is the ability for all the players in the e-Business to make enterprise-wide commitments to creating and managing a complex organization and business system that's better able to fit the needs of the market. Organizations that are doing this today are organizations that are going to own the market in the future.

e-Business Technology

While some organizations are using new EAI-enabled or traditional middleware to tie custom systems together with those of their e-Business members, many others are looking to Enterprise Resource Planning (ERP) packages as points of integration. ERP provides all members in the e-Business with a common application layer to exchange information through well-defined interfaces, business logic, and repositories. Unfortunately, getting all members of the e-Business to run the same ERP application is almost an impossible task.

As noted in previous chapters, ERP systems are designed to provide their owners with a system for planning, controlling, and monitoring an organization's business process. What's more, ERP systems offer easy system-to-system integration through standard mechanisms for communications. They also build a common understanding of what the data represents and a common set of rules (methods) for accessing the data.

However, traditional ERP systems are not necessarily e-Business systems. e-Business systems must deal with the complexity of integrating information from any number of disparate systems that span multiple organizations. While some properties of ERP systems are appropriate for use with the e-Business, others are not. Typically, ERP systems exist within a single organization, using a single database as the point of integration with internal organizations. There is a single database and network protocol standard; thus the enterprise system is able to work with other departmental systems without having to deal with complex integration problems.

When integrating external systems, it's almost impossible to get all member organizations to agree on a set of standards (e.g., network protocol, database architecture, process automation, and so on). Given this difficulty in arriving at a unanimous agreement, the best solution is layers and layers of middleware, gateways, and adapter technology so that information can be moved from system to system. In most cases, very little processing can be shared among the members, and the e-Business system architecture can grow exceedingly complex and confusing.

In this context then, there are two problems to solve. The first is getting all member organizations to agree on a single communications standard and a single database architecture. While it might appear that communications would be an easy problem to solve, some of the member organizations, especially the smaller manufacturing concerns, have to invest a significant amount of money to get their systems ready to link to others in the e-Business. Once everyone is ready, the second problem has to be addressed. All members need to agree on a common communications mechanism and middleware approach, allowing all member systems to seamlessly access processes and data in the extended enterprise.

As difficult as these two problems might appear, implementing the solutions is often even more difficult.

Clearly, these difficulties will not be overcome anytime soon. The value that the new EAI technology brings to this problem domain is the ability to integrate many of these systems without requiring that significant changes be made in the systems owned by the trading partners. Instead of having to change the database, application, and even the network, EAI-enabled middleware is able to adapt each system into the larger system by accounting for the differences in data and methods within a middle tier (see Figure 16.3).

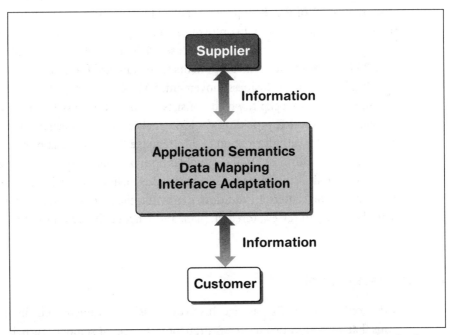

Figure 16.3   **EAI technology is able to link many different systems in the e-Business by not requiring that changes be made to the source or target systems.**

Message brokers and application services represent the middleware best suited for e-Business systems. Because message brokers are message oriented, and so asynchronous in nature, they're able to move information from system to system without requiring that all systems be up and running at the same time.

Data is another issue. While most organizations can agree on relational databases, few can agree on a database model and architecture that can be shared across the e-Business. e-Businesses solve this problem by either forcing a common data architecture among the members or using message brokers or data translation middleware to adapt the data to various models and schemas.

ERPs and e-Business

Many ERP software vendors are addressing these issues along with the concept of e-Business, by opening up interfaces to their systems. For example, as we noted in Chapter 14, which was devoted to SAP, SAP provides opportunities for business-to-business integration through their Business Application Programming Interface (BAPI) standard. Meanwhile, SAP has set its sights on larger game. With release 3.1 of R/3, SAP provides access to R/3's independent business components through BAPIs that conform to an accepted open object standard such as DCOM or CORBA. In addition, release 3.1 is Internet enabled, adding more than 25 Internet application components to its standard framework.

Building on the e-Business movement, SAP offers niche subsystems such as the Supply Chain Cockpit, which consists of the e-Business Engineer and the e-Business Controller, providing decision-makers with a mechanism to gather and analyze relevant information and to manage the supply chain from a single interface. The e-Business Engineer enables both planners and decision-makers to perform graphical maintenance of extended e-Business models, such as plants and distribution centers. In addition, it provides the planner and decision-maker with the ability to review, forecast, plan, and schedule based on the actual status of an e-Business.

e-Businesses Organize

SAP is only a single ERP package. It solves e-Business problems only in organizations that are committed to R/3. A more objective set of standards is being developed by the National Initiative for Supply Chain Integration (NISCI), a nonprofit, private organization that receives backing from the Department of

Commerce. The mission of NISCI is to assist member businesses in understanding and building the most effective methods and technologies to optimize the performance of e-Businesses comprised of more than three members. NISCI will provide thought leadership in e-Business optimization by providing a central repository of information on both problems and solutions. Thus far, organizations have been dependent on large consulting companies to provide both methodology and technology. NISCI is committed to functioning through a board of directors made up of producers, suppliers, and intermediate processors. NISCI will work to improve their member organization by following several objectives, including stimulating value creation, certifying education, and designing chain architecture supporting real-time, consensus decision-making.

Certainly e-Business integration is in its first stages in most organizations, and many organizations have chosen to move forward with "baby steps." While all have an e-Business, few have moved to optimize it through process reengineering, training, and most importantly, technology. The value of such cooperation is only now becoming apparent.

The future is easy to define but much harder to implement. We need to examine our information infrastructure to determine how we are currently doing business. Then we need to look at what it will take to modify the infrastructure to extend the enterprise to other members. Only then will it be possible to tackle the integration issues—which will be innumerable.

CHAPTER SEVENTEEN

XML and EAI

"Internet is so big, so powerful and pointless that for some people it is a complete substitute for life."
—Andrew Brown

With so many vendors promoting XML as the standard integration mechanism—the common data exchange format that everyone can agree upon—any discussion of EAI deserves a discussion of XML. However, while the coupling of XML with EAI exists, it is a tenuous coupling. Still, it is relevant enough to warrant devoting an entire chapter to it and its value within a typical EAI problem domain.

From the outset, it is important to remember that XML is in a state of flux. For more detailed and more current information (mostly pertaining to XML's application to the Web), see www.w3c.org/xml. The site lists the current state of XML, along with a large number of proposals to evolve XML, many looking to expand its use into the enterprise. The site also lists the XML strategies (or lack thereof) employed by middleware vendors. For example, IBM is listed as having an aggressive XML-enablement strategy for MQSeries message-queuing software.

The Rise of XML

XML provides a common data exchange format, encapsulating both metadata and data. This allows different applications

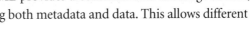

and databases to exchange information without having to understand anything about each other. In order to communicate, a source system simply reformats a message, a piece of information moving from an interface, or a data record as XML-compliant text and moves that information to any other system that understands how to read XML (see Figure 17.1). Simple as one, two, three.

Despite its value to EAI, XML was not originally designed for EAI. XML was created as a mechanism to publish data through the Web without the originator having to understand anything about the system sending the data. As the enterprise integration problem became more evident, EAI architects and developers saw the value of applying XML to the problem domain in order to move information throughout an enterprise. Even more valuable, XML has an application as a common text format to move information between enterprises, supporting supply chain integration efforts. As a result, many are calling XML the next EDI (Electronic Data Interchange).

While its benefit may appear revolutionary, XML itself is anything but revolutionary. It also falls short of being a panacea for the EAI solution. Still, it presents some real value for integration, even though applying this value means stretching XML far from its original intention. The problem is, of course, that if stretched too far, XML may be applied in areas where it has little chance of success. The over-application of XML to so many areas of technology dilutes its real

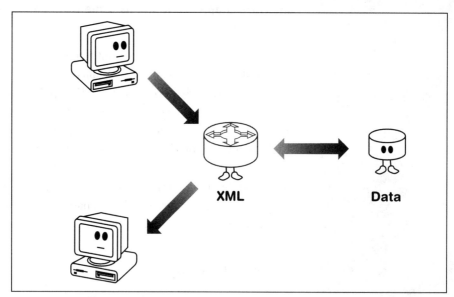

Figure 17.1   XML provides a standard mechanism for data exchange.

value and results in a great deal of unnecessary confusion. Moreover, many vendors are looking to take XML and recast it using their own set of proprietary extensions. While some want to add value to XML, others are seeking only to lock in users.

What's XML?

Like HTML (Hypertext Markup Language), XML is a subset of Standard Generalized Markup Language (SGML), a venerable standard for defining descriptions of structure and content in documents. Unlike HTML, which is limited to providing a universal method to display information on a page (without context or dynamic behavior), XML takes the next step—providing context and giving meaning to data.

XML redefines some of SGML's internal values and parameters while simultaneously removing many of the little-used features that make SGML so complex. XML maintains SGML's structural capabilities, letting middleware users define their own document types. It also introduces a new type of document, one in which it is unnecessary to define a document type at all.

XML has shown great promise in defining vertical market XML vocabularies for a particular industry, vocabularies that define a set of elements and describe where they should fit in the document structure. Both the automobile industry and the health care industry have become prominent players in the new world of XML vocabularies.

The use of industry-specific vocabularies is one of the most promising aspects of EAI and XML. Such vocabularies can define information interchange and even transformation characteristics to fit a specific industry. As a result, EAI solutions, inclusive of metadata and behavior, can be used among verticals. Herein lies the future of EAI—the ability to leverage existing best-practice integration solutions in the same way packaged applications have been leveraged. Sometime in the not too distant future, it will be possible to purchase the best-of-breed integration solution rather than build it from the ground up.

Data Structures

XML is simple to understand and use. XML can take large chunks of information and consolidate them into an XML document—meaningful pieces that provide structure and organization to the information.

The primary building block of an XML document is the element defined by tags (see the example in the next section). An element has both a beginning and an ending tag. All XML documents contain an outermost element known as the **root element**, in which all other elements are contained. XML is also able to support **nested elements**, or elements within elements. Nesting allows XML to support hierarchical structures and, as a result, the use of traditional hierarchical and object-oriented databases for XML document storage. Element names describe the content of the element, and the structure describes the relationship between the elements.

An XML document is considered to be "well formed" (able to be read and understood by an XML parser) if it is in a format that complies with the XML specification, if it is properly marked up, and if elements are properly nested. XML also supports the ability to define attributes for elements and describe characteristics of the elements. This is contained within the beginning tag of an element.

DTDs

The Document Type Definition (DTD) determines the structure and elements of an XML document. When a parser receives a document using a DTD, it makes sure the document is in the proper format.

XML documents can be very simple, with no document type declaration:

```
<?xml version="1.0" standalone="yes"?>
<conversation>
<greeting>Hello, world!</greeting>
<response>Stop the planet, I want to get off!</response>
</conversation>
```

Or they can be more complicated. They may be DTD specified, contain an internal subset, and possess a more complex structure:

```
<?xml version="1.0" standalone="no" encoding="UTF-8"?>
<!DOCTYPE titlepage SYSTEM
   "http://www.frisket.org/dtds/typo.dtd"
[<!ENTITY % active.links "INCLUDE">]>
<titlepage>
<white-space type="vertical" amount="36"/>
<title font="Baskerville" size="24/30"
   alignment="centered">Hello, world!</title>
<white-space type="vertical" amount="12"/>
```

```
<!- In some copies the following decoration is
   hand-colored, presumably by the author ->
<image location="http://www.foo.bar/fleuron.eps"
   type="URL" alignment="centered"/>
<white-space type="vertical" amount="24"/>
<author font="Baskerville" size="18/22"
   style="italic">Munde Salutem</author>
</titlepage>
```
[Source: W3C]

XML Parsers

The fundamental difference between HTML and XML is that, unlike HTML, XML defines the content rather than the presentation. For example, Microsoft Internet Explorer uses an XML parser, which is able to read an XML page and extract the data for access by another program.

Parsers are becoming part of the middleware layer, able to process XML documents. Major middleware vendors, including IBM and BEA, are planning to offer XML parsers as part of their middleware offerings. Most middleware users will leverage these parsers to move XML documents in and out of the middleware layers (see Figure 17.2).

XML Metadata

XML metadata can be any attribute assignable to a piece of data, from the concrete to such abstract concepts as the industry associated with a particular document. XML can also be used to encode any number of existing metadata standards. The binding of data and metadata is a key feature that makes XML most applicable to information-sharing scenarios. This feature is consistent with the concept of a common enterprise metadata repository that's supported throughout an organization. XML is attempting to support common metadata standards throughout the Internet. In that context, supporting metadata standards within the enterprise should not pose an insurmountable problem.

Because XML doesn't depend on any particular type of metadata format, there is little risk that a particular technology vendor will define its own set of metadata tags. In other words, XML cannot be made proprietary to any particular type of data. When the Resource Description Framework (RDF, discussed in the section "RDF and EAI," later in this chapter) brings all the metadata initiatives together, the data can be shared.

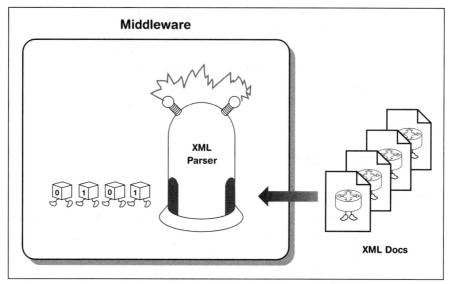

Figure 17.2   Most middleware vendors will provide XML parsers with their products.

XML and Middleware

There is tremendous vendor competition here, with vendors staking early claims to XML dominance. In the process, they seem to be turning XML, which is really just a specification, into a technology, which may not be beneficial to XML at this time.

Each vendor looks at XML in a different way. Some vendors see XML as a common information exchange mechanism. Others see it as a database storage format. Some look to the Web attributes of XML, while the rest see XML as a mechanism to finally get metadata under control.

XML (and the technology that accompanies it) is an excellent text-processing facility. It can follow a set of rules for the creation and organization of documents, resulting in a text format most users are willing to agree on. As a result, users of different types of middleware will be able to share information more easily. These benefits are possibly due to the self-describing nature of XML data.

XML's benefit to middleware is clear. XML provides a generic format for the exchange of information. Middleware simply needs to move messages that encapsulate XML and have those messages understood by any source or target application that understands XML. Seems pretty straightforward. Unfortunately, things are not always as they seem, and a number of downsides have to be considered.

There are XML and middleware "arguments" in which people state the value of moving information from system to system using XML because XML provides a "standard information format." Information coming from the source system is being reformatted into XML (as content and metadata). The XML is being moved using some sort of middleware, and then the information is again reformatted into something understandable by the target system (see Figure 17.3). What's the gain in all this reformatting? Not much.

This process requires reformatting twice, when it should be necessary to reformat only once. Moreover, because XML requires that the metadata come along for the ride with the information, the size of the message is going to be increased. In the end, a lot of redundant and unnecessary information is being passed around with little gain other than the "warm, fuzzy feeling" that accompanies messages using a "standard" text format.

A less warm and fuzzy, but better approach is to translate a message, such as MQSeries or MSMQ, into XML when needed. Most middleware vendors, such as IBM and BEA, are taking this approach.

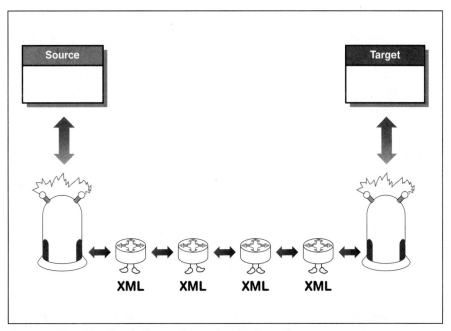

Figure 17.3   Moving information using XML as the common format

Persistent XML

While there are products that provide persistent XML storage, XML itself does not provide a good database format for medium-to-large data sets. XML requires that portions of the XML document exist in memory. Otherwise, the document will be parsed and reparsed, which results in significant performance problems. While this approach may sound reasonable, it demands a large amount of memory over time with typical organic database growth. Moreover, pre- and post-processing is a requirement to take care of special characters (e.g., the ampersand) encapsulated within the XML document.

Database vendors are moving quickly to address this need. Virtually every major relational database vendor, such as IBM and Oracle, is pledging support for XML. Object-oriented database vendors, who have yet to see a significant market for their products, consider XML storage to be their salvation. XML is so easy to incorporate into products, due to the simplicity of the technology, that most vendors can join the XML playing field with minimal effort. There probably won't be a lot of product dollars to be made here by technology vendors, but with XML on the checklists at most major corporations, it cannot be ignored.

Data types represent another limitation of XML. An ASCII text–based format, XML does not provide facilities for complex data types or binary data (e.g., multimedia data). To solve this problem many vendors are proposing new standards to the Worldwide Web Consortium (W3C) to bind XML to binary information. They are also coming out with their own XML hybrids before the W3C is able to react. Of course, the result is a smattering of products without any notion of standardization.

RDF and EAI

RDF (Resource Description Framework), a part of the XML story, provides interoperability between applications that exchange information. RDF is another standard defined for the Web that's finding use everywhere, including EAI. RDF was developed by the W3C to provide a foundation of metadata interoperability across different resource description communities.

RDF uses XML to define a foundation for processing metadata and to provide a standard metadata infrastructure for both the Web and the enterprise. The difference is that XML is used to transport data using a common format, while RDF layers on top of XML—defining a broad category of data. When the XML data is declared to be of the RDF format, applications are then able to understand the data without understanding who sent it.

RDF extends the XML model and syntax to be specific for describing either resources or a collection of information. (XML points to a resource, in order to scope and uniquely identify a set of properties known as the **schema**.)

RDF metadata can be applied to many areas, including EAI, for example, searching for data and cataloging data and relationships. RDF is also able to support new technology (such as intelligent software agents and exchange of content rating).

RDF itself does not offer predefined vocabularies for authoring metadata. However, the W3C does expect standard vocabularies to emerge once the infrastructure for metadata interoperability is in place. Anyone, or any industry, can design and implement a new vocabulary. The only requirement is that all resources be included in the metadata instances using the new vocabulary.

RDF benefits EAI in that it supports the concept of a common metadata layer that's shareable throughout an enterprise or between enterprises. Thus, RDF can be used as a common mechanism for describing data within the EAI problem domain. However, RDF is still in its infancy, and middleware vendors will have to adapt their products to it in order for it to be useful.

XSL and EAI

XSL (Extensible Style Language) is a simple declarative language that programmers use to bind rules to elements in XML documents and so provide behavior. Extensible through JavaScript and written in XML, XSL builds on existing standards, such as the Document Style Semantics and Specification Language (DSSSL) and Cascading Style Sheets (CSS).

The ability to provide a rules-processing layer to XML gives XSL its greatest benefit to EAI because this ability allows for the creation of rules to define routing, flow, and even transformation. However, as with XML, XSL is a Web-born standard, and the value to intra-enterprise information movement is still not clear.

Unlike HTML, XML tags do not support a behavior mechanism for formatting their content. XSL was designed from the ground up to support higher-structured and data-rich XML documents, as well as transformation features. XSL can take an XML document and reformat it, changing both the schema and the content (see Figure 17.4), albeit in a very limited way.

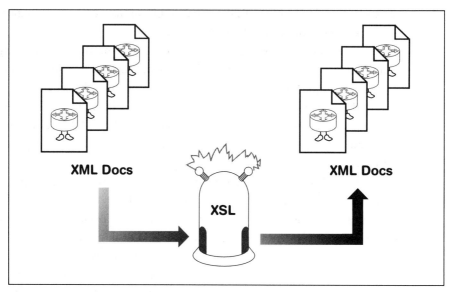

Figure 17.4   XSL can transform an XML document.

XML and EAI

XML will add value to EAI. However, because it is over-applied in so many areas of technology, this new standard is actually devalued. It will be some time before it will be clear where XML best fits within most EAI problem domains. Right now, it is difficult to cut through the hype and misinformation. It remains prudent to understand the features of XML and the possible emergence of XML-related standards (RDF, XSL, and so on) as standard EAI technologies. The trend is clear. We're just not *there* yet.

XML is text based and, therefore, easily understood by all platforms. Although this limits the types of data that can be encapsulated using XML, its simplicity remains its strength. XML's value is its ability to share information with systems that may be beyond the user's control (perhaps in the enterprise but still out of immediate control). In those situations, XML becomes the least common denominator for information, with XML parsers available on most platforms and middleware vendors beginning to support parsers. Still, too many tradeoffs still jeopardize the certainty that XML will dominate the future of EAI.

XML is good at providing a format for messaging and protocols. Therefore XML makes sense because it requires that the data be formatted in a way easily processed by the target systems.

XML's ability to support simple, self-describing messages is a clear advantage in some types of situations. Its use on the Web is a clear fit due to the fact that data is being sent down to a browser that does not know the structure of the data unless it's sent along with the data. Traditional message-oriented middleware rarely provides a self-describing message format. However, most enterprises are usually integrating systems that are tightly coupled, and the format of the data is well defined by the developer using the middleware.

Building on this idea, XML's value is really the ability to share information between loosely-coupled systems. This means supply chain integration or merger and acquisition scenarios. Electronic Data Interchange (EDI, including ANSI X.12) has dominated this type of communication for some time now. However, its complexity and expense could drive many toward XML. This is a shift just waiting to happen. EDI vendors see it coming, and they are scrambling around trying to incorporate XML technology into their core product sets.

CHAPTER EIGHTEEN

Message Brokers—
The Preferred EAI Engine

"Computers make it easier to do a lot of things, but most of the things they make it easier to do don't need to be done."
—Andy Rooney

The business value of message brokers is clear. Using a "hub-and-spoke" architecture, this technology can broker information (messages) between one or more target entities (networks, middleware, applications, and/or systems) with a great deal more ease than traditional methods. What's more, message brokers can accomplish this regardless of how the information is represented or accessed.

They also provide a mechanism to integrate multiple business processes that, until now, have been more isolated than open. They are successful at this, whether the business processes are new, old, legacy, centralized, or distributed. Message brokers bridge many different platforms and application development solutions. They are also able to connect to each application and to route information between applications by using any number of middleware and API mechanisms. Message brokers are capable of more than simply routing information. They can provide enhancements such as hosting business functions that build on the existing business functions of the entities they connect.

Message brokers often provide "message transformation" engines, allowing the message broker to alter the way information is represented for each application (a.k.a. message transformation). Other features of the message broker may include rules-processing capabilities (the ability to apply rules to the transformation and routing of information), and intelligent routing capabilities (the ability to identify messages, as well as the ability to route them to the appropriate location).

The services provided by message brokers can be put into several distinct categories: message transformation, rules processing, intelligent routing, message warehousing, flow control, repository services, directory services, management, APIs, and adapters. These categories, and more, will be discussed later in this chapter.

An advantage to message brokers is that they leave systems "where they are," minimizing change while still allowing data to be shared. In providing greater efficiency and flexibility, message brokers more closely resemble the way business "actually works"—automating functions currently performed manually, for example, sending sales reports through interoffice mail or walking data down the hall on disk. By mirroring "the way business works," the success of message brokers suggests that the EAI solution really addresses a business flow problem, with technology such as message brokers serving as the necessary infrastructure. This notion of the EAI solution as a solution to a process automation problem will be discussed in the next chapter.

Integration, not Perspiration

Message brokers are not new. They've been around, in one form or another, for years. Message broker vendors, such as Active Software, New Era of Networks (NEON), TSI Software, and SAGA Software, are really just transforming this long-standing concept into functional products. (A number of organizations, including the U.S. Department of Transportation and Federal Express, have spent millions of dollars creating customized message brokers that meet their particular business demands. In fact, many organizations have first-generation message brokers in place *and don't even realize it*.) NEON's message broker, MQ Integrator, grew from a project at Goldman Sachs. NEON built a message broker to serve the specific needs of the firm and, by further developing it, began selling it as a product. TSI Software's Mercator message broker was also the result of product evolution, growing out of their EDI-mapping products.

A number of major vendors are entering the message broker field. SAGA Software, for instance, has built a message broker (Sagavista) from the ground up, specifically to address the EAI problem. As the market for message brokers continues to grow, more of the larger vendors will begin to compete. Both Oracle and Microsoft have expressed interest in developing message brokers, but neither has come up with a reasonable approach . . . yet. Traditional middleware vendors, such as BEA (with their Tuxedo TP monitor), are presenting their products as EAI engines in spite of the fact that they are not true message brokers and fail to provide message broker capabilities. However, BEA, along with other transactional middleware vendors, are teaming up with message broker vendors to offer their customers the best of transactional and message brokers middleware—a trend that is going to continue as EAI architects and developers seek to leverage all EAI levels within a single technology and vendor.

While this competition will be interesting to monitor as time goes on, the immediate goal must be to understand the technology so that correct decisions can be made.

Why a New Direction?

Traditional middleware, such as message-oriented middleware (MOM—message-queuing software and pub/sub engines), solves only part of the EAI problem. Message brokers, by building *on top* of existing middleware technology, address the other part. For this reason, it is appropriate to call message brokers the "middleware of middleware" (see Figure 18.1).

A number of components of a business integration solution are neither middleware nor applications. They are routing, reformatting, and flow components. While these can be placed in an application, or middleware, they are a better architectural "fit" when they are placed in message brokers, providing a central point of integration. So, given this, what do message brokers offer? With the technology so new, vendors have taken individual approaches to addressing the message-brokering problem. Despite this lack of standardization, there remain some common components. These are a message transformation layer, a rules engine, and an intelligent routing mechanism (see Figure 18.2), along with a number of features we will discuss later in this chapter.

A message broker is a software system based on asynchronous, store-and-forward messaging. It manages interactions between applications and other information resources, utilizing abstraction techniques. They work simply. An

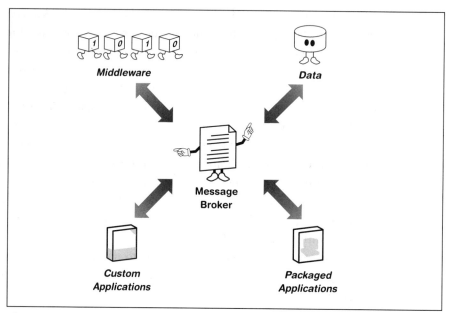

Figure 18.1   Message brokers are able to integrate many different types of middleware, as well as applications and databases.

application puts (publishes) a message to the message broker. Another application gets (subscribes to) the message. In order to work successfully, the applications need not be session connected, which eliminates, from the outset, the primary scalability problem associated with most integration technologies. However, message brokers do even more. They also extend the basic messaging paradigm by mediating the interaction between the applications, allowing the publishers and subscribers of information to remain truly anonymous. They transform and convert data, reformat and reconstitute messages, and route information to any number of targets (determined by centrally defined business rules applied to the message content).

To be the solid foundation necessary for a successful EAI strategy, message brokers must offer genuine "any-to-any" and "many-to-many" capabilities. ("Any-to-any" refers to the ability to connect diverse applications and other information resources, the consistency of approach, and the importance of a common look-and-feel for all connected resources. "Many-to-many" means that, once a resource is connected and publishing information, information is easily reusable by any other application that requires it.) The publish/subscribe

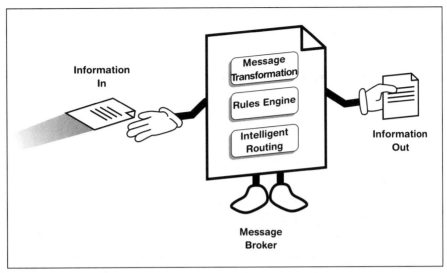

Figure 18.2   Message brokers have three primary components: the message transformation layer, the rules engine, and the intelligent routing mechanism.

messaging model is one technique in use to address this need. Its popularity suggests that it is an effective one.

We have noted that vendors have taken a number of approaches to solving the message-brokering problem. That being the case, it is clear that not all message brokers are alike. A complete message-brokering solution demands an underlying messaging system, a brokering layer (or "rules engine"), a connectivity (adapter) framework, design and development tools, and system management and administration tools. Some products currently on the market provide pieces to the puzzle, but not the puzzle itself. A systems integrator is often needed to combine those pieces with the other pieces necessary to complete the puzzle. The success of the finished "picture" will depend on the design and architecture of the solution—that is, how well the pieces integrate will determine their scalability. IS organizations need to carefully "kick the tires" in order to select the right solution for an EAI initiative.

While message brokers use messages, it's difficult to fit them into the MOM category. This is not to suggest that message brokers don't rely on the concept of a "message." They do. But, more than that, they provide value-added services from the uppermost layer in the ISO model, the application layer. Message brokers are different because of the services they offer above and beyond traditional middleware.

Considering the Source (and Target)

When considering the details of a message broker, the cart is sometimes put ahead of the horse. The first step in evaluating a message broker must include an evaluation of the types of systems to be integrated.

As we have noted in Chapters 1–5, message brokers interface with source and target applications at the data level, the application interface level, the method level, and the user interface level. This reality indicates that source and target systems may be any number of entities—database servers, Web servers, host applications, user screens, distributed objects, ERP applications, as well as custom or proprietary applications. The strength of message brokers is that they are able to link any number of different types of systems, adjusting to the differences between all source and target systems. They are able to do this by exposing an application programming interface, and sometimes an adapter (adapters will be discussed later in this chapter).

It's also important to note here that message brokers adhere to the noninvasive EAI model, where the source and target applications typically don't require a tremendous number of changes in order for message brokers to move information

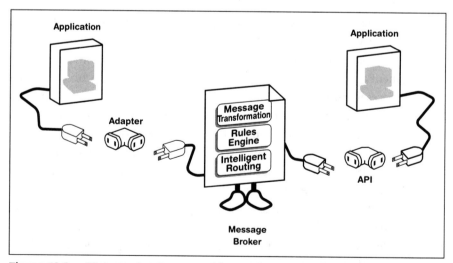

Figure 18.3   **Message brokers provide services to applications through an application programming interface, or an adapter.**

between them. In fact, in many cases, no changes to the source or target applications are required. This is due to the fact that message brokers are able to leverage many points-of-integration that don't require that the application itself change. Examples of these points-of-integration include database access, screen scraping, defined APIs, and middleware.

The application programming interface is nothing more than the mechanism that allows an application to access the services of a message broker (see Figure 18.3). By contrast, adapters are able to link deeply into an application, or data repository, moving information from a source application without having to invoke the native interfaces.

Message Transformation Layer

The message transformation layer understands the format of all messages being passed among the applications and changes (transforms) those messages "on the fly." The data from one message is restructured into a new message that makes sense to the receiving application(s). The message transformation layer is the "Rosetta stone" of the system. It provides a common dictionary that contains information on how each application communicates outside itself (application externalization), as well as which pieces of information have meaning to which applications (see Figure 18.4).

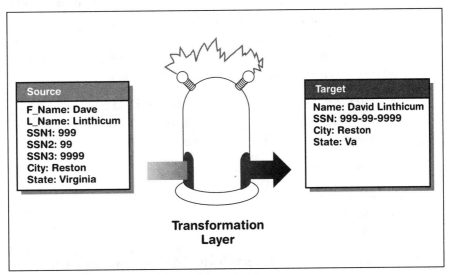

Figure 18.4   The message transformation layer

Message transformation layers generally contain parsing and pattern-matching methods that describe the structure of any message format. Message formats are then constructed from pieces that represent each field encapsulated within a message. Once the message has been broken down to its component parts, the fields may be recombined to create a new message.

Most brokers can handle most types of messages, including fixed, delimited, and variable. Messages are reformatted using an interface the message broker provides, which may be as primitive as an API or as easy to use as a GUI.

Message transformation layers generally store application information in a repository (see the description in the section "Repository Services," later in this chapter) that keeps track of the source system, the format of the message, the target system, and the desired format of the target system. For example, a SAP system tracks customer information in a very different manner than a Baan system. In order to exchange customer information between the two systems, the information must be reformatted. This reformatting, or transformation, may include a schema conversion and data conversion. It is carried out so that consistent application semantics between all integrated source and target applications can be assured.

Schema Conversions

A **schema conversion** is the process of changing the structure of a message, and thus remapping the schema, so that it is acceptable for the target system. Though it's not difficult in and of itself, EAI architects need to understand that this process must occur dynamically within the message broker. For example, if a message containing Accounts Receivable information arrives from a DB2 system existing on a mainframe, it may look something like this:

```
Cust_No.            Alphanumeric  10
Amt_Due             Numeric       10
Date_of_Last_Bill   Date
```

With the following information:

```
AB99999999
560.50
09/17/98
```

The client/server system, created to produce the annual report, receives the information and must store it according to the following schema:

Customer_Number	Numeric	20
Money_Due	Numeric	8
Last_Billed	Alphanumeric	10

As this example clearly shows, the schema found in the client/server system is different from the schema found in the DB2 system. Moving information from the DB2 system (the source system) to the client/server system (the target system) without a schema conversion most likely would result in a system error due to the incompatibility of the formats. In order to communicate successfully, the information in "Cust_No" (which is alphanumeric and holds 10 positions) needs to be converted to all-numeric information, capable of holding 20 digits, or positions. All data that is not numeric (that is, letters) has to be transformed into numeric data. This can be accomplished by either deleting all characters entirely when transforming "Cust_No" to "Customer_Number" or converting characters into numeric representations (that is, A=1, B=2, and so on). This process can be defined within the rules-processing layer of the message broker by creating a rule to transform data dynamically, depending on its content and schema. Moving information from one system to another demands that the schema/format of the message be altered on the fly—as the information is being transferred from one system to the next (see Figure 18.5).

While most message brokers can map any schema to any other schema, it is wise to anticipate extraordinary circumstances. For example, when converting information extracted from an object-oriented database and placing that information in a relational database, the object schema must be converted into a relational representation before the data within the message can be converted. The

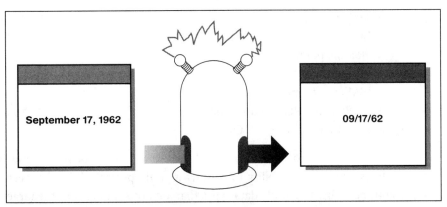

Figure 18.5   Transforming message formats/schemas dynamically

same holds true when moving information from a relational database to an object-oriented database. Most message brokers break the message moving into their environment into a common format and then transform it into the appropriate message format for the target system that's receiving the message. As we have already noted, the rules-processing engine within the message broker allows for appropriate programming to take place.

Data Conversion

In the previous transformation example, information in "Cust_No" (alphanumeric and holding 10 positions) needs to be converted to all-numeric with a capability of 20 positions. The "alpha" component of "Cust_No" (that is, the letters) must be dealt with in another manner—either by being deleted or converted, or by changing the nature of the target application to accept letters. Deleting characters entirely, or converting them into numeric representations, are examples of data conversion. The key in making data conversion successful is to determine the data format of the source and target applications, assess the difference between them (for example, which data elements need to be extracted and converted, and where they ultimately need to be placed). Most message brokers are able to understand most message schemas through message identifications. Therefore, they automatically convert data to a workable format. At times, however, it is necessary to program a rule to address a specific data type conversion problem. The conversion of numeric information to alphanumeric information (and vice versa) generally requires such a programmed rule.

While many formats exist within most EAI problem domains, we will confine our attention to the following:

- Alphanumeric
- Binary integers
- Floating point values
- Bit-fields
- IBM mainframe floating points
- COBOL and PL/I picture data
- Binary large objects (BLOBS)

In addition to these formats, there are a number of formatting issues to address, such as the ability to convert logical operators (bits) between systems and the ability to handle data types that are not supported in the target system.

These issues often require significant customization in order to facilitate successful communication between systems.

Within the domain of data conversion, values are managed in two ways: carrying over the value from the source to the target system without change or modifying the data value on the fly. Modifying, or changing, data value can be accomplished through the use of either an algorithm or a "look-up" table. One or more of the source application attributes may use an algorithm to change the data or to create new data. For example, attributes in the source application may represent "Amount Sold" and hold the value 8. Another attribute, "Cost of Goods Sold," may contain the value 4. However, in the target application, these attributes may have to populate a new attribute, "Gross Margin," which is the amount sold less the cost of the goods sold. In order to make this communication successful, the algorithm "Amount Sold" − "Cost of Goods Sold" has to be applied.

Algorithms of this type represent nothing more than the type of data conversions that have been done for years when populating data warehouses and data marts. Now, in addition to these simple algorithms, it is possible to aggregate, combine, and summarize the data in order to meet the specific requirements of the target application.

When using the look-up table scenario, it might be necessary to convert to an arbitrary value. "ARA" in the source system may refer to a value in the Accounts Receivable system, but before determining this, it must be checked against the look-up table. For instance, a message broker may use a currency conversion table to convert dollars to yen. This table may be embedded in a simple procedure or, more likely, in a database connected to the message broker. It's also possible for the message broker to invoke a remote application server function to convert the amount.

The EAI architect or developer may encounter special circumstances that have to be finessed. For example, the length of a message attribute may be unknown, or the value may be in an unknown order. In cases like these, it is necessary to use the rules-processing capability of the message broker to convert the problem values into the proper representation for the target system.

Intelligent Routing

Intelligent routing, sometimes referred to as "flow control" or "content-based routing," builds on the capabilities of both the rules layer and the message trans-

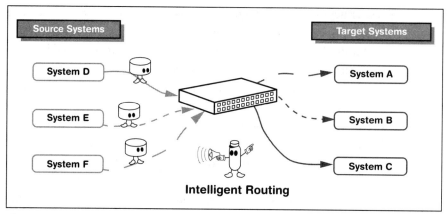

Figure 18.6 **Intelligent routing means identifying the message and sending it on to the proper destination.**

formation layer. In this scenario, the message broker can identify a message coming from the source application and route it to the proper target application, transforming it if required. For example, when a message arrives at the message broker, it is analyzed and identified as coming from a particular system and/or subsystem. Once the message is identified, and the message schema is understood, the applicable rules and services are applied to the processing of the message, including message transformation. Once processed, the message broker, based on how it is programmed, will route the message to the correct target system (see Figure 18.6). This all happens virtually instantaneously, with as many as a thousand of these operations simultaneously.

Rules Processing

The rules-processing engine, found within most message brokers, provides the EAI architect and developer with the ability to create rules to control the processing and distribution of messages. In short, rules processing is an application development environment supported by the message broker to address the special requirements of integrating applications. By using rules engines, it becomes possible to implement intelligent message routing and transformation. For example, at times a message may be required by a second target application. At other times a message will have to be routed to two or more applications. In order to address each situation, messages should be able to be routed to any number of target applications that extract and transform data from any number of source applications. A truly flexible solution requires a rules engine to make these formatting and routing decisions dynamically. Combining a rules engine with a message transformation layer allows for such a solution to be realized.

A rules engine is, in effect, an application between applications, one that does nothing more than provide the logic for sharing information. Each rules engine solves an intelligent routing and transformation problem differently. Most have the capability of testing a message to determine fields and values. Most often, rules engines use traditional Boolean logic (IF, ELSE, and OR) and high-level languages to create rules and to associate actions to each rule found to be true.

The rules-processing capabilities of message brokers should not be confused with traditional application servers. Application servers provide a full spectrum of element environments and tools. Most rules-processing engines only provide features sufficient to move a message from any number of source systems to any number of target systems. However, as message brokers mature, they are providing rules-processing services that rival those of application servers. As mentioned previously, vendors have gone so far as to integrate application servers with message brokers. This strategy combines the "best of both worlds" while addressing method-level EAI.

Rules processing generally relies on scripting languages rather than more complex programming languages (such as Java and C++), and interpreters rather than compilers. However, the way in which each message broker processes rules varies from vendor to vendor and from message broker to message broker.

Rules are created through either the rules editor (like a program editor) or a wizard. The program editor creates rules by allowing commands to be entered into the message broker. These commands may be stored as a simple text file, or, in more sophisticated message brokers, they may be stored within the repository. The rules wizard guides the user through the selection of each rule that is being applied to a particular message, group of messages, or events. For example, the wizard may ask if the message should be processed as soon as it comes into the message broker or at a particular time of day. Such an option is especially useful for things like updating customer information in a database, when such updates might be better made during off-peak hours. The wizard may also inquire regarding the transformation of information between the source and target systems, including the logic that may be required. It may create the opportunity to take many things into account at the same time, such as checking for states and events that other systems may provide. For example, it may not be advisable to update the SAP database, if the last update to the database produced an error message or an unstable state. Or certain users might have to be logged on before proceeding with a certain type of message processing. It may be beneficial to wait for a specific event before extracting information from a source system.

Because rules processing is truly programming, the "sky is the limit" as to what can be done. Messages can be generated based on sales events over a million dollars. Other applications based on the monitoring of events for states can be invoked. Anything that can be programmed can be made part of the rules processing. With rules engines becoming more powerful, and vendors providing easier mechanisms to create rules, the "sky" is certainly attainable.

Message Warehousing

Another feature of message brokers is **message warehousing**. A message warehouse is a database that, as an option, is able to store messages that flow through the message broker (see Figure 18.7). In general, message brokers provide this message persistence facility to meet several requirements: message mining, message integrity, message archiving, and auditing.

Message mining implies that the message warehouse is a quasi-data warehouse, allowing for the extraction of business data to support decisions. For example, it is possible to use the message warehouse to determine the characteristics, and amount, of new customer information that is being processed through the message broker. All new sales orders for a given period of time can be displayed. Off-the-shelf data mining and reporting tools work wonderfully for such applications.

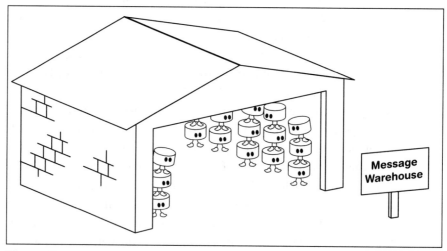

Figure 18.7   Message warehousing

In most instances, the messages that are stored in the message warehouse are stored without modifications. However, in some cases, the messages go through a data warehouse like they would an aggregation, or transformation process. In other words, the data is combined and altered so that it will make sense to the average business user. In general, EAI architects and application programmers accomplish this through the rules-processing mechanism of the message broker, or they may employ an outside application to alter the message for storage.

Message warehousing is able to provide services such as message integrity because the warehouse itself provides a natural, persistent state for message traffic. If the server goes down, the message warehouse may act as a **persistent buffer**, or **queue**, to store messages that would otherwise be lost. Messages may then be resent or compared with other message warehouses on the network to insure message transfer integrity. The underlying principle here is that of persistent message queuing supported by traditional message-oriented middleware. This also provides stateful messaging, or the ability to maintain states between two or more systems even when using asynchronous messaging, which by definition is a cohesive, not coupled, mechanism.

Message archiving provides the message broker user with the ability to store months of message traffic in an archive for auditing or other purposes. For example, it might be useful at one point in the future to be able to look back and examine the message traffic of a particular day. Message archiving allows information to be restored for analysis. In most cases, EAI administrators maintain message archives for just over a year, although no actual standard currently exists.

Auditing means using the message warehouse to determine the health of the EAI solution, and provides the ability to solve problems. For example, by using the auditing facilities of a message broker, one can determine message traffic loads, message content variations, and the number of messages requiring transformation. Auditing also tracks messages that change, the state before the transformation, and the state following.

Repository Services

Today, many message brokers embrace the concept of a repository, a database of information about source and target applications, which may include data elements, inputs, processes, outputs, and the inter-relationships among applications. Although many experts view repositories as part of the world of application development, they do not question their value to the world of EAI.

EAI-enabled repositories, in their simplest form, provide the message broker user with a database of information pertaining to:

- Location of system (directory)
- Security parameters
- Message schema information
- Metadata
- Enabling technology
- Transformation information
- Rules and logic for message processing
- Design and architecture information (e.g., UML)
- Object information

The goal is to provide a sophisticated repository that is capable of keeping track of not only rudimentary information (such as directory data), but more sophisticated information about the source and target systems (such as metadata, message schemas, and even security and ownership). The repository should provide all the information required by the EAI architect and programmer to locate any piece of information within the enterprise, and to link it to any other piece of information. In essence, the repository is the master directory for the entire EAI problem domain.

Many of the concepts regarding repositories have been borrowed from the application development world. Rules, logic, objects, and metadata are still tracked within a repository. The difference is that, by using the repository with a message broker, other less sophisticated information such as encrypted passwords, network addresses, protocol translation services, and even error code translations and maintenance information is also being tracked.

Within more sophisticated message brokers, the repository is becoming the "center of the universe," able to go to both the source and target systems in order to discover necessary information such as metadata and available business processes. Engaged in this "auto-discovery," the message broker will be able to populate the repository with this information, as well as any other information that may be required. Ultimately, the repository will become the enterprise metadata repository, able to track all systems and databases connected to the message broker.

With the foregoing being the case, the value of a repository is clear. With the repository as a common reference point for all connected processes and databases, integrating data and methods is as straightforward as finding their equivalents and joining them together. The repository can also track the rules that the EAI architect and developer apply within the EAI problem domain. Moreover, because the repository knows the schema of both the source and the target systems, it also contains information for the proper transformation of messages flowing from source to target. In many cases, this transformation can be automatically defined, never requiring the user to be involved in the definition of the transformation procedure.

Repositories are, however, only the storage mechanisms in this scenario. The message broker must read the information out of the repository and carry out the appropriate process. In addition to the message broker engine, the graphical user interface that accompanies most message brokers provides EAI architects and developers with a mechanism to alter the repository and so alter the behavior of the message broker.

Graphical User Interface

One of the wonderful realities of the message broker is that it is middleware "with a face"—or, at least, with a graphical user interface. This interface allows the user to create rules, link applications, and define transformation logic (see Figure 18.8).

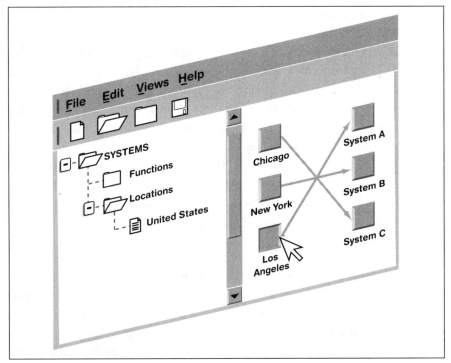

Figure 18.8   The message broker graphical user interface

While the features and functions of interfaces vary from vendor to vendor, all vendors make the claim that they simplify the EAI process. While some provide only the most basic features for justifying this claim—such as scripting and rudimentary administration—the newest versions include such features as wizard systems to define rules and transformation, along with an interface that allows the user to drill down to any level of detail within any connected system. These interfaces can depict an EAI solution, including connected systems, rules, and message routing, using diagrams that bring the entire solution to light. More than simply setting up the solution, these graphical user interfaces also provide administration features, such as the capability to monitor message traffic, the performance of the message brokers, the status of connected systems, and mechanisms to route around problems.

Directory Services

Because message brokers deal with distributed systems, they require directory services to locate, identify, use, and authorize network resources for those systems. The benefit of directory services is that they provide a single point of entry for applications and middleware (e.g., message brokers). They also support the use of a shared set of directory and naming service standards. Directory services act as guides among the thousands of resources available to applications and middleware.

Using directory services, the message broker or EAI developer can build applications that can intelligently locate resources anywhere on the network. Directories know where to find these resources on behalf of applications. They track them as they are reconfigured, moved, or deleted. For example, an e-mail application can locate a user group, a word-processing application can find a printer, and a client/server application can find a database—no matter where these resources exist on the network. Application objects exist on the network rather than on certain servers. It is, therefore, essential that developers have a common infrastructure for locating the object.

Directory services are nothing more than a way to classify resources on the network in a way consistent with any other method of classification. In biology, biologists classify living things according to kingdom, phylum, class, order, family, genus, and species. Directory services identify and classify all computer systems by moving down a hierarchy, using a naming system to determine the direction at the branches.

In the world of networks, there are directory services such as the Domain Name System (DNS), Novell's NetWare Directory System and Directory Services,

Netscape Communications' Directory Server, Microsoft's Active Directory, and X.500. DNS gives all Internet users the ability to resolve server names. It has been a tremendous resource for years, but it is limited to that one, simple function.

Management

Administration and management of the EAI problem domain is primarily the responsibility of the management layer of the message broker. Unfortunately, too many message brokers are marketed with little or no management. This is due to the level of the technology's maturity and the fact that several enterprise management tools are currently available on the market. However, many of these general-purpose management tools, such as BMC's Patrol and Computer Associate's UniCenter, fail to address the management requirements of EAI, which include the ability to monitor message traffic, message integrity, and the coordination of the distribution of messages among target applications.

EAI solutions require the ability to start and stop source and target applications, as well as the ability to monitor important statistics, such as performance, message integrity, and the general functioning of the entire EAI problem domain. Message broker vendors who are anticipating the needs of EAI management are creating separate products to address the specific needs of EAI management while enabling existing enterprise management tools to handle the special needs of EAI. While it is too early to predict with certainty, it appears that a new generation of management tools built specifically for the EAI marketplace is on the horizon. However, until that generation arrives, the user must either depend on what is bundled with the message broker or create his or her own management infrastructure.

Adapters

The notion of adapters for message brokers has been considered for years; however, as with so many other things, each vendor has had its own concept of exactly what an adapter should be. To date, there is no standard. (EAI architects should note that, regardless of vendor, the capabilities of many adapters are exaggerated.)

Adapters are layers between the message broker interface and the source or target application—for example, a set of "libraries" that map the differences between two distinct interfaces—the message broker interface and the native interface of the source or target application—and that hide the complexities of that interface from the end user or even from the EAI developer using the message broker. For instance , a message broker vendor may have adapters for several different source and target applications (such as SAP R/3, Baan, and PeopleSoft) or adapters for certain types of databases (such as Oracle, Sybase, or DB2), or even adapters for specific brands of middleware. As time marches on, adapters are becoming more sophisticated, trading a set of libraries that developers must play around with for binary interfaces that require little, if any, programming. Adapters are also getting smarter, with intelligence placed within the adapter and with adapters running at the source and target systems in order to better capture events.

There are two types of adapters in the world of message brokers: thin adapters and thick adapters; and adapters may behave in two different ways: dynamic and static.

Thin Adapters

Thin adapters are offered by the most popular message brokers today. In most cases, they are simple API wrappers, or binders, that map the interface of the source or target system to a common interface supported by the message broker (see Figure 18.9). In other words, they simply perform an API binding trick, binding one API to another.

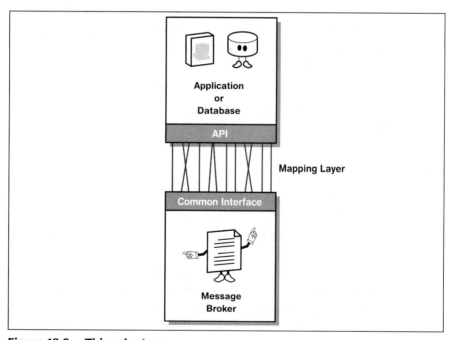

Figure 18.9   Thin adapters

Wrappers Are Also Thin Adapters

Other examples of thin adapters are wrapping application interfaces using open interface standards, such as CORBA or COM. Here again, one interface is being traded off for another. However, in this case, there is the advantage of providing a common, open interface.

Most ERP vendors are seeking to create open interfaces to their applications, at both the data and process levels, making integration easier to implement with traditional tools, while reducing the risk of proprietary interfaces. For example, SAP is seeking to provide interfaces based on CORBA and Java. This is clearly a move in the right direction.

Thin adapters have the advantage of simplicity in implementation. Because there is no additional "thick" layer of software between source and target applications, there is greater granular control. They have a number of disadvantages, though. Because nothing more than trading one interface software for another is being accomplished, thin adapters impact performance without increasing functionality. Quite a bit of programming is still required. Complicating matters is the fact that common APIs that are being mapped are almost always proprietary.

Thick Adapters

Thick adapters, in contrast to thin adapters, provide a lot of software and functionality between the message broker infrastructure and the source or target applications. The thick adapter's layer of abstraction makes managing the movement or invoking processes painless (see Figure 18.10). Because the abstraction layer and the manager manage the difference between all the applications requiring integration, there is almost no need for programming.

Thick interfaces are capable of accomplishing this because they provide a layer of sophisticated software that hides the complexities of the source and target application interfaces from the message broker user. The user sees only a business-like representation of the process and the metadata information as managed by the abstraction layer and the adapter. In many cases, the user connects many systems through this abstraction layer and the graphical user interface, without ever having to resort to hand-coding.

Repositories play a major role in the thick adapter scenario. As we have noted, the repository is able to understand much of the information about the

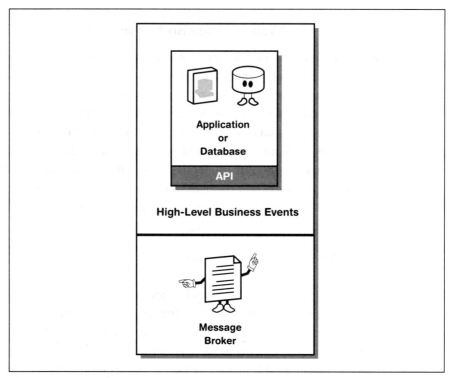

Figure 18.10   Thick adapters place an abstraction layer on top of the application interfaces.

source and target applications and is able to use that information as a mechanism to interact with those applications on behalf of the message broker.

Moreover, several abstraction layers may be created around the types of applications to be integrated. For example, there may be an abstraction for common middleware services (such as distributed objects, message-oriented middleware, and transactional middleware). There may also be an abstraction layer for packaged applications and another layer that is able to address the integration of relational and nonrelational databases. However, the complexities of the interfaces that each entity (middleware, packaged applications, and databases) employs are hidden from the end user.

Message broker vendors are moving toward thick adapters. Progress is slowed by the fact that thick adapters require an inordinate amount of time to develop, as much as six times the time a thin adapter might take. But, as EAI becomes more sophisticated, enterprises will continue to look for more sophisticated solutions,

---

Centralized versus Distributed Adapters

Two distinct architectures are emerging in the world of adapters: distributed and centralized. **Centralized adapters**, as the name suggests, are adapters that run with the message broker. Generally, these are thin adapters that only bind the message broker's API to the API of the source or target application.

Just as centralized adapters are thin adapters, **distributed adapters** are thick adapters that exist on the message broker as well as on the source or target application. Running an adapter on the application being integrated allows many processes about the source or target application to be better determined, processes like capturing events, monitoring states, or even restarting the application as required. More to the point, because the adapter is really in two parts, it is better able to coordinate the transfer of information between the message broker and the source or target application.

---

solutions that require no programming and provide an easy, business-like method to view the integration of the enterprise. Thick adapters are the future.

Static and Dynamic Adapters

In addition to thick versus thin, there is also the notion of static versus dynamic adapters. **Static adapters**, the most common today, have to be manually coded with what's contained within the source and the target systems. For example, static adapters have no mechanism for understanding anything about the schema of connected databases and therefore must be configured by hand to receive information from the source schema. What's more: if the connected database schema changes, static adapters have no mechanism for updating their configuration with the new schema.

In contrast, dynamic adapters are able to "learn" about the source or target systems connected to them through a discovery process that the adapters go through when first connected to the application or data source. This discovery process typically means reading the database schema, information from the repository, or perhaps the source code to determine the structure, content, and application semantics of the connected system. In addition to simply learning about the connected system, dynamic adapters are also able to relearn if something changes within the connected system over time. For instance, changing the customer number attribute name will automatically be understood by a dynamic adapter.

Using an API

In addition to adapters, message brokers leverage APIs as a mechanism to access the services of source and target applications, which is really nothing special. A message broker API is very much like the API of a traditional message-oriented middleware product. The advantage is that, with a message broker, many applications can be integrated. Traditional message-oriented middleware, as we have noted, is best for linking one application with another.

Topologies

As we have noted, message brokers use a hub-and-spoke topology. The message broker, as hub, rests between the source and target applications being integrated in a configuration that resembles a star (see Figure 18.11). While this configuration is the most traditional one, it is possible to leverage message brokers using other topologies, such as a bus or multihub.

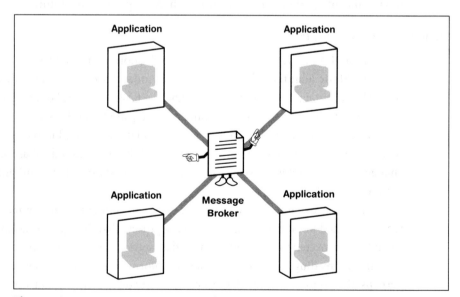

Figure 18.11   Hub-and-spoke configuration

In the bus configuration, the message broker sits on the network bus and provides message broker services to other systems on the bus (see Figure 18.12). This scenario is effective when message brokers play a smaller role within the EAI problem domain.

In the multihub configuration, a number of message brokers are linked, with the source and target applications linked to any of the brokers in the configuration (see Figure 18.13). The advantage of this configuration is the ability to scale, making it possible to integrate a virtually unlimited number of source and target applications. As more applications than a single message broker can handle need to be integrated, then more message brokers can be added to the network.

As message brokers mature and become more sophisticated, there is a clear movement away from the simple hub-and-spoke configuration toward the multihub configuration. However, the transition is not a smooth one. Some message brokers are able to support multihub configurations, while others are unable to intelligently share the message-processing load between them. The message brokers able to exist in a multihub configuration are successful by learning to "share the load" with the other message brokers on the network. Load-balancing mechanisms that are able to off-load message-processing work to message brokers with available capacity help make it possible to simply add message brokers to the network. They locate the broker, configure it, replicate the repository, and put the message broker to work.

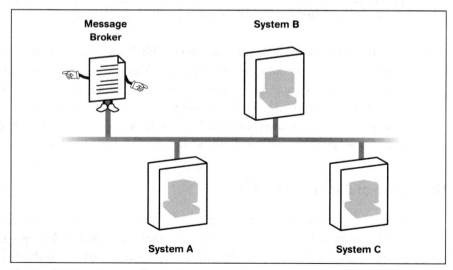

Figure 18.12   Bus configuration

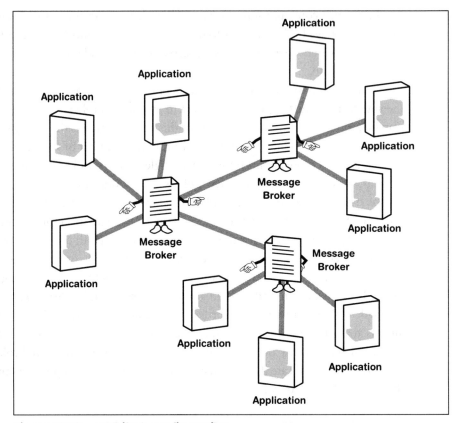

Figure 18.13   Multihub configuration

In addition to the ability to scale, the multihub configuration provides a fail-safe service as well. Because several message brokers share the network load, if one should fail, others are able to continue processing the messages. However, these fail-safe features vary from vendor to vendor, with some more effective than others. Still, with the message broker the heart of the enterprise in the context of EAI, it makes sense to incorporate sound mechanisms to protect it from failure.

The Future of EAI and Brokers

Are message brokers the next generation of middleware? Message brokers fill a need that many larger companies have and that traditional middleware is incapable of solving. However, as with any new technology that is introduced into an enterprise, there is a certain degree of initial confusion.

Most message-brokering products on the market address solutions to the same problems very differently. It would be a great idea for the vendors to "get on the same sheet of music" and offer a standardized product. At this time, it is easier to promote the concept of the message broker than it is to promote a particular product.

Message brokers, at least the core engine, are destined to become commodity products because many perform only rudimentary functions. In an effort to differentiate their product, many message broker vendors are putting layer upon layer of value-added software on top of the core message broker engine. Thin adapters are giving way to thick adapters. Vendors are learning that it is better to hide the complexities of enterprise systems behind abstraction layers and put a business face on all the "geeky" little details.

These abstraction layers save the end user from having to deal with the complexities of the technology and put them in a better position to take care of the business at hand. Given this reality, when all is said and done, message brokers may turn out to be more about business automation than middleware.

CHAPTER NINETEEN

Process Automation and EAI

"Any sufficiently advanced bug is indistinguishable from a feature."
— Rick Kulawiec

We have clearly defined EAI as the science of integrating many applications and data stores so that they provide value to one another. **Process automation (sometimes referred to as "workflow") is the science of managing the movement of data and the invocation of processes in the correct and proper order. Process automation provides another layer of easily defined and centrally managed processes (or workflows) that exist on top of an existing set of processes and data contained within a set of enterprise applications.**

The goal of our discussion is to define a mechanism to tie together any relevant existing enterprise processes so that they support the flow of information and logic between them, obtaining the maximum amount of value from each other. Process automation views middleware, or the "plumbing," as a commodity and generally provides easy-to-use visual interfaces for binding these processes together and, along the way, creating visual process automation or workflow models.

While some may dispute the relevance of process automation and EAI, we would argue that process automation is ultimately where EAI is heading—although there is still a long way to go to get the plumbing (the middleware) right. In spite of the existing difficulties, many EAI vendors are busily promoting process automation as a part of their EAI technology offering. Their strategy is clear—they are anxious to join the world of high-end process automation modeling tools with the new offering of EAI-enabled middleware, such as message brokers and application servers.

What *Is* Process Automation?

Most business processes have already been automated. That's the good news. The bad news is that they tend to be loosely coupled and to exist on different systems. For example, adding a customer to a packaged accounting application may establish the customer in one system, while it is necessary to use another system entirely to perform a credit check on the customer and still another to process an invoice (see Figure 19.1). Clearly, not only do these systems need to share information, but they need to share that information in an orderly and efficient manner.

The goal of process automation, and of EAI as a whole, is to automate the data movement and process flow so that another layer of process automation will

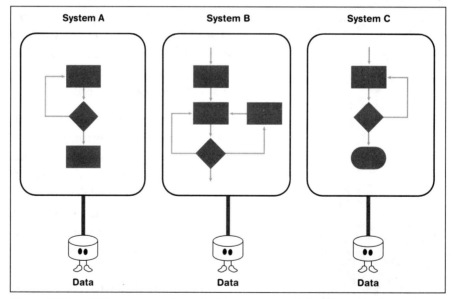

Figure 19.1   While many automated processes exist within most organizations, they tend to be loosely coupled or not coupled at all.

exist over and above the processes encapsulated in existing systems (see Figure 19.2). In other words, process automation completes EAI, allowing the integration of systems not only by sharing information readily, but also by managing the sharing of that information with easy-to-use tools.

Process automation is best defined as the passing of information from participating system to participating system and applying appropriate rules in order to achieve a business objective. This is true whether or not the business processes are automated. For example, the processing of an insurance claim or the verification of an expense report are business events that can be automated with process automation.

The process flow logic, generally, only has to do with process flow and is not a traditional programming logic (such as user interface processing, database

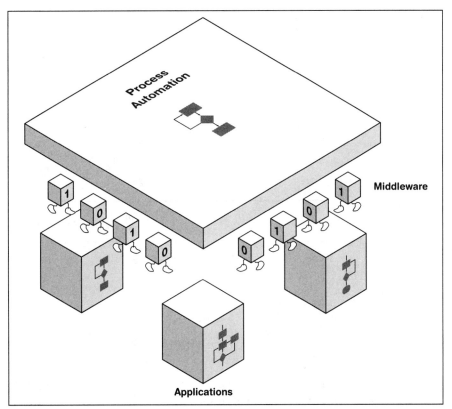

Figure 19.2 Process automation is another layer of process and data movement management that exists on top of the existing enterprise processes.

updates, or the execution of transactions). In most process automation scenarios, the process logic is separated from the application logic. It functions solely to coordinate or manage the information flow between many source and target applications (see Figure 19.3). For example, before process automation, in order for an expense report to be processed, an employee first had to enter it into the expense reporting system. The employee then printed the expense report and submitted it to his or her manager for approval. After checking the report, the manager signed the report (when he or she found the time) and sent it to accounting for processing (with their packaged accounting system). If accounting discovered a problem, the report would be kicked back to the employee for correction.

It is hard to imagine a more inefficient and time-consuming process. Unfortunately, it is an equally credible process, one that many, many people would recognize.

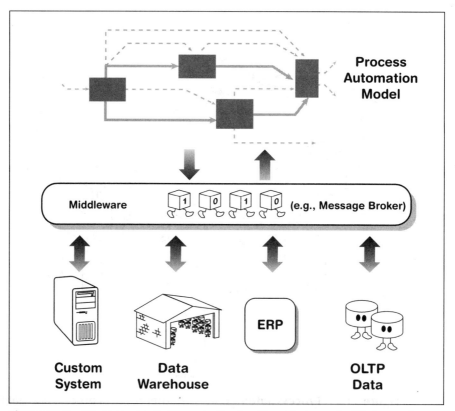

Figure 19.3   **The process logic coordinates the movement of information between many connected applications or data stores.**

With process automation in place, the information in the expense report example could be moved directly from the employee's expense-reporting system to the manager (perhaps via intra-enterprise e-mail) who could approve the expense. Even better, the system may be built in such a way that the manager need not view the report at all. If the report passes a set of predetermined criteria (procedural rules), then it could be automatically approved by the process automation layer and sent along to the accounting system for processing. The manager could receive automatic notice of the approval, and the employee could receive a notice that the check is on the way.

Such a system operates on three levels of technology (see Figure 19.4). At the uppermost layer is the process automation or workflow level. This is where the process automation–modeling tools and workflow engines exist, where the method of information movement is defined.

The next level down is the transformation, routing, and rules-processing layer. This is where the information movement and formatting actually occurs. Typically this layer is a message broker, but transaction-oriented middleware and distributed objects are applicable as well. This layer also applies rules to information moving from one system to the next, reformatting the information as required and reading and writing from the source or target systems interfaces, either through direct calls or through adapters.

The messaging system exists at the lowest level. This is the system responsible for moving information between the various connected applications. Although application servers and other enterprise middleware work here, it is typically message-oriented middleware such as IBM's MQSeries, JMS, or Microsoft's MSMQ.

What this schema clearly shows is that the most primitive layers rest toward the bottom while the more sophisticated layers are at the top. Information moves

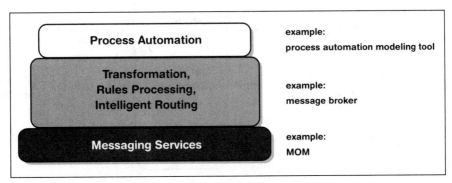

Figure 19.4   The three layers of process automation

up the layers from the source systems, where it is processed, and down the layers to the target system, where it is delivered.

Process automation saves steps and time. A process similar to the previous expense report example might take days or weeks, but with a good process automation approach, it could take mere seconds. Over the years, many business processes that have existed within organizations (on stovepipe systems) have been automated with fair success, but as we have seen with the EAI problem, there has not been a great deal of thought given to how all of these systems will share information.

Process Automation and EAI Levels

If process automation is defined as a mechanism to coordinate the movement of information among various connected systems, as well as the application of business logic, how does process automation relate to already established levels of EAI? In short, it encapsulates all levels, providing process management at the data, interface, method, and user interface levels (see Figure 19.5).

Process automation is application independent and should also be independent of the various types of application interfaces. At times access to applications

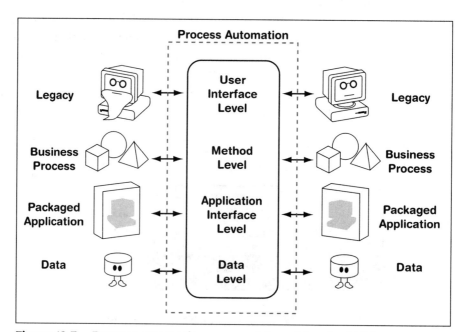

Figure 19.5   Process automation encapsulates all levels of EAI.

will be gained using the database as a point of integration, thus employing data-level EAI. In other cases, application interfaces or user interfaces will provide the point of integration, application interface level and user interface level, respectively.

At the method level, process automation extends method-level integration, building on the existing methods contained in existing applications. Method level represents the primary point of integration for process automation because creating a process automation layer really means creating additional program logic.

The marriage of method-level integration and process automation is the clear direction of EAI. As applications are integrated at the data and application interface levels (including user interface–level EAI), the next logical step is method-level EAI. Although more costly, method-level EAI will provide a better—and more permanent—solution for most problem domains. The nirvana of EAI rests with the marriage of method-level EAI with state-of-the-art process automation techniques and technology.

Implementing Process Automation

Integrating business applications into a process automation solution means removing the flow dependency from the application. The routing feature found in most process automation solutions allows relevant information to be extracted from any source or target application or data store. The benefit of this solution is that when a change in process flow or logic is required, only the model itself needs to be changed, not the applications that are a part of the process model. Moreover, using this type of approach, it is possible to reuse any source or target systems from model to model.

Like most things, implementing process automation solutions might seem relatively straightforward. It isn't. In many respects, it is similar in function to traditional business process re-engineering (BPR) solutions, only with a layer of automation.

Here are a few steps to consider:

1. Business processes that exist within the organization must be documented. This means that you have to understand all processes as well as data contained within the source and target enterprise systems. This step has to be done regardless of the type of EAI solution you are considering applying.

2. The missing processes required to tie the existing processes together must be defined. This means understanding not only how each process works, but also how each must leverage the other to create a more efficient set of processes.

3. The processes using process automation technology to tie these processes together must be executed.

Documenting Processes

While it would be nice if a unified approach existed to properly document the processes found in source and target systems, it is not the reality. Approaches will vary depending on many technical and political issues. There are, however, some commonalities. They include:

- Reading application documentation, including system and application design graphics and text
- Reading application interface documentation
- Reviewing database schemas for applications
- Reading source code

Defining Processes

Most process automation solutions provide a way to graphically represent processes, clearly depicting business activities, defining how information flows between them, and showing the logic that controls that flow.

Executing Processes

There are only a few approaches to executing processes. They include logical, physical read-only, and physical read-write (see Figure 19.6).

The **logical approach** refers to executing the process automation model without actually changing states (e.g., invoking processes or changing the database) at the source or target applications. This is a good approach for testing the process automation model without absorbing the risk of making real changes inside critical enterprise systems. Of course, this approach does not solve the problem at hand, but it does provide simple modeling of some future, desired state.

The **physical read-only** approach means that the process automation tool is only able to read information from the source systems. While this protects the systems from a process layer gone wrong, it grants the ability to only read and move information, not update target systems. This approach is low risk, and it is underpowered, because reading and processing information typically does little good unless you're able to affect a target system.

The **physical read-write** approach means that the process automation software has full access to the source and target systems. While this is the most desir-

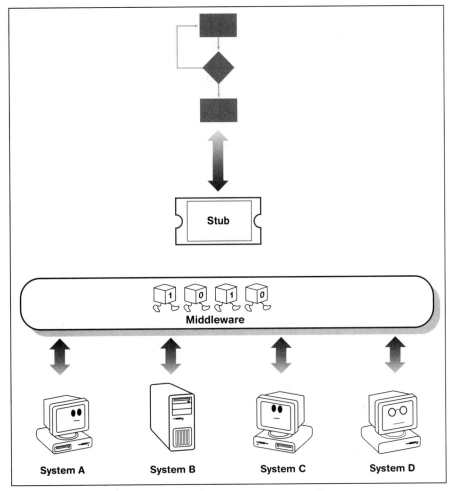

Figure 19.6   Logical versus physical process automation

able approach, it also carries the greatest risk. A flaw in the process model could result in a source or target system left in an unstable or incorrect state. This may be avoided by leveraging test systems independent of the mission-critical enterprise systems. While the cost is great, the ability to mediate risks provides an even greater cost savings in the long run.

Tools and Approaches

As with every type of EAI, a set of technologies and tools may be used to approach the problem. With process automation, a modeling tool provides the user with the technology to depict process automation or workflow graphically (see Figure 19.7).

There are three components of a process automation model:

- The processes and applicable logic
- Real entities, such as organizations or people
- The source and target systems

Each process- or workflow-modeling tool provides a different approach, but they generally model the preceding components. The process-modeling tool binds the components together in order to create the final solution. The process model is able to model:

- The processes, either automated or manual
- The sequence of the processes

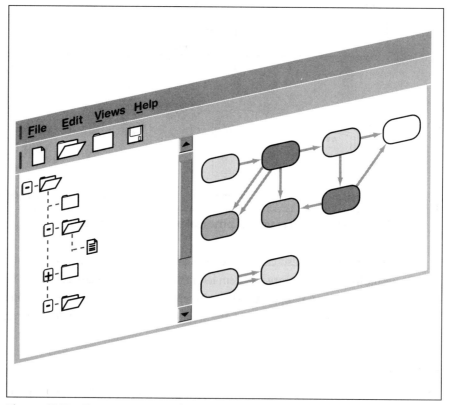

Figure 19.7   Process automation modeling tool

- The human resources involved in the processes, if any of the activities can take place at the same time
- The data found in all involved processes

Process Modeling

Creating the model using the process automation tool generally means drawing a diagram that depicts the processes, resources (systems and people), logic, and the movement of information between the systems. If the process becomes too complex, subprocesses can be defined and even reused from model to model. For example, a credit check may be a complex subprocess that is included within many separate processes. This is analogous to traditional structured programming, where subprograms or subroutines can be reused.

Drawing a process using a process automation–modeling tool is just a matter of selecting items (e.g., resource, process, and data) from a palate and pasting them on a diagram. Once the graphic diagram is in place, it is simply a question of defining the processes' connections and sequence. Using this model, it is possible to further define the process automation logic or the process logic that is being layered on top of the existing process logic.

Not surprisingly, each process automation tool approaches this generic description of activities in very different ways. However, as time goes on, de facto approaches will emerge, and each tool will align itself behind a commonly accepted approach.

Middleware Interfaces

A process automation tool is just that: a tool. Without the proper connections to the source or target systems, the process model that is created using such tools is incapable of executing a new model. In order to make those connections, it is necessary to employ traditional EAI-enabled middleware such as message brokers, application servers, and other middleware solutions.

To tell the truth, there is a disconnect between the high-end process-modeling tools and the middleware. For example, while there exist today message brokers that may certainly support an advanced process automation tool, they generally support more rudimentary tools that come with the message broker product. Advanced process automation tools do support middleware, but they require a fair amount of custom development work to occur on the back-end to integrate the applications. This is precisely the tradeoff that many EAI architects and developers are confronting today.

Things are slowly changing—in both directions. The middleware vendors are looking to incorporate sophisticated process automation within their products, either by building their own product or by licensing a tool from a process automation tool vendor. In addition, process automation tool vendors are either building or licensing the middleware. The value of both technologies is clear. This is the direction of EAI technology and EAI itself.

Workflow Standards

As with any technology, process automation has a standards body working in the background to create a common approach to process automation, as well as interfaces to the technology they access to execute the workflow models. While there are a few efforts afoot, the most significant of them is the Workflow Management Collation (WfMC) (www.aiim.org/wfmc).

The WfMC is a consortium of workflow/process automation vendors that is seeking to create a common approach and mechanisms to process automation. Until now, it has focused on the models themselves. Now it is focusing more on the plumbing that actually drives the models.

The WfMC is creating an Interoperability Specification (also known as "Interface 4") to define standards requests and responses to workflow engines. This specification defines how all requests and responses are encoded and transported over the enterprise network. These standards define requests and responses as well as the inputs and outputs. In short, they define how all workflow engines must interact with external systems, as well as other workflow engines. The standards also define the functions that all workflow engines must support, and how to define the coding needed to transport the requests.

Process Automation and EAI

Process automation is going to be a part of almost all EAI solutions, although the evolution of middleware has a long way to go to enable process automation to work. However, once it is understood how to connect any data and process point to any other data and process point, then workflow is certain to be the way the movement or flow of information is managed within or between enterprises.

Most EAI middleware vendors have experienced the process automation "vision" and have begun to create workflow and process automation–modeling tools to augment their existing middleware solutions. While this is a step in the right direction, most client organizations will want to pick and choose from the best-of-the-breed solutions. This means mixing and matching middleware, adapters, and process automation–modeling tools. While this is not possible today, once the industry responds with standard interfaces, definitions, and workflow engines, mixing and matching should be easy to accomplish to find the ultimate solution to a particular problem domain.

The customization of process automation models for particular vertical industries is another direction development is taking. For example, because information moves in rather the same way within banks, it is possible to create models that define best practices in process automation and integration within any set of banking systems (see Figure 19.8). Although shareable vertical market process models are still a few years away, the benefit is clear.

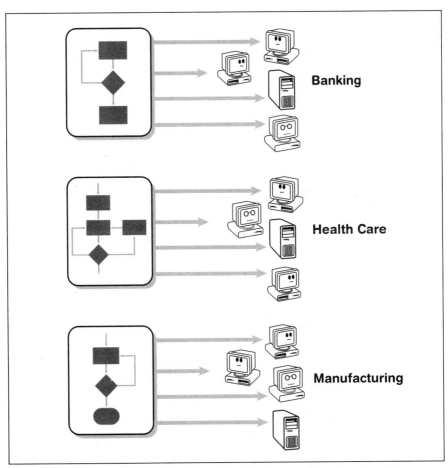

Figure 19.8   Process automation models will eventually be shared across verticals.

The question remains, "How will the next generation process automation tools and technology add value to a typical enterprise?" As businesses rapidly change over time, the need for a flexible information movement and integration infrastructure increases. While state-of-the-art EAI solutions, such as message brokers, provide flexible solutions today, a lot of work still remains to be done to bind systems together at the back-end. Every time things change, similar "plumbing" work must be repeated. Process automation provides the ultimate in flexibility because the user is removed from having to deal with the plumbing.

CHAPTER TWENTY

EAI Moving Forward

"**program**: *n.* A magic spell cast over a computer allowing it to turn one's input into error messages. *v. tr.* To engage in a pastime similar to banging one's head against a wall, but with fewer opportunities for reward."

—Unknown

As we conclude, let's look at the state of the art in EAI technology, as it exists now and where it is likely to be going in the next few years. If you're considering an EAI approach in your organization, now might be the time to "lay your cards on the table" and solidify some decisions.

EAI is clearly a complex problem. However, as with any complex problem, once it is broken down to its component parts, the solution becomes simply the aggregation of a number of solution sets. In this case, the solution sets include a combination of a variety of approaches and several types of technology.

As in the world of technology at large, the world of EAI is changing rapidly. The problem that EAI seeks to solve is morphing from the very simple to the very complex, even as it moves from a departmental problem to an enterprise-wide problem. As a result, few companies have been able to get ahead of the "EAI curve." They have yet to discover the full potential of EAI. As the problem grows, so does the potential benefit to the solution. So the technology continues to respond. The nirvana of EAI has yet to be created. In short, there's a great deal of work ahead of us.

Problem Domains Change

As EAI evolves, the problem domains are changing. No sooner is a "traditional" EAI problem solved (such as application-to-application and database-to-database integration), then EAI expertise and technology is being applied to more complex, but more rewarding, business issues.

This is both natural and smart. As systems are integrated within the enterprise, it is just good business to take that experience and technology and apply it to other opportunities that influence the bottom line.

Moving from Intra- to Inter-Enterprise Application Integration

Although supply chain integration, or Inter-Enterprise Application Integration, was covered earlier in Chapter 16, it's important to recall here that supply chain integration is an old issue, one well served by new EAI tricks. Using familiar approaches and technologies, it is possible to bring together very different systems that exist in different companies and allow these systems to share information easily.

Using automation to integrate the supply chain is nothing new. However, the application of new technology and standards, such as message brokers and XML, provides many additional opportunities to address this challenge effectively and efficiently (see Figure 20.1). What's surprising is that most EAI vendors don't seem to share this vision. They are still concentrating on enterprise integration, satisfied to solve most external integration problems by exposing systems with Web servers. While Web integration is always critical, the heavy lifting occurs at the back-end, where system binding ultimately needs to occur.

EDI (Electronic Data Interchange) represents a sound solution, but its complexity and expense have largely doomed it—although EDI will remain a point-of-integration for some time. XML provides a much more simplistic approach and, as such, is less expensive to employ. However, many organizations have chosen not to use either XML or EDI. They have gone with some other message standard (e.g., JMS) or a proprietary communications mechanism. As a result, a hodgepodge of technologies and standards will remain in place even as we seek to address the supply chain integration problem.

Ultimately, you need to select a middleware product to move this information. Although message brokers seem to provide the most flexible solution, in

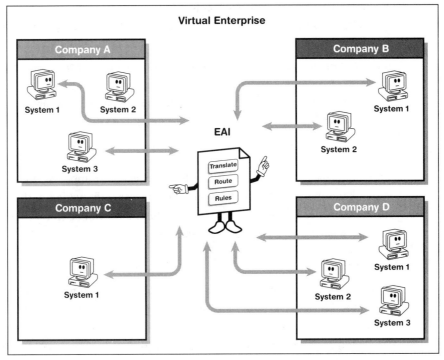

Figure 20.1   **EAI technology and approaches are easily adaptable to the supply chain integration problem.**

many instances transactional middleware (e.g., application servers and TP monitors) is the better fit. Middleware is sold primarily for enterprise integration, but the application of this technology to supply chain integration is also occurring and will grow in importance.

Moving from Data-Level to Application-Level Integration

Another clear trend is the movement from data-level to application-level (application interface–level and method-level EAI) integration. As noted previously, data-level integration provides an inexpensive mechanism to integrate applications because, in most instances, there is no need to change the applications. While data-level integration provides a rudimentary solution for most EAI problem domains, the integration of both application services and application methods generally provides more value in the long run. The downside, at least with method level, is that it is necessary to change the source and target applications or even, in many instances, create a new application (composite applications).

This approach is consistent with the "baby step" approach most enterprises take in implementing solutions to integration problems. Often EAI solutions are created in a series of small, low-risk steps. This type of implementation works from the department to enterprise but never from the enterprise to department. Data-level EAI provides most organizations with the opportunity to get EAI under control, with low risk, then to plot a strategy to move to application-level integration, as more time and money become available and the appetite for risk increases.

Loose Ends

Unfortunately, any discussion of EAI tends to leave a number of "loose ends"—issues that don't really fit into the context of any other discussion of the EAI solution but that need to be considered before the subject can be closed. These issues include: security, performance, and administration.

Security

Too often, security seems to be an afterthought to the implementation of new technology. In order to address security properly, it is necessary to build the system or, in this case, the integration solution from the ground up. While a detailed discussion of security is beyond the scope of this book, it's important to remember that whenever information is sent or received from enterprise systems, when interfaces to the systems are built, or when middleware is being implemented, security must be considered. The vulnerabilities of any enterprise remain only a handful of mouse clicks away—a very sobering thought when money and time are on the line. A few mouse clicks and an enterprise's most valuable asset, its information, could be laid bare to the predatory desires of a competitor.

Security must be considered early in the EAI project process. In most cases, EAI security will be built on top of an already existing security structure within the source and target applications (e.g., Top Secret, RACF, or Windows NT security) to be integrated. Therefore, in addition to integrating applications, EAI will need to integrate the security systems.

Performance

Just as with security, performance issues must be part of the EAI design from the ground up to insure that a set of integrated systems is going to perform well. Many organizations, sensitive to the security risks of integration, do consider security during the EAI development process. However, many of these same organizations fail to adequately address performance until it is too late.

Such complex issues as message rates, transactions-per-second, and interface performance must be taken into account when considering performance engineering and EAI. The most reliable approach to performance in the design of an integration solution is to select the technology and then do a simulation model to make an educated assessment of how the solution will perform. Using simulation tools, it is possible to determine the time it will take for a message or a transaction to move between applications. This simulation must test the various entities of the system at the component (e.g., server) and system level (e.g., integrated systems) to ensure the overall performance of the EAI solution (see Figure 20.2). Just as a chain is no stronger than its weakest link, an integration solution is no more efficient than its slowest performing component. Testing identifies problem components before the solution is actually implemented.

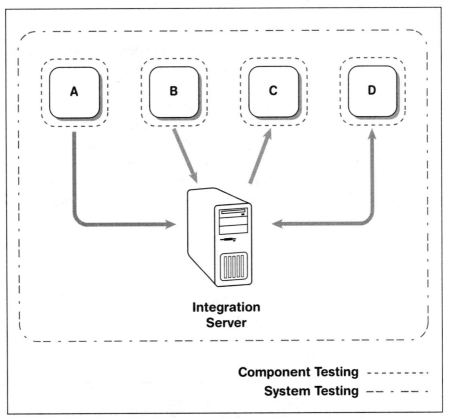

Figure 20.2 **In order to ensure an EAI solution that performs well, the solution must be tested at the component and system levels.**

Administration

The administration of the EAI solution must also be considered. Within typical EAI problem domains application servers, message brokers, TP monitors, and even new composite applications are being implemented to integrate the enterprise. These all represent new technology that must be maintained. Such maintenance includes performance management, disaster recovery (backup and restore), security administration, and configuration management. Over time, in most problem domains, more money will be budgeted for administration than for creating the original solution. For this reason, creating an EAI solution with an eye to administrative efficiency is in the best interest of the bottom line. Of course, solutions that are easy to administer generally provide more up time and a better user experience.

Vendor Approaches

While the majority of our attention has been devoted to various approaches to EAI, you'll discover as you shop for solutions that each EAI vendor has its own take on what EAI is. Who's right? Who's wrong? Unfortunately, as with everything else in the EAI domain, the answer is not black and white.

EAI is a combination of problems, and each organization has its own set of integration issues to address. As a result, it is virtually impossible to find a single technological solution set that can be applied universally. A particular enterprise's EAI solution will generally require products from several different vendors. At this time, and in the foreseeable future, one-step shopping is simply not an EAI reality.

Although vendors' approaches to EAI vary considerably, it is possible to create some general categories. These include:

- Data oriented
- Application integration oriented
- Process automation oriented
- Transaction oriented
- Distributed object oriented

You should note that these vendor solutions are independent of the levels of EAI (database, method, application interface, and user interface), and may inhabit one, two, or three of the levels of EAI.

Data-Oriented

Vendors that promote the data-oriented approach to EAI make the case that integration should occur between the databases—that is, databases should be viewed as the primary points of integration; thus they believe in data-level EAI. Even within data-level EAI, there are many approaches, and each vendor is quick to promote its particular solution. Data-level solutions can be categorized into two categories: data replication and data federation.

Data Replication

Data replication means moving data between two or more databases, databases that can come from the same vendor or many vendors, or even databases that employ different models. The trick with database replication is to account for the differences between database models and database schemas by providing the infrastructure to exchange data. Such solutions are plentiful and inexpensive. Most relational database vendors, including Sybase and Oracle, provide database replication services within their own product offering. These replication engines typically exist within the database engines, at either end (see Figure 20.3).

Many database-oriented middleware solutions are on the market that provide database replication services as well. This is accomplished by placing a layer of software between two or more databases. On one side, the data is extracted from the source database or databases, and on the other side, the data is placed in the target database or databases. Many of these solutions provide transformation services as well—the ability to adjust the schemas and the content so they make sense to the target database (see Figure 20.4).

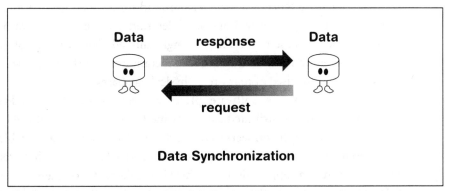

Figure 20.3   Database replication solutions are offered by most major database vendors.

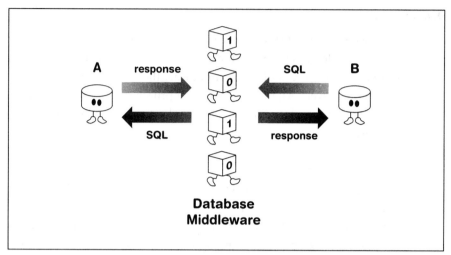

Figure 20.4 Database-oriented middleware solutions provide database replication solutions as well.

The primary advantages of database replication are simplicity and low cost. Database replication is easy to implement, and the technology is cheap to purchase and install. Unfortunately, data replication loses value if methods need to be bound to the data or if methods are shared along with the data. To accomplish these things, method sharing solutions such as transaction-oriented or application integration–oriented EAI must be considered (see the discussion of these solutions later in this chapter).

Data Federation

Although database federation has been around for awhile, the solution set has been perfected only recently. Database federation is the integration of multiple databases and database models into a single, unified view of the databases (see Figure 20.5). Put another way, database federations are virtual enterprise databases that are comprised of many real physical databases.

Database federation software places a layer of software (middleware) between the physical distributed databases and the applications that will be viewing the data. This layer connects to the back-end databases using available interfaces and maps the physical databases to a virtual database model that exists only in the software. The application uses this virtual database to access the required information, and the database federation handles the collection and distribution of the data as needed to the physical databases.

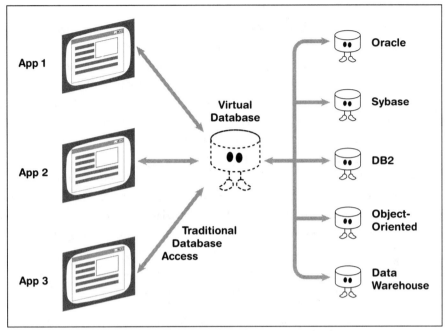

Figure 20.5   Data federation software is middleware that allows an application to view a number of databases through a single view.

The advantage of using database federation software is the ability to bind many different data types into one unified enterprise-wide model.

Database federation allows access to any connected database in the enterprise through a single well-defined interface. This nails the data-level EAI problem, providing the most elegant solution. While this solution, unlike replication, does not require changes to the source or target applications, changes do have to be made at the application level to support federated database software. This is due to the fact that different interfaces are being used to access a different database model (the virtual database).

Application Integration–Oriented

Application integration–oriented product solutions focus on the integration of both packaged and custom applications by using well-defined application interfaces, and supports the data, method, application interface, and user interface EAI levels. Right now, the interest in integrating popular ERP applications (e.g., SAP, PeopleSoft, and Baan) has made this the most exciting EAI sector. (While distributed object and transaction-oriented solutions may be applied to this space—because here you program your way to success—message brokers vendors are promoting their products as the preferred solution.)

Message brokers support application integration–oriented solutions by connecting into as many custom or packaged applications as possible through adapters. They also connect into technology solutions that include middleware and screen scrapers as points of integration (see Figure 20.6).

The advantage of using application integration–oriented products is the efficient integration of many different types of applications. In just a matter days, it is possible to connect a SAP R/3 application to a Baan application, with the application integration–oriented solution accounting for the differences between schema, content, and application semantics by translating on the fly the information moving between the systems. Moreover, this type of solution can be used as a database replication solution, which is also able to connect to application interfaces.

The downside to using application interface–oriented products is that there is little regard for business logic and methods that may exist within the source or

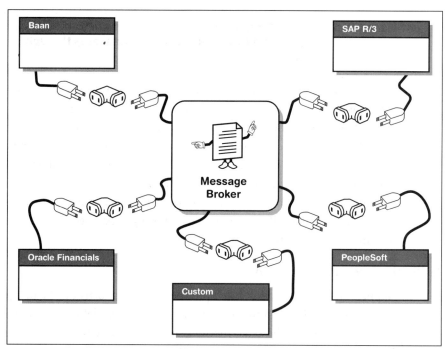

Figure 20.6   **Application integration–oriented solutions link to packaged or custom applications or other points of integration to integrate applications.**

target systems, logic and methods that may be relevant to a particular integration effort. In such a case, transaction- or distributed object–oriented solutions
(composite applications or a pure method-level approach) are probably a better
choice. Ultimately, application interface–oriented technology will learn to share
methods as well as information, perhaps by joining forces with transaction-
oriented or distributed object–oriented solutions. However, for now you will
have to make an either/or decision.

Process Automation–Oriented

Process automation–oriented products, as covered in the previous chapter, are
those solutions that layer a set of easily defined and centrally managed processes,
or workflow solutions, on top of an existing set of processes contained within a
set of enterprise applications (see Figure 20.7).

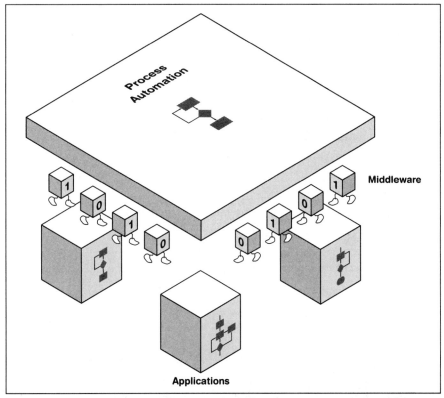

Figure 20.7 **Process automation–oriented products layer a set of centrally
managed processes on top of an existing set of enterprise
processes.**

The focus is to bring together any relevant enterprise processes to obtain the maximum amount of value while supporting the flow of information and logic between these processes. These products view the middleware or the plumbing as a commodity and provide easy-to-use visual interfaces for binding these processes together.

In reality, process automation is another layer of value on top of existing EAI solutions, solutions that include message brokers, application servers, distributed objects, and other middleware layers. They offer a mechanism to bind disparate processes together and to create workflow solutions that automate tasks once performed manually. However, by diminishing the importance of the plumbing, they miss the larger picture. In reality, no single EAI vendor has solved the plumbing issues. Ultimately, the solution to these issues will be delivered by a combination of process automation and middleware vendors. That being the case, it is clear that the binding of middleware and process automation tools represents the future of EAI.

Transaction-Oriented

Transaction-oriented products are those middleware products that use the notion of a transaction, with connectors to back-end systems, to integrate applications, a clear method-level EAI approach. Examples of these products include TP monitors and application services. Although transaction-oriented products can be used for data integration, method-level integration is where these products shine. With these products, it is possible to create common methods (transactions, really) and share those methods among many connected applications (see Figure 20.8).

The advantages of transaction-oriented products are scalability and reliability. However, success with these products requires a tremendous amount of coding. As time marches on, transaction-oriented middleware will combine forces with messaging and message brokers, providing EAI architects and developers with the best of method-level, data-level, and application interface–level EAI.

Distributed Object–Oriented

Like transaction-oriented products that exist at the method level, distributed objects (such as those based on the COM or CORBA standards) also provide EAI architects and developers with an opportunity to share methods. The elegance of the distributed object architecture, the built-in communications, and the ability

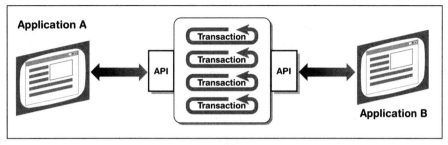

Figure 20.8   Transaction-oriented EAI products allow for the sharing of methods.

to support the distributed model has led many to believe that this is the ultimate EAI technology. However, distributed objects have a long way to go before they can support most large-scale EAI projects. They still fall short when it comes to supporting transactionality, messaging, and easy-to-use tools for building and deploying distributed object EAI solutions. A great deal of custom coding will be required to leverage the power of distributed objects within an EAI solution.

It's important to note that the distributed object standards are moving in the right direction by including built-in support for transaction and integration with Web standards such as Java. Still, it will take some time and momentum in order for distributed objects and EAI to fit together. At this time, it doesn't appear that distributed objects have the luxury of either.

Technologies Join Forces

Although these technologies represent different approaches to EAI, most EAI problem domains will discover that they use most levels of EAI (method, application interface, data, and user interface) when integrating an enterprise. Therefore it is important to select the appropriate technology that works at each level. Wishing for a single technology and a single vendor for all levels is just that—wishing.

Developers and architects may pass information between databases, supporting data-level EAI, using any number of tools. These include newer message brokers, as well as more traditional data replication software. At the application interface level, message brokers seem to do a better job connecting to and moving information in and out of packaged applications. Moreover, at the user interface level, message brokers seem to provide a better event-driven approach, including connectors to most traditional screen-scraping technology. That said, it's in implementing method-level EAI, or creating composite applications, where all message brokers fall short.

Message brokers are not designed to house or share application logic. Rather, they provide rudimentary rules engines to support operations such as the identification, transformation, and routing of messages to the appropriate systems. If this is the type of EAI required, then application servers are the correct choice, providing the ability to integrate many different systems by sharing common business logic and, thus, information.

It should be clear that message brokers and application servers are complementary and converging. While message brokers do a more-than-adequate job in providing event-driven, asynchronous access to many different types of systems, application servers do a much better job in providing the infrastructure to share common logic. Both technologies integrate the enterprise—solve the EAI problem—but do so in very different ways. Although both application servers and message brokers use the middle-tier integration approach, application servers are front-end and are application development focused where message brokers are back-end and operations and process oriented.

Application server and message broker vendors believe the adage, "If you can't beat 'em, join 'em." That's precisely where the application server and message broker vendors are going. Most message broker vendors are partnering with application server vendors to ensure that, at least in the short term, they'll have a solution at the method level. The end result of these partnerships is sure to be the creation of hybrid products that support both application server and message-brokering features. The speed and approach will vary greatly from vendor to vendor, with larger message broker vendors purchasing smaller, more vulnerable application servers and larger application server companies consuming the smaller message broker players. At the same time, some application server vendors will incorporate message-brokering features in their products, and some message broker vendors will learn to provide products more like application servers .

The integration of application servers and message brokers results in a hybrid "super" product that may be called an "application and integration server." This product will offer a location for shared application logic and the ability to build composite applications (see Figure 20.9), as well as the ability to access any system using a synchronous or asynchronous communications model. Moreover, this new product will be able to account for the difference in application semantics, schema, and content.

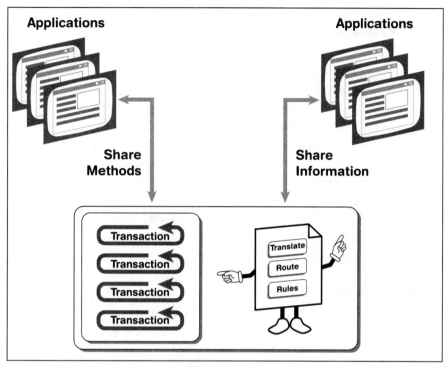

Figure 20.9   Application and integration servers combine the best features of application servers with message brokers.

Future Directions

A discussion of the existing technology is comparatively simple when viewed against the future. Here, reason, guesswork, and a good crystal ball have to suffice. First we must consider approach. There are two elements that must be improved within the enterprise: architecture and application design.

Importance of the Architecture

Anyone who suggests that enterprise architecture is a lost art is just plain wrong. In order for it to be "lost," it would have had to be "found" once, and that has never been the case. Within most enterprises, technology has been implemented for years without considering how it would all someday have to fit together. Ultimately, this is the source of the EAI problem—bad architecture. Many organizations have a problem with architecture because it requires discipline. A technology and business plan has to be created and adhered to, avoiding the temptations of using new and more trendy technology unless it is able to prove its value within the enterprise.

The new interest in architecture is led by the newly conceived role of architect, which now exists within many enterprises. Today, the architect coordinates the installation and configuration of technology, assuring that the enterprise is using the best solution to add the most value to the business. Enterprise architects also manage the network and systems, and the integration of all technologies, typically by leveraging an enterprise architecture or master plan.

Unfortunately, the simple fact is that, within most enterprises, the damage has already been done. Indeed, the enterprise architects are going to be in repair mode for years. EAI is only one of the many problems they will be called upon to solve, finally bringing together applications that were never designed to communicate information in the first place. Given the importance of the solution, the interest in enterprise architecture will clearly grow over time.

Importance of Application Design

If architecture is an enterprise issue, then application design is certainly a system-level issue. Although applications have been designed well for years, the failure has been with applications not designed to interact with other applications. In the future, application architects will pay more attention to designing and building the mechanisms that are necessary to move information in and out of an application.

Middleware is only one part of the application integration story. While middleware does a good job moving information from one application to the next, the ability to externalize both processes and information from any application comes with its own set of problems as well as opportunities. The name for this concept varies from organization to organization, but the term "application externalization" is the most descriptive. This is the process of changing or enabling an existing application so that other layers of technology can take advantage of it.

At issue is the fact that most applications are not built to work with other applications or technology, and thus are not able to externalize both processes and data encapsulated within a given application. While we've traditionally focused on middleware and the technology employed to connect applications together, it may be just as important to focus on the science of enabling these applications, both new and old, to communicate outside of themselves.

EAI and the Modern Enterprise

EAI would not be so important now if the "ball" had not been dropped in the past. As technology paradigms shifted over the years, applications were built around the new paradigm. These shifts included centralized, client/server, and distributed computing, Web-enabled applications, and packaged applications. Now, all these applications are in place, and we have discovered that integrating logic and data is a daunting proposition. Enter EAI, along with an opportunity to finally integrate all of these disparate systems with a minimum impact on the applications and the way an enterprise does business. Unfortunately, the approaches and technology behind EAI are still in their infancy. The knowledge necessary to fully integrate an enterprise is lacking. Indeed, as it functions now, EAI tends to be a stopgap measure to avoid creating new systems. The ultimate goal of EAI is to bind all enterprise systems together in such a way that any application can access any method or any piece of data without delay. It will take some time before this goal is achieved, but don't fear, we'll get there some day!

Glossary

Note: Some terms taken directly from www.messageq.com with permission.

Advanced Program-to-Program Communication (APPC): IBM's solution for program-to-program communications, distributed transaction processing, and remote data access across the IBM product line.

application interface–level EAI: Refers to the leveraging of interfaces exposed by custom or packaged applications. Developers leverage these interfaces to access both business processes and simple information. Using these interfaces, developers are able to bundle together many applications, allowing them to share business logic and information. The only limitations that developers face are the specific features and functions of the application interfaces.

Application Link Enabling (ALE): A SAP R/3 technology that's able to combine business process with middleware. ALE provides a robust distributed architecture for SAP, giving transparent distributed access to both SAP data and processes. The ALE architecture is also essential for moving information to non-SAP systems and, ultimately, supporting the entire EAI effort.

application programming interface (API): An interface that enables different programs to communicate with each other.

application servers: Servers that provide not only for the sharing and processing of application logic, but also the connections to back-end resources. These resources include databases, ERP applications, and even traditional mainframe applications. Application servers also provide user interface development mechanisms. Additionally, they usually provide mechanisms to deploy the application to the platform of the Web.

asynchronous communications: A form of communications by which sending and receiving applications can operate independently so that they do not have to be running or available simultaneously. An application sends a request and may or may not wait for a response. See also *nonblocking communications.*

automatic binding: Describes the action when an *RPC* client stub locates a specific server on a list of servers.

backbone: A series of connections that forms a major communications pathway within a network.

bandwidth: The amount of data that can be sent through a connection; usually measured in bits per second. A fast modem can move about 15,000 bits in one second (about a page of English text).

binding: The association of a client and a server.

blocking communications: A synchronous messaging process whereby the requestor of a service must wait until a response is received.

buffered queue: A message queue that resides in memory.

Business Application Programming Interfaces (BAPIs): Provide an object-oriented mechanism to get at the underlying proprietary SAP middleware technology, such as *RFCs*. In addition to providing access to the data and processes, a benefit once only possible by means of specific methods, a BAPI allows access to the SAP Business Objects held in the Business Object Repository (BOR), encapsulated in their data and processes.

Business Component API: Allows internal and external applications to invoke business rules encapsulated within PeopleSoft as well as simple access data. This interface provides a high-level abstraction layer hiding the complexities of the PeopleSoft system from those that invoke the Business Component API.

business process management: The concept of shepherding work items through a multistep process. The items are identified and tracked as they move through each step, with either specified people or applications processing the information. The process flow is determined by process logic, and the applications (or processes) themselves play virtually no role in determining where the messages are sent.

common business model: The aggregation and high-level model of all objects, methods, properties, procedural logic, batch processing, and everything else in the enterprise that processes information.

Common Object Request Broker Architecture (CORBA): An object model standard maintained by the *OMG*. It is a competing object model of COM/*DCOM* and JavaBeans.

Common Programming Interface-Communications (CPI-C): IBM's *SNA* peer-to-peer *API* that can run over *SNA* and *TCP/IP*. It masks the complexity of *APPC*.

communications middleware: Software that provides interapplication connectivity based on communications styles such as *message queuing*, *ORBs*, and *publish/subscribe*.

communications protocol: A formally defined system for controlling the exchange of information over a network or communications channel.

Component Object Model (COM): Microsoft's standard for distributed objects, an object encapsulation technology that specifies interfaces between component objects within a single application or between applications. It separates the interface from the implementation and provides *APIs* for dynamically locating objects and for loading and invoking them. See also *Distributed Component Object Model*.

Computer Aided Software Engineering (CASE): An automated set of tools that allows a system designer to model a computer system or database before actually programming the system or creating the physical database.

connectionless communications: Communications that do not require a dedicated connection or session between applications.

data-level EAI: The process—and the techniques and technology—of moving data between data stores. This can be described as extracting information from one database, perhaps processing that information as needed, and updating it in another database. While this sounds direct and straightforward, in a typical EAI-enabled enterprise, implementing EAI might mean drawing from as many as one hundred databases and several thousands of tables. It may also include the transformation and application of business logic to the data that is being extracted and loaded.

data-level integration: A form of *EAI* that integrates different data stores to allow the sharing of information among applications. It requires the loading of data directly into the database via its native interface and does not involve the changing of business logic.

data transformation: A key requirement of *EAI* and *message brokers*. There are two basic kinds of data transformation: syntactic translation changes one data set into another (such as different date or number formats), while semantic transformation changes data based on the underlying data definitions or meaning.

data warehouse: A database that receives relevant information from several operational databases. Data warehouses are almost exclusively used for decision support.

database middleware: Allows clients to invoke *SQL*-based services across multivendor databases. This middleware is defined by de facto standards such as *ODBC*, *DRDA*, and *RDA*.

Distributed Component Object Model (DCOM): Microsoft's protocol that enables software components to communicate directly over a network in a reliable, secure, and efficient manner. DCOM is based on the *DCE-RPC* specification and works with both Java applets and ActiveX components through its use of the *COM* object model.

Distributed Computing Environment (DCE): From the Open Software Foundation, DCE provides key distributed technologies such as *RPC*, distributed naming service, time synchronization service, distributed file systems, and network security .

directory services: A way for clients to locate services. Usually contained in a single system image of available servers.

Electronic Data Interchange (EDI): A standard for sharing information between trading partners in support of supply chain integration.

Entity Relation Diagram (ERD): A graphical representation of a conceptual or physical database design.

Enterprise Application Integration (EAI): The unrestricted sharing of information between two or more enterprise applications. A set of technologies that allow the movement and exchange of *information* between different applications and business processes within and between organizations.

eXtensible Markup Language (XML): Like *HTML*, a subset of Standard Generalized Markup Language (SGML), a standard for defining descriptions of structure and content in documents. However, where *HTML* is concerned with the presentation of information on a Web page (without context or dynamic behavior), XML provides context and gives meaning to data.

Extensible Style Language (XSL): A simple, declarative language that programmers use to bind rules to elements in *XML* documents and so provide behavior.

fault-tolerance: The ability for a system to recover from typical system problems, such as network or processor failures.

gateway: A hardware and/or software setup that performs translations between disparate protocols.

groupware: A collection of technologies that allows the representation of complex processes that center around collaborative human activities. It is a model for client/server computing based on five foundation technologies: multimedia document management, workflow, e-mail, conferencing, and scheduling.

heterogeneity: A typical enterprise information system today includes many types of computer technology, from PCs to mainframes. These technologies include a wide variety of different operating systems, application software, and in-house developed applications. *EAI* solves the complex problem of making a heterogeneous infrastructure more coherent.

Hypertext Markup Language (HTML): The set of markup symbols inserted in a file intended for display on a World Wide Web browser. The markup instructs the Web browser how to display a Web page.

information: Machine-readable content or data that is in the correct format to be processed by an application or system.

integrity: In a client/server environment, integrity means that the server code and server data are centrally maintained and therefore secure and reliable.

intelligent routing: Sometimes referred to as "flow control" or "content-based routing," intelligent routing builds on the capabilities of both the rules layer and the message translation layer. In this scenario, the message broker can identify a message coming from the source application and route it to the proper target application, translating it if required.

Intermediate Document (IDOC): A structured information set providing a standard format for moving information in and out of a SAP system. In this regard, it represents a similar concept to EDI, but IDOC is not a standard. It is possible to invoke an *RFC* at the SAP level and get an IDOC as a result.

Internet Inter-ORB Protocol (IIOP): A standard that ensures interoperability for objects in a multivendor *ORB* environment.

Inter-Process Communication (IPC): A mechanism allowing one or more applications to communicate one to another at the process level.

invasive integration: An implementation approach that requires changes or additions to existing applications—opposite of *noninvasive integration.*

load balancing: Automatic balancing of requests among replicated servers to ensure that no server is overloaded.

Logical Unit 6.2 (LU6.2): IBM's device-independent process-to-process protocol provides the facilities for peer-to-peer communications between two programs and also supports asynchronous networking.

message broker: A key component of *EAI*, a message broker is an intelligent intermediary that directs the flow of messages between applications, which become sources and consumers of information. Message brokers provide a very flexible communications backbone and such services as *data transformation, message routing,* and *message warehousing.*

Message-Oriented Middleware (MOM): Used for connecting applications running on different operating systems, most commonly through the use of *message queuing.*

message queuing: A form of communications between programs. Application data is combined with a header (information about the data) to form a message. Messages are stored in queues, which can be buffered or persistent. Message queuing is an *asynchronous communications* style and provides a loosely coupled exchange across multiple operating systems. See also *buffered queue* and *persistent queue.*

message routing: A super-application process where messages are routed to applications based on business rules. A particular message may be directed based on its subject or actual content.

message warehousing: A central repository for temporarily storing messages for analysis or transmission.

method-level EAI: The sharing of the business logic that may exist within the enterprise. For example, the method for updating a customer record may be accessed from any number of applications, and applications may access each other's methods without having to rewrite each method within the respective application.

middleware: Software that facilitates the communications between two applications. It provides an *API* through which applications invoke services, and it controls the transmission of the data exchange over the network. There are three basic types: *communications mid-*

dleware, database middleware, and *systems middleware.*

nonblocking communications: An asynchronous messaging process whereby the requestor of a service does not have to wait until a response is received from another application.

noninvasive integration: An implementation approach that does not require changes or additions to existing applications.

object middleware: Allows clients to invoke methods or objects that reside on a remote server. This middleware revolves around *OMG's CORBA* and Microsoft's *DCOM.*

Open Database Connectivity (ODBC): A Windows standard *API* for *SQL* communications.

Open Integration Framework (OIF): Clearly outlines the options that are available to those looking to integrate with PeopleSoft, including up-to-date mechanisms such as XML and their latest Business Component API appearing with PeopleTools 8.

Object Management Group (OMG): A consortium of object vendors and the founders of the *CORBA* standard.

Object Request Broker (ORB): Software that allows objects to dynamically discover each other and interact across machines, operating systems, and networks.

OpenDoc: A set of shared class libraries with platform-independent interfaces.

patterns: Formalize and streamline the idea of EAI—to build once at the application level and then reuse throughout the solution domain. Patterns describe recurring design problems that appear in certain design contexts. They describe generic schemes for the solution of the problems, solution schemes created by defining their components, responsibilities, and relationships.

persistent queue: A message queue that resides on a permanent device, such as a disk, and can be recovered in case of system failure.

process automation: Sometimes referred to as "workflow," process automation is the science of managing the movement of data and the invocation of processes in the correct and proper order. Process automation provides another layer of easily defined and centrally managed processes (or workflows) that exist on top of an existing set of processes and data contained within a set of enterprise applications.

publish/subscribe (pub/sub): A style of interapplication communications. Publishers are able to broadcast data to a community of information users or subscribers who have issued the type of information they wish to receive (normally defining topics or subjects of interest). An application or user can be both a publisher and subscriber.

Remote Data Access (RDA): The ability to link to a database residing on a remote system, and requesting information from that database.

Relational Database Management System (RDBMS): A type of database that represents physical data storage as a set of tables with columns and rows, and is able to link (create a relation) through columns that two or more tables have in common.

Remote Function Call (RFC): An interface for SAP callable from a multitude of platforms, development environments, and applications. The R/3 Automation Software Development Kit provides RFC libraries and RFC Dynamic Link Libraries (DLLs), user dialogs, in addition to an error-processing facility. Documentation and sample programs for RFCs are included in this software, allowing access to SAP processes and data from standard software such as MS Excel, PowerBuilder, Visual Basic, C++, and Java. Even more beneficial is the ability to access RFCs using other, more "standard" Microsoft interfaces such as COM, COM+, and OLEDB.

Remote Procedure Call (RPC): A form of application-to-application communications that hides the intricacies of the network by using an ordinary procedure call mechanism. It is a tightly coupled synchronous process.

Resource Description Framework (RDF): A part of the XML story, provides interoperability between applications that exchange information.

router: A special-purpose computer or software package that handles the connection of two or more networks. Routers check the destination address of the packets and decide the route to send them.

scalability: The ability of an information system to provide high performance as greater demands are placed upon it, through the addition of extra computing power.

server: A computer or software package that provides specific capabilities to client software running on other computers.

sockets: A portable standard for network application providers on *TCP/IP* networks.

Structured Query Language (SQL): The standard database query language for relational databases.

SQR: A reporting tool that's a part of all PeopleSoft applications.

straight through processing (STP): Occurs when a transaction, once entered into a system, passes through its entire life cycle without any manual intervention. STP is an example of a *zero latency process*, but one specific to the finance industry, which has many proprietary networks and messaging formats.

stored procedure: A program that creates a named collection of *SQL* or other procedural statements and logic that is compiled, verified, and stored in a server database.

synchronous communications: A form of communications that requires the sending and receiving applications to be running concurrently. An application issues a request and waits until it receives a response from the other application.

System Network Architecture (SNA): A network architecture from IBM found in the more traditional mainframe technology.

systems middleware: Software that provides value-add services as well as interprogram communications. An example is transaction processing monitors that are required to control local resources and also cooperate with other resource managers to access non-local resources.

TP monitors: Based on the premise of a transaction. A transaction is a unit of work with a beginning and an end. The reasoning is that if an application logic is encapsulated within a transaction, then the transaction either completes or is rolled back completely. If the transaction has been updating remote resources, such as databases and queues, then they too will be rolled back if a problem occurs.

transactional middleware: Provides an excellent mechanism for method sharing; it is not as effective when it comes to simple information sharing, the real goal of EAI. For instance, transactional middleware typically creates a tightly coupled EAI solution, where messaging solutions are more cohesive in nature.

Transmission Control Protocol/Internet Protocol (TCP/IP): The network protocol for the Internet that runs on virtually every operating system. IP is the network layer, and TCP is the transport layer.

trigger: A stored procedure that is automatically invoked on the basis of data-related events.

two-phase commit: A mechanism to synchronize updates on different machines or platforms so that they all fail or all succeed together. The decision to commit is centralized, but each participant has the right to veto. This is a key process in real-time transaction-based environments.

Unified Modeling Language (UML): A standard set of notations and concepts to approach object-oriented analysis and design.

user interface–level EAI: Using this scenario, architects and developers are able to bundle applications by using their user interfaces as a common point of integration (which is also known as "screen scraping"). For example, mainframe applications that do not provide database- or business process–level access may be accessed through the user interface of the application.

workflow: Software used to automatically route events or work-items from one user or program to another. Workflow is synonymous with "process flow," although traditionally "workflow" has been used in the context of person-to-person information flows.

XA interface: Set of function calls, split between the transaction manager and the resource manager. Allows the resource manager to tell the transaction manager whether it is ready to work with a transaction or whether it is in an unresponsive "resting state."

X/Open: An independent open systems organization. Its strategy is to combine various standards into a comprehensive integrated systems environment called Common Applications Environment, which contains an evolving portfolio of practical *APIs*.

zero latency: No delay between an event and its response.

Zero Latency Enterprise (ZLE): An enterprise in which all parts of the organization can respond to events as they occur elsewhere in the organization, using an integrated IT infrastructure that can immediately exchange information across technical and organizational boundaries.

zero latency process: An automated process with no time delays (i.e., no manual re-entry of data) at the interfaces of different information systems. *Straight-through processing (STP)* is an example.

Bibliography

Aberdeen Group, "Advanced Technologies and a Sense of Process," *Aberdeen Group Report,* Boston, Mass., 1998.

Berson, A., *Client/Server Architecture,* New York: McGraw-Hill, 1992.

Black, U.D., *Data Communications and Distributed Networks,* 2d edition, Englewood Cliffs, N.J.: Yourdon Press, Prentice-Hall, 1987.

Boar, B.H., *Implementing Client/Server Computing, A Strategic Approach,* New York: McGraw-Hill, 1993.

Booch, G., *Object-Oriented Analysis and Design with Applications,* 2d edition, Menlo Park, Calif.: Benjamin/Cummings, 1994.

Chorafas, D.N., *Systems Architecture & Systems Design,* New York: McGraw-Hill, 1989.

Claybrook, B., *OLTP, Online Transaction Processing Systems,* New York: John Wiley & Sons, 1992.

Coad, P., and E. Yourdon, *Object-Oriented Analysis,* 2d edition, Englewood Cliffs, N.J.: Prentice-Hall, 1991.

Date, C.J., *An Introduction to Database Systems,* vol. I, 3rd edition, Reading, Mass.: Addison-Wesley, 1991.

———, *An Introduction to Database Systems,* vol. II, Reading, Mass.: Addison-Wesley, 1985.

Firesmith, D.G., *Object-Oriented Requirements Analysis and Logical Design, A Software Engineering Approach,* New York: John Wiley & Sons, 1993.

Freedman, A., *Computer Glossary,* 6th edition, New York: American Management Association, 1993.

Gartner Group, "Application Integration: Better Ways to Make Systems Work Together," *Gartner Group Conference Proceedings,* Stamford, Conn., 1998.

Goldberg, A., and D. Robson, *Smalltalk-80: The Language and Its Implementation,* Reading, Mass.: Addison-Wesley, 1983.

Green, J.H., *Local Area Networks, A User's Guide for Business Professionals,* Glenview, Ill.: Scott, Foresman and Company, 1985.

Gray, J., and A. Reuter, *Transaction Processing: Concepts and Techniques,* San Mateo, Calif.: Morgan Kaufmann Publishers, 1993.

Hackathorn, R.D., *Enterprise Database Connectivity,* New York: John Wiley & Sons, 1993.

Helzerman, C., "XML Does for Data What HTML Does for Display," available online: http://www.claritycnslt.com/home/WhatsNew.asp, 1999.

Hutchison, D., *Local Area Network Architectures,* Reading, Mass.: Addison-Wesley, 1988.

Ianella, Renato, "An Idiot's Guide to the Resource Description Framework," available online: http://www.dstc.edu.au/cgi-bin/redirect/rd.cgi?http://archive. dstc.edu.au/RDU/reports/RDF-Idiot/, 1999.

Kerninghan, B.W., and D.M. Ritchie, *The C Programming Language,* 2d edition, Englewood Cliffs, N.J.: Prentice-Hall, 1988.

Krol, E., *The Whole Internet User's Guide and Catalog,* Cambridge, Mass.: O'Reilly & Associates, 1992.

Linthicum, D.S., *David Linthicum's Guide to Client/Server and Intranet Development,* New York: John Wiley & Sons, 1997.

———, "Client/Server Protocols: Choosing the Right Connection," *DBMS Magazine* 7, no. 1 (1994): 60.

———, "Moving Away from the Network, Using Middleware," *DBMS Magazine* 7, no. 1 (1994): 66.

———, "Operating Systems for Database Servers," *DBMS Magazine* 7, no. 2 (1994): 62.

———, "Client/Server Strategy," *DBMS Magazine* 7, no. 4 (1994): 46.

———, "4GLs: Productivity at What Cost?" *DBMS Magazine* 7, no. 5 (1994): 22.

———, "A Better RPC?" *DBMS Magazine* 7, no. 7 (1994): 24.

———, "Defending OOP with VisualAge," *DBMS Magazine* 7, no. 9 (1994): 22.

———, "CASE Does Powerbuilder," *DBMS Magazine* 7, no. 10 (1994): 24.

———, "Lockheed Succeeds with C/S," *DBMS Magazine* 7, no. 13 (1994): 26.

———, "A Multiplatform Power Tool," *DBMS Magazine* 8, no. 1 (1995): 20.

———, "System Architect 3.0," *DBMS Magazine* 8, no. 1 (1995): 62.

————, "Reconsidering Message Middleware," *DBMS Magazine* 8, no. 3 (1995): 24.

————, "EOF—A Next Step for C/S," *DBMS Magazine* 8, no. 4 (1995): 26.

————, "Rethinking C++," *DBMS Magazine* 8, no. 5 (1995): 23.

————, "Symantec Enterprise Developer 2.0," *DBMS Magazine* 8, no. 7 (1995): 22.

————, "Delphi 1.0," *DBMS Magazine* 8, no. 7 (1995): 28.

————, "Putting TP Monitors in Their Place," *DBMS Magazine* 8, no. 8 (1995): 22.

————, "Breaking Up is Easy to Do," *DBMS Magazine* 8, no. 9 (1995): 22.

————, "One-Stop Shopping with Oracle," *DBMS Magazine* 8, no. 10 (1995): 28.

————, "Travel Like a Native," *DBMS Magazine* 8, no. 11 (1995): 24.

————, "Keeping an Eye on Your Database Server," *DBMS Magazine* 8, no. 12 (1995): 60.

————, "Banking on Delphi," *DBMS Magazine* 8, no. 13 (1995): 26.

————, "The Client/Server Internet," *DBMS Magazine* 9, no. 1 (1996): 26.

————, "Visual Basic 4.0: Ready for the Enterprise?" *DBMS Magazine* 9, no. 1 (1996): 44.

————, "ProtoGen+ Goes Virtual," *DBMS Magazine* 9, no. 2 (1996): 24.

————, "Moving Towards Remote Controlled OLE," *DBMS Magazine* 9, no. 3 (1996): 28.

————, "Cruising the Galaxy," *DBMS Magazine* 9, no. 4 (1996): 30.

————, "Battle of the Visual Masters," *DBMS Magazine* 9, no. 4 (1996): 91.

————, "Rise of the Intranet," *DBMS Magazine*, Vol. 9, no. 5 (1996): 24.

————, "The Successes and Failures of Application Development Tools," *DBMS Magazine* 9, no. 5 (1996): 71.

————, "DCE Lightens its Load," *DBMS Magazine* 9, no. 7 (1996): 24.

————, "Partitioning Power," *DBMS Magazine* 9, no. 8 (1996): 28.

————, "Selecting a Client/Server Application Development Tool," *DBMS Magazine* 9, no. 8 (1996): 41.

————, "Selecting a DBMS," *DBMS Magazine* 9, no. 8 (1996): 48.

————, "Here Comes the Java Tools," *DBMS Magazine* 9, no. 9 (1996): 24.

————, "C++ Tools for Client/Server Development," *DBMS Magazine* 9, no. 9. (1996): 89.

————, "The Staying Power of C++," *DBMS Magazine* 9, no. 10 (1996): 24.

————, "Objects Meet Data," *DBMS Magazine* 9, no. 10 (1996): 72.

————, "The ABCs of SAP R/3," *DBMS Magazine* 9, no. 11 (1996): 28.

———, "Tool Time," *DBMS Magazine* 9, no. 11 (1996): 15.

———, "The JDBC Connection," *DBMS Magazine* 9, no. 11 (1996): 21.

———, "Distributed Objects Get New Plumbing," *Internet Systems* 10, no. 1 (1997): 4.

———, "OLE-Enabled Middleware," *DBMS Magazine* 10, no. 1, (1997): 26.

———, "Reevaluting Distributed Objects," *DBMS Magazine* 10, no. 1 (1997): 44.

———, "The Good, the RAD, and the Ugly," *DBMS Magazine* 10, no. 2 (1997): 22.

———, "Moving to N-Tier RAD," *DBMS Magazine* 10, no. 3 (1997): 24.

———, "Complexity Revisited," *Internet Systems* 10, no. 4 (1997): 4.

———, "The Java APIs," *Internet Systems* 10, no. 4 (1997): 16.

———, "Driving Development," *DBMS Magazine* 10, no. 4 (1997): 36.

———, "Visual Basic 5.0," *DBMS Magazine* 10, no. 4 (1997): 50.

———, "Building in Java," *Internet Systems* 10, no. 5 (1997): 0.

———, "Another Tool, Another Repository," *DBMS Magazine* 10, no. 5 (1997): 26.

———, "Microsoft Repository 1.0," *DBMS Magazine* 10, no. 7 (1997): 27.

———, "Performance Anxiety," *DBMS Magazine* 10, no. 8 (1997): 26.

———, "The Midas Touch," *DBMS Magazine* 10, no. 9 (1997): 22.

———, "Fun with Partitioning,", *DBMS Magazine* 10, no. 10 (1997): 24.

———, "Next-Generation Middleware," *DBMS Magazine* 10, no. 10 (1997): 69.

———, "Patterns Demystified," *DBMS Magazine* 10, no. 11 (1997): 26.

———, "Get the Message," *DMS Magazine* 10, no. 12 (1997): 24.

———, "Mixing Tuples and Objects," *DBMS Magazine* 10, no. 13 (1997): 22.

———, "Finding Your Way," *DBMS Magazine* 10, no. 12 (1997): 55.

———, "The Magical Framework Myth," *DBMS Magazine* 11, no. 1 (1998): 22.

———, "Crossing the Streams," *DBMS Magazine* 11, no. 2 (1998): 24.

———, "Getting Along," *DBMS Magazine* 11, no. 3 (1998): 26.

———, "Integrating Enterprise Applications," *DBMS Magazine* 11, no. 3 (1998): 38.

———, "Java Realities," *DBMS Magazine* 11, no. 4 (1998): 24.

———, "Conducting Components," *DBMS Magazine* 11, no. 5 (1998): 26.

———, "Emerging Solutions," *DBMS Magazine* 11, no. 6 (1998): 32.

———, "Please Move to the Middle," *DBMS Magazine* 11, no. 7 (1998): 22.

———, "Middleware Performance," *DBMS Magazine* 11, no. 8 (1998): 22.

———, "Database-enabled Java Tools," *Software Development* (August 1998): 50.

———, "Site Building," *Computer Shopper* 18, no.8. (1998): 476.

————, "Profiting from the Year 2000," *Computer Shopper* 18, no. 8 (1998): 0.

————, "Standards Smooth Software Development," *Network World* 15, no. 32 (1998): 31.

————, "Message Brokers Rising," *DBMS Magazine* 11, no. 9 (1998): 20.

————, "Site Building: Building Web Sites with SMIL," *Computer Shopper* 18, no. 9 (1998): 478.

————, "Site Building: Microsoft Provides New Interfaces for IIS," *Computer Shopper* 18, no. 10 (1998): 469.

————, "Site Building: Understanding Internet Application Servers," *Computer Shopper* 18, no. 11 (1998): 447.

————, "Site Building," *Computer Shopper* 18, no. 12 (1998): 441.

————, "Site Building: Understanding Directory Services," *Computer Shopper* 19, no. 1 (1999): 453.

————, "Intershop 3 Merchant Edition," *PC Magazine* 18, no. 1 (1999).

————, "AbleCommerce Developer 2.6," *PC Magazine* 18, no. 1 (1999).

————, "Site Building," *Computer Shopper* 19, no. 2 (1999): 423.

————, "Site Building," *Computer Shopper* 19, no. 3 (1999): 411.

————, "Enterprise Application Integration from the Ground up," *Software Development* (April 1, 1999).

————, "Site Building," *Computer Shopper* 19, no. 4 (1999): 271.

————, "Site Building: Getting Your Site Ready for the 5.0 Browsers," *Computer Shopper* 19, no. 5 (1999): 270.

————, "Mastering Message Brokers," *Software Development* (June 1, 1999).

————, "Site Building: Getting Yourself and Your Site Ready for P3P," *Computer Shopper* 19, no. 6 (1999): 216.

————, "Integrating with PeopleSoft," *EAI Journal* 1, no. 2 (1999): 22.

————, "Site Building," *Computer Shopper* 19, no. 7 (1999): 266.

————, "Tag Your Site for High Visibility," *Computer Shopper* 19, no. 8 (1999): 246.

Mann, J., "Workflow and Enterprise Application Integration," available online: *http://www.messageq.com/workflow/approaches_to_EAI_2.html*, 1998.

Object Management Group: *The Common Object Request Broker: Architecture and Specification*, OMG document no. 91.12.1, revision 1.1, 1992.

Object Management Group: *CORBAservices: Common Object Services Specification*, OMG document no. 95-3-31, 1995.

Orfali, R., and D. Harkey, *Client/Server Programming with OS/2 Extended Edition*, New York: Van Nostrand Reinhold, 1991.

Orfali, R. et al., *The Essential Client/Server Survival Guide*, 2d edition, New York: John Wiley & Sons, 1996.

Renaud, P.E., *Introduction to Client/Server Systems*, New York: John Wiley & Sons, 1993.

Rumbaugh, J. et al., *Object-Oriented Modeling and Design*, Englewood Cliffs, N.J.: Prentice-Hall, 1991.

Sagavista Technology Team, "SAP ALE IDoc Interface and Sagavista IDoc Importer," Reston, Va.: SAGA Software, 1999.

Salemi, J., *PC Magazine Guide to Client/Server Databases*, Emeryville, Calif.: Ziff-Davis Press, 1993.

Shlaer, S., and S.J. Mellor, *Object-Oriented Systems Analysis—Modeling the World in Data*, Englewood Cliffs, N.J.: Prentice-Hall, 1988.

Slater, A., "Extracting Operational Information from SAP's R/3," available online: http://www.messageq.com/erp_integration/extracting_SAP_info.html, 1998.

Smith, J.D., *Reusability & Software Construction: C and C++*, New York: John Wiley & Sons, 1990.

Smith, P., *Client/Server Computing*, Carmel Ind., Sams Publishing, 1992.

Tanenbaum, A.S., *Distributed Operating Systems*, Englewood Cliffs, N.J.: Prentice-Hall, 1995.

Wirfs-Brock, R. et al., *Designing Object-Oriented Software*, Englewood Cliffs, N.J.: Prentice-Hall, 1990.

Webster's New World Dictionary of Computer Terms, Englewood Cliffs, N.J.: Prentice-Hall, 1988.

World Wide Web Consortium, "W3C Issues Recommendation for Resource Description Framework (RDF)," available online: http://www.w3.org/Press/1999/RDF-REC, 1999.

Index

Addison-Wesley Computer and Engineering Publishing Group

How to Interact with Us

1. Visit our Web site

http://www.awl.com/cseng

When you think you've read enough, there's always more content for you at Addison-Wesley's web site. Our web site contains a directory of complete product information including:

- Chapters
- Exclusive author interviews
- Links to authors' pages
- Tables of contents
- Source code

You can also discover what tradeshows and conferences Addison-Wesley will be attending, read what others are saying about our titles, and find out where and when you can meet our authors and have them sign your book.

2. Subscribe to Our Email Mailing Lists

Subscribe to our electronic mailing lists and be the first to know when new books are publishing. Here's how it works: Sign up for our electronic mailing at **http://www.awl.com/cseng/mailinglists.html**. Just select the subject areas that interest you and you will receive notification via email when we publish a book in that area.

3. Contact Us via Email

cepubprof@awl.com
Ask general questions about our books.
Sign up for our electronic mailing lists.
Submit corrections for our web site.

bexpress@awl.com
Request an Addison-Wesley catalog.
Get answers to questions regarding your order or our products.

innovations@awl.com
Request a current Innovations Newsletter.

webmaster@awl.com
Send comments about our web site.

mary.obrien@awl.com
Submit a book proposal.
Send errata for an Addison-Wesley book.

cepubpublicity@awl.com
Request a review copy for a member of the media interested in reviewing new Addison-Wesley titles.

We encourage you to patronize the many fine retailers who stock Addison-Wesley titles. Visit our online directory to find stores near you or visit our online store: **http://store.awl.com/** or call 800-824-7799.

Addison Wesley Longman
Computer and Engineering Publishing Group
One Jacob Way, Reading, Massachusetts 01867 USA
TEL 781-944-3700 • FAX 781-942-3076